Puritanism
in Early
America

PROBLEMS IN
AMERICAN CIVILIZATION

Under the editorial direction of
Edwin C. Rozwenc
Amherst College

Puritanism in Early America

Second Edition

Edited and with an introduction by
George M. Waller
Butler University

D. C. HEATH AND COMPANY
Lexington, Massachusetts   Toronto   London

CONTENTS

INTRODUCTION

Our generation is no stranger to the hope and conviction that man can change his lot for the better. Those who came to the English colonies, whether to New England or elsewhere, were "voting with their feet." By moving they sought to change their condition—political, religious, economic, or social. May not we sympathize and identify with them today, no matter whether our search for an ideal is framed in notions of violent protest, traditional reform, or slow, conservative evolution?

Certainly the people who came to New England by the thousands beginning in 1630 were, in the view of many historians, typical of all Englishmen who came to America in the days of early settlement. For one reason or another they found society in England unsatisfactory and the promise of America alluring. Historians may disagree over the quest. Were the Puritans seeking a new way of life, or to reestablish an old one which had been disrupted by changes in the mother country? But is not the central question for our time the solution of the same problem the Puritans faced—how to establish a social order that reconciles freedom and responsibility, that attains the opportunities for individualism and self-realization along with stability and order?

What was the Puritan ideal? Who were the Puritans? To what extent did they share a common dream, how successful were they in carrying it out, and how did the effort affect the development of New England?

In searching for answers to these questions it is no longer necessary to concern ourselves unduly with those writers of the early part of this century who condemned the Puritans, and certainly not with the nineteenth century's "filiopietistic" New Englanders who uncriticially praised their Puritan "ancestors." A generation of recent scholarship has revealed new dimensions in the theology, political structure, social organization, and behavior of colonial New Englanders.

The older questions on the nature of Puritanism and its influence on American life may have validity. One cannot escape the conclusion that the Puritan heritage constitutes an important strain in American civilization and that the "New England Way" provided a distinctive difference in its own day between the northern colonies and the other English colonies in America. But the question of what that influence was and whether for good or ill, while it whets an endless curiosity about these settlers, has produced arguments and interpretations almost impossible to reconcile, and almost as varied as the historians who make them. Too often the questions have been too broad, the consequences assumed, and the underlying assumptions unexplored. They led to dispute rather than understanding.

Now, more recent scholarship has raised new questions and suggested new approaches to traditional materials. No general agreement has resulted. Perhaps Puritanism contains paradoxes and contradictions, as some have suggested, both in its religious outlook and in the society it sought to establish, making generalizations extremely difficult.

But a number of writers have set themselves to the task of understanding a complex theology, its relation to its parent Calvinism, to religious reformers in England and to other Reformed churches and their theologians, as well as to denominational groups that were close to, and, in the view of some scholars, part of Puritanism. Such queries involve other problems. Was New England a Puritan orthodoxy? Did the leaders agree, and did the populace generally follow and accept? Was religion the dominant force in their lives, extending to their political structure, their economic behavior, their social organization? Was New England a "Bible Commonwealth," a theocracy in which the will of the ministers governed the actions of the civil rulers?

If it was neither completely orthodox nor under theocratic sway, was New England's government, nevertheless, an oligarchy? What was the relation between the people and their governments? Where was the locus of authority? To what extent did they reconcile the traditional conflict between freedom and authority? Were the seeds of democracy or at least individualism evident in church organization, town meeting, social mobility, or economic opportunity, even if not in the intent of the ruling magistrates? Was the government arbitrary, society disciplined, striving for utopian goals, or did the people seek a consensus molded by varying and changing purposes? In the readings that follow, the first group of selections lets the New Englanders speak for themselves, reflecting their own attitudes. John Winthrop and Thomas Shepard provide evidence about the purpose and religious beliefs of respected leaders. Winthrop and John Cotton deal with the problem of authority. The comments of William Bradford, viewing the Massachusetts Bay Colony from neighboring Plymouth, point up the problem of social control, as do the strictures of Increase Mather about dancing. The poetry of Anne Bradstreet and Edward Taylor illustrates the sensitivity, literary grace, and piety attained by some thoughtful New Englanders. Thomas Brattle, a wealthy Bostonian, indicates his concern as a prominent layman with the Salem witchcraft proceedings. Additional expressions of the Puritans themselves are quoted in some of the discussions that follow this part.

Paramount among those who have searched for understanding about the Puritans is Perry Miller, selections from whose works are presented next in the readings. Miller devoted himself to the most extensive examination of American Puritan thought ever undertaken, and he is the acknowledged leader of the "Harvard school" who have attempted to know the meaning of "Puritanism" for New England. With Samuel Eliot Morison, Kenneth Murdock, and others, Miller sought to rebut those who had found the Puritans repressive, intellectually sterile, and altogether an adverse influence on later America. Others of this school, not represented in this volume of readings but widely recognized for their impressive contributions, build on Miller while modifying his conclusions. One is Edmund S. Morgan, who finds no oligarchy but rather government by consensus in support of an orthodox ideal. Another, Bernard Bailyn, in an important book on the New England merchants, finds Miller's emphasis on ideas inadequate to explain the economic life of the northern colonies.

In *Law and Authority in Early Massachusetts,* published in 1960, George Lee Haskins, professor of law at the University of Pennsylvania, traced the development of the Massachusetts legal code of 1648. Although agreeing with Miller that the Bay Colony was an oligarchy, he maintained that it was no "Bible Commonwealth," since though the Bible furnished much that went into its law code, the colony drew also on English law, tradition, and custom, and the practical experience of New World conditions. Not represented in these readings, this study is now being revised to represent more recent conclusions of its author.

Developing these issues further, the selection from David D. Hall agrees in general with Miller that New England was initially a Puritan experiment with a fairly well-formed, consistent, and enforced body of beliefs, laws, and practices. He goes beyond Miller in recognizing the contradictory and changing nature of New England's Puritanism; he sees a less American kind of Puritanism than did Miller or Haskins, tracing its relations to European reformed religions, and its concern not with all but only with certain dominant theological questions. He calls for an examination of specific economic, social, and political events that brought change, rejecting Miller's exclusive concern with ideas that produced a static picture of Puritanism.

Taking sharp issue with the interpretations of the Millerites is the selection by Clifford K. Shipton. Independent towns, civil authority separate from the religious, and local differences between churches indicate for Shipton no theocracy, no oligarchy, and little orthodoxy. For him, New England exhibits an early New World shift toward individualism, freedom of the mind if not of action, and anticipation of civil rights.

Darrett B. Rutman has, perhaps, differed most bluntly among recent writers about colonial New England. Calling on a broader range of materials than the writings of the leaders or the laws of the magistrates, he finds an absence of ordered social structure and concludes that there was no single "New England Way."

Another approach to the nature of New England society is represented in the next section of the readings. Turning from the differing analyses of general characteristics, a group of historians has concentrated its attention on local records in an effort to discover more particularized information. Sumner Chilton Powell, in a pioneering study of a single town—Sudbury—used the traditional methods of local history and genealogy to establish the institutional roles of the town's various groups. Although his interpretations are not always those of the "quantifiers" in the later readings, his evidence tends to support some of the views of that school.

The second excerpt by Darrett B. Rutman examines the society of Boston not as Winthrop envisioned it but as research in a wide variety of records showed it to be. Instead of the ideal of unity, Rutman sees only "action, reaction, and interaction" in a town "fragmented from almost the very beginning" *(Winthrop's Boston,* viii), to which the adjective *Puritan* and the arguments about it cannot be applied in any meaningful way.

One of the most exciting avenues of history now opening up is the employment of the techniques of the behavioral scientists— sociological concepts, demographic analysis, psychology, and anthropology. The approaches of these disciplines complement the earlier emphasis on intellectual history. It is not strange that our current attempts to understand urban problems, generational differences, racial tensions, and behavioral problems have advanced methods that the historian hopes may enlighten us about man's behavior in the past. Is not man's nature constant enough to hope that the tools we are now using to understand our own culture may help us know more about the New England Way, the hopes and disappointments of those people, the tensions and the fruits of the Puritans' endeavors—and through them, in turn, to understand ourselves better?

The selections from Philip J. Greven, John J. Waters, and Kenneth A. Lockridge are examples of the work of "quantifiers," as they have been called. Greven and Lockridge use the techniques of behavioral science and statistical analysis to illuminate colonial life. Waters draws his data from more traditional genealogical methods. They each raise new questions and provide a start toward some new answers that have escaped the traditional historical approach. These new interdisciplinary methods may tell us more about the actual life of the people, their family structure, behavior, interpersonal relations, and social groupings, helping to indicate the relative influence of patterns carried over from England, the ideas of the leaders, and the impact of problems peculiar to the new environment. With quantified information about individual towns, these historians expect to provide a better basis for generalizations.

Another approach utilizing the methods of behaviorial science is represented in the selections from John Demos and Chadwick

Hansen dealing with the Salem witchcraft frenzy of 1692. Both writers find in this episode evidence that tends to support the studies of Lockridge, Waters, and others, who see, in late seventeenth-century New England, change and resulting instability that affected the New England Way. This did not mean that it "failed" as some writers have claimed, but that it merely was modified by new economic, social, and political currents. For this reason the readings in this volume do not treat the issue of "declension" in Puritanism directly, although some of the writers do refer to its supposed decline. Most recent writers are concerned with a more meaningful problem: the identification of factors that brought alterations in the structure of New England society, and the precise effects on New England and, for that matter, on American colonial development as a whole. But this issue arose late in the seventeenth century and is too large a topic to be dealt with in a volume devoted primarily to illuminating whatever pattern New England may have shown when its "experiment" was at its height.

So, finally, what may we conclude about those who came to New England? Do they furnish an example for those in any age who strive for something different, and, in their eyes, better? What obstacles do dissenters meet when they become the rulers and their ideal encounters, in turn, dissent? What was Puritanism like, if such an entity ever was? How was New England molded by its settlers and what they believed? What were these people up to, and how well did they succeed?

I THE PURITANS SPEAK

Theology and Purpose

John Winthrop (1588–1649)
A MODELL OF CHRISTIAN CHARITY

A Puritan from his youth, Winthrop was one of the signers of the Cambridge Agreement by which the stockholders of the Massachusetts Bay Company pledged themselves to go to New England. He had attended Trinity College, Cambridge, was trained in the law, and had been a justice of the peace and lord of the manor of Groton, in Suffolk, a center of the East Anglian Puritan movement. Winthrop was elected governor before he sailed for America and served as governor or deputy governor almost continuously until his death, the most influential of the Bay Colony's leaders.

The following excerpt is taken from a lecture delivered to his fellow passengers on the Arbella *before reaching America and is one of the most straightforward statements of purpose we have from the Puritan leadership.*

2ly. for the worke wee haue in hand, it is by a mutuall consent through a speciall overruleing providence, and a more then an ordinary approbation of the Churches of Christ to seeke out a place of Cohabitation and Consorteshipp vnder a due forme of Government both ciuill and ecclesiasticall. In such cases as this the care of the publique must oversway all private respects, by which not onely conscience, but meare Ciuill pollicy doth binde vs; for it is a true rule that perticuler estates cannott subsist in the ruine of the publique.

3ly. The end is to improue our liues to doe more seruice to the Lord the comforte and encrease of the body of christe whereof wee are members that our selues and posterity may be the better preserued from the Common corrupcions of this euill world to serue the Lord and worke out our Salvacion vnder the power and purity of his holy Ordinances.

4ly. for the meanes whereby this must bee effected, they are 2fold, a Conformity with the worke and end wee aime at, these wee see are extraordinary, therefore wee must not content our selues with vsuall ordinary meanes whatsoever wee did or ought to haue done when

From *Winthrop Papers*, II, Massachusetts Historical Society (Boston, 1931). Used by permission of the Massachusetts Historical Society.

wee liued in England, the same must wee doe and more allsoe where wee goe: That which the most in theire Churches maineteine as a truthe in profession onely, wee must bring into familiar and constant practice, as in this duty of loue wee must loue brotherly without dissimulation, wee must loue one another with a pure hearte feruently wee must beare one anothers burthens, wee must not looke onely on our owne things, but allsoe on the things of our brethren, neither must wee think that the lord will beare with such faileings at our hands as hee dothe from those among whome wee haue liued. . . .

Thus stands the cause betweene God and vs, wee are entered into Covenant with him for this worke, wee haue taken out a Commission, the Lord hath giuen vs leaue to drawe our owne Articles wee haue professed to enterprise these Accions vpon these and these ends, wee haue herevpon besought him of favour and blessing: Now if the Lord shall please to heare vs, and bring vs in peace to the place wee desire, then hath hee ratified this Covenant and sealed our Commission, [and] will expect a strickt performance of the Articles contained in it, but if wee shall neglect the observacion of these Articles which are the ends wee haue propounded, and dissembling with our God, shall fall to embrace this present world and prosecute our carnall intencions seekeing great things for our selues and our posterity, the Lord will surely breake out in wrathe against vs be revenged of such a periured people and make vs knowe the price of the breache of such a Covenant.

Now the onely way to avoyde this shipwracke and to provide for our posterity is to followe the Counsell of Micah, to doe Justly, to loue mercy, to walke humbly with our God, for this end, wee must be knitt together in this worke as one man, wee must entertaine each other in brotherly Affeccion, wee must be willing to abridge our selues of our superfluities, for the supply of others necessities, wee must vphold a familiar Commerce together in all meekenes, gentlenes, patience and liberallity, wee must delight in eache other, make others Condicions our owne reioyce together, mourne together, labour, and suffer together, allwayes haueing before our eyes our Commission and Community in the worke, our Community as members of the same body, soe shall wee keepe the vnitie of the spirit in the bond of peace, the Lord will be our God and delight to dwell among vs, as his owne people and will commaund a blessing vpon vs in all our wayes, soe that wee shall see much more of his wisdome power goodnes and truthe then formerly wee haue beene acquainted with, wee shall finde that the God of Israell is among vs, when tenn of vs shall be able to resist a thousand of our enemies, when hee shall make vs a prayse and glory, that men shall say of succeeding plantacions: the lord make it like that of New England: for wee must Consider that wee shall be as a Citty vpon a Hill, the eies of all people are vppon vs; soe that if wee shall deale falsely with our god in this worke wee haue vndertaken and soe cause him to withdrawe his present help from vs, wee shall be made a story and a by-word through the world, wee shall open the mouthes of enemies to speake euill of the wayes of god and all professours for Gods sake; wee shall shame the faces of many of gods worthy seruants, and cause theire prayers to be turned into Cursses vpon vs till wee be consumed out of the good land whether wee are goeing: and to shutt vpp this discourse with that exhortacion of Moses that faithfull seruant of the Lord in his last farewell to Israell Deut. 30. Beloued there is now sett before vs life, and good, deathe and euill in that wee are Commaunded this day to loue the Lord our God, and to loue one another to walke in his wayes and to keepe his Commaundements and his Ordinance, and his lawes, and the Articles of our Covenant with him that wee may liue and be multiplyed, and that the Lord our God may blesse vs in the land whether wee goe to possesse it. But if our heartes shall turne away soe that wee will not obey, but shall be seduced and worshipp . . . other Gods our pleasures, and proffitts, and serue them; it is propounded vnto vs this day, wee shall surely perishe out of the good Land whether wee passe over this vast Sea to possesse it;

> Therefore lett vs choose life,
> that wee, and our Seede,
> may liue; by obeyeing his
> voyce, and cleaueing to him,
> for hee is our life, and
> our prosperity.

Thomas Shepard (1605–1649)

THE COVENANT OF GRACE

Shepard came to Massachusetts Bay in 1635 and became the much-loved minister of Newtown (now Cambridge), where he gained a reputation for vital, solid mastery of theology, though he was never as well known as John Cotton or his predecessor at Newtown, Thomas Hooker. He had attended Emmanuel College, Cambridge.

The "Covenant theology" or "federal theology" as it is sometimes called, has been identified with American Puritan thought by Perry Miller, who saw it as easing the stark belief in predestination which Puritans held in common with Calvin's thought and Reformed Churches in general. Miller has called it "an idiom . . . to make a bit more plausible the mysteries of the Protestant creed" (introduction to "The Marrow of Puritan Divinity" in Errand Into the Wilderness).

Below, Shepard explains the Covenant, God's special relationship to man, and the avenue of salvation.

The blessed God hath evermore delighted to reveal and communicate Himself by way of Covenant. He might have done good to man before his fall, as also since his fall, without binding Himself in the bond of Covenant; Noah, Abraham, and David, Jews, Gentiles, might have had the blessings intended, without any promise or Covenant. But the Lord's heart is so full of love (especially to His own) that it cannot be contained so long within the bounds of secrecy—viz. from God's eternal purpose to the actual accomplishment of good things intended—but it must aforehand overflow and break out into the many streams of a blessed Covenant. The Lord can never get near enough to His people, and thinks He can never get them near enough unto Himself, and therefore unites and binds and fastens them close to Himself, and Himself unto them, by the bonds of a Covenant. And therefore when we break our Covenant, and that will not hold us, He takes a faster bond and makes a sure and everlasting Covenant, according to Grace, not according to Works; and that shall hold His people firm unto Himself, and hold Himself close and fast unto them, that He may never depart from us.

Oh! the depth of God's grace herein: that when sinful man de-

From preface to Peter Bulkeley, *The Gospel Covenant; or the Covenant of Grace Opened,* 2nd ed. (London, 1651).

serves never to have the least good word from Him, that He should open His whole heart and purpose to him in a Covenant; that when he deserves nothing else but separation from God, and to be driven up and down the world as a vagabond, or as dried leaves fallen from our God, that yet the Almighty God cannot be content with it, but must make Himself to us, and us to Himself, more sure and near than ever before! And is not this Covenant then (Christian reader) worth thy looking into and searching after? Surely never was there a time wherein the Lord calls His people to more serious searching into the nature of the Covenant than in these days.

For are there not some who cut off the entail to children of those in Covenant, and so lessen and shorten the riches of grace in the Lord's free Covenant, and that in the time of more grace under the Gospel than He was wont to dispense under the Law? Are there not others who preach a new, or rather another Gospel or Covenant— viz. that actual remission of sins and reconciliation with God (purchased indeed in redemption by Christ's death) is without, nay, before faith . . . ? Is it not time for the people of God now to pry into the secret of God's Covenant—which He reveals to them that fear Him (Psal. 25. 14)—when, by clipping of it and distinguishing about it, the beautiful countenance of it begins to be changed and transformed by those angels of "new light" [from that] which once it had when it began to be published in the simplicity of it by the Apostles of Christ (II Cor. 11. 3)? Nay, is not the time come wherein the Lord of hosts seems to have a quarrel against all the world, and especially His churches and people, whom He goes on to waste by the sharpest sword that (almost) was ever drawn out? And is it not the duty of all that have the least spark of holy fear and trembling to ask and search diligently what should be the reason of this sore anger and hot displeasure, before they and theirs be consumed in the burning flames of it?

Search the scriptures, and there we shall find the cause, and see God Himself laying His finger upon that which is the sore and the wound of such times: for so it is said (Isa. 24. 1–5), "Behold, the Lord maketh the earth empty and waste, and turns it upside down, and scattereth abroad the inhabitants thereof; and it shall be as with the people, so with the priest; and the land shall be utterly spoiled." Why? "For the earth is defiled under the inhabitants thereof." Why so? "Because they have transgressed the laws, changed the ordinance, and broken the everlasting Covenant." And therefore when the Lord shall have wasted His church, and hath made it as Adnah and Zeboim, when heathen nations shall ask, "Wherefore hath the Lord done all this against this land? What meaneth the heat of His great anger?", the answer is made by the Lord Himself expressly (Deut. 29. 25): viz. "Because they have forsaken the Covenant of the Lord God of their fathers." And no wonder, for they that reject the Covenant of Grace, they break the league of peace between God and themselves. And hence, if acts of hostility in desolating kingdoms, churches, families and persons break out from a long-suffering God, they may easily see the cause, and that the cause and quarrel of God herein is just.

As all good things are conveyed to God's people not barely by common providence but by special Covenant (Isa. 16. 8, 9), so all the evils they meet with in this world (if in them the face of God's anger appears), upon narrow search, will be found to arise from breach of Covenant, more or less. So that if it be the great cause of all the public calamities of the church and people of God, and those calamities are already begun, and God's hand is stretched out still—was there then ever a more seasonable time and hour to study the Covenant, and so see the sin, repent of it, and at last to lay hold of God's rich grace and bowels in it, lest the Lord go on and fulfill the word of His servants, and expose most pleasant lands to the doleful lamentation of a very little remnant, reserved as a few coals in the ashes, when all else is consumed?

As particular persons, when they break their Covenant, the Lord therefore breaks out against them: so, when whole churches forsake their Covenant, the Lord therefore doth sorely visit them. Sins of ignorance the Lord Jesus pities (Heb. 5. 2) and many times winks at, but sins against light He cannot endure (II Pet. 2. 21). Sins against light are great, but sins against the purpose and Covenant, nay God's Covenant, are by many degrees worse, for the soul of man rusheth most violently and strongly against God when it breaks through all the light of the mind and purposes of the will that stand in his way to keep him from sin. And is not this done by breach of Covenant? And therefore no wonder if the Lord makes His people's chain heavy by sore affliction, until they come to consider and behold this sin, and learn more fear (after they are bound to their good behavior) of breaking Covenant with God again.

It is true, the Covenant effectually made can never be really broke, yet externally it may. But suppose God's churches were in greatest peace, and had a blessed rest from all their labors round about them: yet what is the child's position, but his legacy left him, written with the finger of God his father, in the New Covenant, and the blood of Jesus Christ his redeemer, in His last will and testament? What is a Christian's comfort, and where doth it chiefly lie, but in this: that the Lord hath made with him an everlasting Covenant, in all things stablished and sure? Which were the last breathing of the sweet singer of Israel, and the last bubblings up of the joy of his heart (II Sam. 23. 5).

God the Father's eternal purposes are sealed secrets, not immediately seen, and the full and blessed accomplishments of those purposes are not yet experimentally felt. The Covenant is the midst between both God's purposes and performances, by which and in which we come to see the one before the world began, and by a blessed faith (which makes things absent, present) to enjoy the other, which shall be our glory when this world shall be burned up and all things in it shall have an end. For in God's Covenant we see with open face God's secret purpose for time past—God's purposes toward His people being, as it were, nothing else but promises concealed, and God's promises in the Covenant being nothing else but His purposes revealed. As also, in the same Covenant and promises we see performances for [the] future, as if they were accomplishments at present. Where then is a Christian's comfort but in that Covenant, wherein two eternities (as it were) meet together, and whereby he may see accomplishments (made sure to him) of eternal glory, arising from blessed purposes of eternal grace? In a word, wherein he fastens upon God, and hath Him from everlasting to everlasting, comprehended at hand near and obvious in His words of a gracious Covenant?

The Church of God is therefore bound to bless God much for this food in season, and for the holy judicious and learned labors of this aged, experienced and precious servant of Christ Jesus, who hath taken much pains to discover—and that not in words and allegories but in the demonstration and evidence of the Spirit—the great mystery of godliness wrapped up in the Covenant, and hath now fully opened sundry knotty questions concerning the same, which happily have not been brought so fully to light until now. Which cannot but be of singular and seasonable use, to prevent apostasies from the simplicity of the Covenant and Gospel of Christ. The sermons were preached in the remote ends of the earth and, as it were, set under a bushel, a church more remote from the numerous society of others of the saints; if now, therefore, the light be set upon a hill, 'tis where it should stand, and where Christ surely would have it put. The good Lord enlighten the minds of all those who seek for the truth by this and such like helps; and the Lord enlighten the whole world with His glory, even with the glory of His Covenant, grace and love, that His people hereby may be sealed up daily unto all fulness of assurance and peace, in these evil times.

Authority—
Government and Church

John Cotton (1584–1652)
LETTER TO LORD SAY AND SEAL, 1636

Cotton entered Trinity College, Cambridge when he was thirteen, took an M.A. at Emmanuel and became a Fellow there. Highly regarded for his ministry in England, where powerful protectors permitted him to express Puritan views, he preached the farewell sermon to Winthrop's settlers, and followed them to Boston in 1633. His was the outstanding reputation for piety and intellect among the New England clergy, his sermons and writings the standard for orthodoxy. As a friend and sympathizer he was almost drawn into the Antinomian group led by Anne Hutchinson but managed to extricate himself.

As teacher in the church at Boston he reflected the views of the government as well as the religious ideas of the leaders. Here he defends the practice of the New England churches in restricting church membership as well as political authority to an orthodox "elect" who can demonstrate that they are the recipients of God's gift of grace.

Right honourable,

. . . I am very apt to believe, what Mr. Perkins hath, in one of his prefatory pages to his golden chaine, that the word, and scriptures of God doe conteyne a short *upoluposis,* or platforme, not onely of theology, but also of other sacred sciences, (as he calleth them) attendants, and handmaids thereunto, which he maketh ethicks, eoconomicks, politicks, church-government, prophecy, academy. It is very suitable to Gods all-sufficient wisdome, and to the fulnes and perfection of Holy Scriptures, not only to prescribe perfect rules for the right ordering of a private mans soule to everlasting blessednes with himselfe, but also for the right ordering of a mans family, yea, of the commonwealth too, so farre as both of them are subordinate to spiritual ends, and yet avoide both the churches usurpation upon civill jurisdictions, *in ordine ad spiritualia,* and the commonwealths

From Thomas Hutchinson, *History of Massachusetts Bay,* I, Appendix III (1764).

invasion upon ecclesiasticall administrations, *in ordine* to civill peace, and conformity to the civill state. Gods institutions (such as the government of church and of commonwealth be) may be close and compact, and co-ordinate one to another, and yet not confounded. God hath so framed the state of church government and ordinances, that they may be compatible to any common-wealth, though never so much disordered in his frame. But yet when a commonwealth hath liberty to mould his owne frame (*scripturæ plenitudinem adoro*) I conceyve the scripture hath given full direction for the right ordering of the same, and that, in such sort as may best mainteyne the *euexia* of the church. Mr. Hooker doth often quote a saying out of Mr. Cartwright (though I have not read it in him) that noe man fashioneth his house to his hangings, but his hangings to his house. It is better that the commonwealth be fashioned to the setting forth of Gods house, which is his church: than to accommodate the church frame to the civill state. Democracy, I do not conceyve that ever God did ordeyne as a fitt government eyther for church or commonwealth. If the people be governors, who shall be governed? As for monarchy, and aristocracy, they are both of them clearly approoved, and directed in scripture, yet so as referreth the soveraigntie to himselfe, and setteth up Theocracy in both, as the best forme of government in the commonwealth, as well as in the church.

The law, which your Lordship instanceth in (that none shall be chosen to magistracy among us but a church member) was made and enacted before I came into the country; but I have hitherto wanted sufficient light to plead against it. 1st. The rule that directeth the choice of supreame governors, is of like æquitie and weight in all magistrates, that one of their brethren (not a stranger) should be set over them, Deut. 17. 15. and Jethroes counsell to Moses was approved of God, that the judges, and officers to be set over the people, should be men fearing God, Exod. 18. 21. and Solomon maketh it the joy of a commonwealth, when the righteous are in authority, and their mourning when the wicked rule, Prov. 29. 21. Jab 34. 30. Your Lordship's feare, that this will bring in papal excommunication, is just, and pious: but let your Lordship be pleased againe to consider whether the consequence be necessary. *Turpius ejicitur quam non admittitur:* nonmembership may be a just cause of non-admission to the place of magistracy. A godly woman, being to make choice of an husband, may justly refuse a man that is eyther cast out of church fellowship, or is not yet receyved into it, but yet, when shee is once given to him, shee may not reject him then, for such defect. Mr. Humfrey was chosen for an assistant (as I heare) before the colony came over hither: and, though he be not as yet ioyned into church fellowship (by reason of the unsetlednes of the congregation where he liveth) yet the commonwealth doe still continue his magistracy to him, as knowing he waiteth for oppertunity of enioying church fellowship shortly.

When your Lordship doubteth, that this corse will draw all things under the determination of the church, *in ordine ad spiritualia* (seeing the church is to determine who shall be members, and none but a member may have to doe in the government of a commonwealth) be pleased (I pray you) to conceyve, that magistrates are neyther chosen to office in the church, nor doe governe by directions from the church, but by civill lawes, and those enacted in generall corts, and executed in corts of iustice, by the governors and assistants. In all which, the church (as church) hath nothing to doe: onely, it prepareth fitt instruments both to rule, and to choose rulers, which is no ambition in the church, nor dishonor to the commonwealth, the apostle, on the contrary, thought it a great dishonor and reproach to the church of Christ, if it were not able to yield able judges to heare and determine all causes amongst their brethren, I Cor. 6. 1. to 5. which place alone seemeth to me fully to decide this question: for it plainely holdeth forth this argument: It is a shame to the church to want able judges of civill matters (as v. 5.) and an audacious act in any church member voluntarily to go for judgment, otherwhere than before the saints (as v. 1.) then it will be noe arrogance nor folly in church members, nor prejudice to the commonwealth, if voluntarily they never choose any civill judges, but from amongst the saints, such as church members are called to be. But the former is cleare: and how then can the latter be avoyded. If this therefore be (as your Lordship rightly conceyveth one of the maine objections if not the onely one) which hindereth this commonwealth from the entertainment of the propositions of those worthy gentlemen, wee intreate them, in the name of the Lord Jesus, to consider, in meeknes of wisdome, it is not any conceite or will of ours, but the holy counsell and will of the Lord Jesus (whom they seeke to serve as well as wee) that overruleth us in this case: and we trust will overrule them also, that the Lord onely may be exalted amongst all his servants. What pittie and griefe were it, that the observance of the will of Christ should hinder good things from us!

But your Lordship doubteth, that if such a rule were necessary, then the church estate and the best ordered commonwealth in the world were not compatible. But let not your Lordship so conceyve. For, the church submitteth itselfe to all the lawes and ordinances of men, in what commonwealth soever they come to dwell. But it is one thing, to submit unto what they have noe calling to reforme: another thing, voluntarily to ordeyne a forme of government, which to the best discerning of many of us (for I speake not of myselfe) is expressly contrary to rule. Nor neede your Lordship feare (which yet I speake with submission to your Lordships better judgment) that this corse will lay such a foundation, as nothing but a mere democracy can be built upon it. Bodine confesseth, that though it be *status populairs,* where a people choose their owne governors; yet the government is not a democracy, if it be administred, not by the people, but by the governors, whether one (for then it is a monarchy, though elective) or by many, for then (as you know) it is aristocracy. In which respect it is, that church government is iustly denyed (even by Mr. Robinson) to be democratical, though the people choose their owne officers and rulers.

Nor neede wee feare, that this course will, in time, cast the commonwealth into distractions, and popular confusions. For (under correction) these three things doe not undermine, but doe mutually and strongly mainteyne one another (even those three which wee principally aime at) authority in magistrates, liberty in people, purity in the church. Purity, preserved in the church, will preserve well ordered liberty in the people, and both of them establish well-ballanced authority in the magistrates. God is the author of all these three, and neyther is himselfe the God of confusion, nor are his wayes the wayes of confusion, but of peace. . . .

Now the Lord Jesus Christ (the prince of peace) keepe and bless your Lordship, and dispose of all your times and talents to his best advantage: and let the covenant of his grace and peace rest upon your honourable family and posterity throughout all generations.

Thus, humbly craving pardon for my boldnesse and length, I take leave and rest,

Your Honours to serve in Christ Jesus,

J. C.

John Winthrop
SPEECH TO THE GENERAL COURT

Often called his "Little Speech," this statement, delivered to the General Court in July 1645, followed Winthrop's vindication after he had been accused of exceeding his authority. The affair had involved resistance by some of the leaders of the town of Hingham to an order of the General Court and was merged with the opposition of Dr. Robert Child and his Presbyterian followers to Winthrop and his fellow magistrates. This speech is a classic statement of the orthodox view of authority and, indeed, a model statement of conservative political theory in England and America throughout the colonial period.

I suppose something may be expected from me, upon this charge that is befallen me, which moves me to speak now to you; yet I intend not to intermeddle in the proceedings of the court, or with any of the persons concerned therein. Only I bless God, that I see an issue of this troublesome business. I also acknowledge the justice of the court, and, for mine own part, I am well satisfied, I was publicly charged, and I am publicly and legally acquitted, which is all I did expect or desire. And though this be sufficient for my justification before men, yet not so before the God, who hath seen so much amiss in my dispensations (and even in this affair) as calls me to be humble. For to be publicly and criminally charged in this court, is matter of humiliation, (and I desire to make a right use of it,) notwithstanding I be thus acquitted. If her father had spit in her face, (saith the Lord concerning Miriam,) should she not have been ashamed seven days? Shame had lien upon her, whatever the occasion had been. I am unwilling to stay you from your urgent affairs, yet give me leave (upon this special occasion) to speak a little more to this assembly. It may be of some good use, to inform and rectify the judgments of some of the people, and may prevent such distempers as have arisen amongst us. The great questions that have troubled the country, are about the authority of the magistrates and the liberty of the people. It is yourselves who have called us to this office, and being called by you, we have our authority from God, in way of an ordinance, such as hath the image of God eminently stamped upon it, the contempt and violation whereof hath been vindicated with examples of divine

From *Winthrop's Journal*, ed. James Savage, I (Boston, 1825).

vengeance. I entreat you to consider, that when you choose magistrates, you take them from among yourselves, men subject to like passions as you are. Therefore when you see infirmities in us, you should reflect upon your own, and that would make you bear the more with us, and not be severe censurers of the failings of your magistrates, when you have continual experience of the like infirmities in yourselves and others. We account him a good servant, who breaks not his covenant. The covenant between you and us is the oath you have taken of us, which is to this purpose, that we shall govern you and judge your causes by the rules of God's laws and our own, according to our best skill. When you agree with a workman to build you a ship or house, etc., he undertakes as well for his skill as for his faithfulness, for it is his profession, and you pay him for both. But when you call one to be a magistrate, he doth not profess nor undertake to have sufficient skill for that office, nor can you furnish him with gifts, etc., therefore you must run the hazard of his skill and ability. But if he fail in faithfulness, which by his oath he is bound unto, that he must answer for. If it fall out that the case be clear to common apprehension, and the rule clear also, if he transgress here, the error is not in the skill, but in the evil of the will: it must be required of him. But if the case be doubtful, or the rule doubtful, to men of such understanding and parts as your magistrates are, if your magistrates should err here, yourselves must bear it.

For the other point concerning liberty, I observe a great mistake in the country about that. There is a twofold liberty, natural (I mean as our nature is now corrupt) and civil or federal. The first is common to man with beasts and other creatures. By this, man, as he stands in relation to man simply, hath liberty to do what he lists; it is a liberty to evil as well as to good. This liberty is incompatible and inconsistent with authority, and cannot endure the least restraint of the most just authority. The exercise and maintaining of this liberty makes men grow more evil, and in time to be worse than brute beasts: omnes sumus licentia deteriores. This is that great enemy of truth and peace, that wild beast, which all the ordinances of God are bent against, to restrain and subdue it. The other kind of liberty I call civil or federal, it may also be termed moral, in reference to the covenant between God and man, in the moral law, and the politic covenants and constitutions, amongst men themselves. This liberty is the proper end and object of authority, and cannot subsist without it; and it is a liberty to that only which is good, just, and honest. This liberty you are to stand for, with the hazard (not only of your goods, but) of your lives, if need be. Whatsoever crosseth this, is not authority, but a distemper thereof. This liberty is maintained and exercised in a way of subjection to authority; it is of the same kind of liberty wherewith Christ hath made us free. The woman's own choice makes such a man her husband; yet being so chosen, he is her lord, and she is to be subject to him, yet in a way of liberty, not of bondage; and a true wife accounts her subjection her honor and freedom, and would not think her condition safe and free, but in her subjection to her husband's authority. Such is the liberty of the church under the authority of Christ, her king and husband; his yoke is so easy and sweet to her as a bride's ornaments; and if through frowardness or wantonness, etc., she shake it off, at any time, she is at no rest in her spirit, until she take it up again; and whether her lord smiles upon her, and embraceth her in his arms, or whether he frowns, or rebukes, or smites her, she apprehends the sweetness of his love in all, and is refreshed, supported, and instructed by every such dispensation of his authority over her. On the other side, ye know who they are that complain of this yoke and say, let us break their bands, etc., we will not have this man to rule over us. Even so, brethren, it will be between you and your magistrates. If you stand for your natural corrupt liberties, and will do what is good in your own eyes, you will not endure the least weight of authority, but will murmur, and oppose, and be always striving to shake off that yoke; but if you will be satisfied to enjoy such civil and lawful liberties, such as Christ allows you, then will you quietly and cheerfully submit unto that authority which is set over you, in all the administrations of it, for your good. Wherein, if we fail at any time, we hope we shall be willing (by God's assistance) to hearken to good advice from any of you, or in any other way of God; so shall your liberties be preserved, in upholding the honor and power of authority amongst you.

FIGURE 1. Portrait of John Cotton (1585–1652) or Increase Mather (1639–1723). This portrait, originally of Cotton, appears to have a portrait of Mather, his son-in-law, painted over it. (Courtesy Connecticut Historical Society)

Society and Social Control

William Bradford (1590–1657)
HISTORY OF PLYMOUTH PLANTATION

Bradford was the second and thereafter almost permanent governor, during his lifetime, of the little band of extreme Puritans, the Separatists, who settled at Plymouth in 1620. Here he reflects, in passages from his famous History, *on the problems his northern neighbors in Massachusetts Bay were having in regulating behavior according to their ideal.*

He realistically and sensibly concludes that the effort to detect and punish wrongdoing is admirable and necessary, according to the Bay Colony's purposes, but acknowledges that full success in controlling man's natural inclinations is unlikely.

[1642] Marvilous it may be to see and consider how some kind of wickednes did grow and breake forth here, in a land wher the same was so much witnesed against, and so narrowly looked unto, and severly punished when it was knowne; as in no place more, or so much, that I have known or heard of; insomuch as they have been somewhat censured, even by moderate and good men, for their severitie in punishments. And yet all this could not suppress the breaking out of sundrie notorious sins, (as this year, besids other, gives us too many sad presidents and instances,) espetially drunkennes and unclainnes; not only incontinencie betweene persons unmarried, for which many both men and women have been punished sharply enough, but some maried persons allso. But that which is worse, even sodomie and bugerie, (things fearfull to name,) have broak forth in this land, oftener then once. I say it may justly be marveled at, and cause us to fear and tremble at the consideration of our corrupte natures, which are so hardly bridled, subdued, and mortified; nay, cannot by any other means but the powerfull worke and grace of Gods spirite. But (besids this) one reason may be, that the Divell may carrie a greater spite against the churches of Christ and the gospell hear, by how much the more they indeaour to pre-

From William Bradford, *History of Plymouth Plantation,* ed. Worthington C. Ford (Boston, 1912).

serve holynes and puritie amongst them, and strictly punisheth the contrary when it ariseth either in church or comone wealth; that he might cast a blemishe and staine upon them in the eyes of [the] world, who use to be rash in judgmente. I would rather thinke thus, then that Satane hath more power in these heathen lands, as som have thought, then in more Christian nations, espetially over Gods servants in them.

2. An other reason may be, that it may be in this case as it is with waters when their streames are stopped or dammed up, when they gett passage they flow with more violence, and make more noys and disturbance, then when they are suffered to rune quietly in their owne chanels. So wikednes being here more stopped by strict laws, and the same more nerly looked unto, so as it cannot rune in a comone road of liberty as it would, and is inclined, it searches every wher, and at last breaks out wher it getts vente.

3. A third reason may be, hear (as I am verily perswaded) is not more evills in this kind, nor nothing nere so many by proportion, as in other places; but they are here more discoverd and seen, and made publick by due serch, inquisition, and due punishment; for the churches looke narrowly to their members, and the magistrats over all, more strictly then in other places. Besids, here the people are but few in comparison of other places, which are full and populous, and lye hid, as it were, in a wood or thickett, and many horrible evills by that means are never seen nor knowne; wheras hear, they are, as it were, brought into the light, and set in the plaine feeld, or rather on a hill, made conspicuous to the view of all. . . .

Increase Mather (1639–1723)

AN ARROW AGAINST PROFANE AND PROMISCUOUS DANCING

The most influential of the second generation of Puritan clergymen, Increase Mather took a B.A. at Harvard, an M.A. at Trinity College, Dublin, came to the Second Church in Boston, and was president of Harvard College from 1685 to 1701. He was sent to England by the Massachusetts government to negotiate the new charter of 1692, an exception to the usual rule that ministers did not act in governmental capacities.

He was the son of Richard Mather of the Boston area clergy, married the daughter of John Cotton, and was the father of the equally famous Cotton Mather.

This little essay on dancing reflects a later defender of orthodoxy, concerned as many of the ministers were with declining commitment to the ideals of the founders.

Concerning the Controversy about *Dancing,* the Question is not, whether all *Dancing* be in it self sinful. It is granted, that *Pyrrhical* or *Polemical Saltation:* i.e. when men vault in their Armour, to shew their strength and activity, may be of use. Nor is the question, whether a sober and grave *Dancing* of Men with Men, or of Women with Women, be not allowable; we make no doubt of that, where it may be done without offence, in due season, and with moderation. The Prince of Philosophers has observed truly, that *Dancing* or *Leaping,* is a natural expression of joy: So that there is no more Sin in it, than in laughter, or any outward expression of inward Rejoycing.

But our question is concerning *Gynecandrical Dancing,* or that which is commonly called *Mixt* or *Promiscuous Dancing,* viz. of Men and Women (be they elder or younger persons) together: Now this we affirm to be utterly unlawful, and that it cannot be tollerated in such a place as *New-England,* without great Sin. And that it may appear that we are not transported by Affection without Judgment, let the following Arguments be weighed in the Ballance of the Sanctuary.

Arg. 1. *That which the Scripture condemns is sinful.* None but Atheists will deny this *Proposition:* But the Scripture condemns

From Increase Mather, *An Arrow Against Profane and Promiscuous Dancing* . . . (Boston, 1698).

Promiscuous Dancing. This *Assumption* is proved, 1. *From the Seventh Commandment.* It is an Eternal Truth to be observed in expounding the Commandments, that whenever any sin is forbidden, not only the highest acts of that sin, but all degrees thereof, and all occasions leading thereto are prohibited. Now we cannot find one Orthodox and Judicious Divine, that writeth on the Commandments, but mentions *Promiscuous Dancing,* as a breach of the seventh Commandment, as being an occasion, and an incentive to that which is evil in the sight of God. Yea, this is so manifest as that the *Assembly* in the *larger Catechism,* do expresly take notice of *Dancings,* as a violation of the Commandments. It is sad, that when in times of Reformation, Children have been taught in their C[a]techism, that such *Dancing* is against the Commandment of God, that now in *New-England* they should practically be learned the contrary. The unchast Touches and Gesticulations used by *Dancers,* have a palpable tendency to that which is evil. Whereas some object, that they are not sensible of any ill motions occasioned in them, by being Spectators or Actors in such *Saltations;* we are not bound to believe all which some pretend concerning their own Mortification. . . .

Now they that frequent Promiscuous Dancings, or that send their Children thereunto, walk disorderly, and contrary to the Apostles Doctrine. It has been proved that such a practice is a *Scandalous Immorality,* and therefore to be removed out of Churches by Discipline, which is the Broom of Christ, whereby he keeps his Churches clean. . . .

And shall Churches in *N*[ew] *E*[*ngland*] who have had a Name to be stricter and purer than other Churches, suffer such a scandalous evil amongst them? if all that are under Discipline be made sensible of this matter, we shall not be much or long infested with a *Choreutical Dæmon.* . . .

The Catechism which Wicked men teach their Children is to Dance and to Sing. Not that Dancing, or Musick, or Singing are in themselves sinful: but if the Dancing Master be wicked they are commonly abused to lasciviousness, and that makes them to become abominable. But will you that are Professors of Religion have your Children to be thus taught? the Lord expects that you should give the Children who are Baptized into his Name another kind of Education, that you should bring them up in the nurture and admonition of the Lord: And do you not hear the Lord Expostulating the case with you, and saying, you have taken my Children, the Children that were given unto me; the Children that were solemnly engaged to renounce the Pomps of Satan; but is this a light matter that you have taken these my Children, and initiated them in the Pomps and Vanities of the Wicked one, contrary to your Covenant? What will you say in the day of the Lords pleading with you? we have that charity for you as to believe that you have erred through Ignorance, and not wickedly: and we have therefore accounted it our Duty to inform you in the Truth. If you resolve not on Reformation, you will be left inexcusable. However it shall be, we have now given our Testimony and delivered our own Souls. *Consider what we say, and the Lord give you understanding in all things.*

Poetry

Anne Bradstreet (1612–1672)
TO MY DEAR AND LOVING HUSBAND

Mrs. Bradstreet was the daughter of Thomas Dudley, who had been governor of the Massachusetts Bay Colony. She was a housewife with a large family to provide for. Her husband became a governor of the colony and served on the governor's council.

Love of life and her religious faith are reflected in her poetry. Her lines sing and her imagery indicates that pious New Englanders fully appreciated the glories of nature in the New World.

> If ever two were one, then surely we.
> If ever man were lov'd by wife, then thee;
> If ever wife was happy in a man,
> Compare with me ye women if you can.
> I prize thy love more then whole Mines of gold,
> Or all the riches that the East doth hold.
> My love is such that Rivers cannot quench,
> Nor ought but love from thee, give recompence.
> Thy love is such I can no way repay,
> The heavens reward thee manifold I pray.
> Then while we live, in love lets so persever,
> That when we live no more, we may live ever.

From Anne Bradstreet, *Several Poems Compiled . . . by a Gentlewoman . . .* (Boston, 1678).

Edward Taylor

PREFACE TO GOD'S DETERMINATIONS TOUCHING HIS ELECT
and
HUSWIFERY

Taylor came to Massachusetts as a young man, graduated from Harvard in 1671, and took up his ministry in the little village of Westfield on the western edge of the colony, where he also served as physician.

His poetry was not published. Deposited in Yale College Library by his grandson, Ezra Stiles, a president of Yale, it did not come to light until 1937.

Taylor's work indicates that a Puritan poet could express a strong religious sense while yet phrasing his thought in imagery that is colorful, worldly, even frivolous and joyful.

Preface

Infinity, when all things it beheld
In Nothing, and of Nothing all did build,
Upon what Base was fixed the Lath, wherein
He turned this Globe, and riggall'd it so trim?
Who blew the Bellows of his Furnace Vast?
Or held the Mould wherein the world was Cast?
Who laid its Corner Stone? Or whose Command?
Where stand the Pillars upon which it Stands?
Who Lac'de and fillited the earth so fine,
With Rivers like green Ribbons smaragdine?
Who made the Sea's its Selvedge and its locks
Like a Quilt Ball within a Silver Box?
Who spread its Canopy? Or Curtains spun?
Who in this Bowling Alley bowld the Sun?
Who made it always when it rises set
To go at once both down and up to get?
Who th' Curtain rods made for this Tapistry?
Who hung the twinkling Lanthorns in the sky?
Who? Who did this? or who is he? Why, *know*
It's onely Might Almighty this did doe.
His hand hath made this noble worke which stands
His Glorious Handywork not made by hands.
Who spake all things from nothing; and with ease
Can speake all things to nothing, if he please.

The *Preface* and *Huswifery* from the manuscripts of "Edward Taylor's Poetical Writings" in the Beinecke Rare Book and Manuscript Library of Yale University Library. Used by permission of the Yale University Library.

Whose little finger at his pleasure can
Out mete ten thousand worlds with halfe a span;
Whose Might Almighty can by halfe a looks
Root up the rocks and rock the hills by the roots,
Can take this mighty World up in his hande,
And shake it like a Squitchen or a Wand,
Whose single frown will make the Heavens shake
Like as an aspen leafe the Winde makes quake.
Oh, what a might is this whose single frown
Doth shake the world as it would shake it down?
Which All from Nothing fet, from Nothing All;
Has All on Nothing set, lets Nothing fall.
Gave All to nothing Man indeed whereby
Through nothing man all might him Glorify.
In Nothing is imbosst the brightest Gem
More precious than all preciousness in them.
But Nothing man did throw down all by sin,
And darkened that lightsom Gem in him.
    That now his Brightest Diamond is grown
    Darker by far than any Coalpit Stone.

Huswifery

Make mee, O Lord, thy Spinning Wheele compleat.
    Thy Holy Worde my Distaff make for mee.
Make mine Affections thy Swift Flyers neate.
    And make my Soule thy Holy Spoole to bee.
    My Conversation make to be thy Reele,
    And reele the yarn thereon spun of thy Wheele.

Make me thy Loome then, knit thereon this twine:
    And make thy Holy Spirit, Lord, winde quills.
Then weave the Web thyselfe. The yarn is fine.
    Thine ordinances make my Fulling Mills.
    Then dy the same in Heavenly Colours Choice,
    All pinkt with Varnisht Flowers of Paradise.

Then cloath therewith mine Understanding, Will,
    Affections, Judgment, Conscience, Memory
My Words and Actions, that their shine may fill
    My wayes with glory and thee glorify.
    Then mine apparell shall display before yee
    That I am Cloathed in Holy robes for glory.

Witchcraft

Thomas Brattle (1658–1713)
THE WITCHCRAFT DELUSION

A wealthy Bostonian, Brattle graduated from Harvard and served the college as treasurer for many years. He was cosmopolitan and widely traveled, with an interest in science. He helped establish the Brattle Street Church, a rival to the Mathers' Second Church and deemed by them much too liberal.

It is not surprising that he was critical of the way authorities handled the Salem outbreak, but like the Mathers, who also did not approve of the conduct of the witchcraft trials, he dared not, even as an influential townsman, speak out openly against the court. His letter, reprinted below, was privately circulated.

. . . This Salem philosophy, some men may call the new philosophy; but I think it rather deserves the name of Salem superstition and sorcery, and it is not fit to be named in a land of such light as New-England is. I think the matter might be better solved another way; but I shall not make any attempt that way, further than to say, that these afflicted children, as they are called, do hold correspondence with the devil even in the esteem and account of the S[alem] G[entlemen]; for when the black man, i.e. say these gentlemen, the devil, does appear to them, they ask him many questions, and accordingly give information to the inquirer; and if this is not holding correspondence with the devil, and something worse, I know not what is.

But furthermore, I would fain know of these Salem justices what need there is of further proof and evidence to convict and condemn these apprehended persons, than this look and touch, if so be they are so certain that this falling down and arising up, when there is a look and a touch, are natural effects of the said look and touch, and so a perfect demonstration and proof of witchcraft in those persons. What can the jury or judges desire more, to convict any man of witchcraft, than a plain demonstration, that the said man is a witch?

From *Collections of the Massachusetts Historical Society*, series I, V, 61 (Boston, 1798).

Now if this look and touch, circumstanced as before, be a plain demonstration, as their philosophy teaches, what need they seek for further evidences, when, after all, it can be but a demonstration? But let this pass with the S. G. for never so plain and natural a demonstration; yet certain is it, that the reasonable part of the world, when acquainted herewith, will laugh at the demonstration, and conclude that the said S. G. are actually possessed, at least, with ignorance and folly.

I most admire that Mr. N[icholas] N[oyes] the Reverend Teacher at Salem, who was educated at the school of knowledge, and is certainly a learned, a charitable, and a good man, though all the devils in Hell, and all the possessed girls in Salem, should say to the contrary; at him, I say, I do most admire; that he should cry up the above mentioned philosophy after the manner that he does. I can assure you, that I can bring you more than two, or twice two, (very credible persons), that will affirm, that they have heard him vindicate the above mentioned demonstration as very reasonable.

Secondly, with respect to the confessors, as they are improperly called, or such as confess themselves to be witches, (the second thing you inquire into in your letter), there are now about fifty of them in prison; many of which I have again and again seen and heard; and I cannot but tell you, that my faith is strong concerning them, that they are deluded, imposed upon, and under the influence of some evil spirit; and therefore unfit to be evidences either against themselves, or any one else. . . .

The great cry of many of our neighbours now is, What, will you not believe the confessors? Will you not believe men and women who confess that they have signed to the devil's book? that they were baptized by the devil; and that they were at the mock-sacrament once and again? What! will you not believe that this is witchcraft, and that such and such men are witches, although the confessors do own and assert it?

Thus, I say, many of our good neighbours do argue; but methinks they might soon be convinced that there is nothing at all in all these their arguings, if they would but duly consider of the premises. . . .

Now for the proof of the said sorcery and witchcraft, the prisoner at the bar pleading not guilty.

1. The afflicted persons are brought into court; and after much patience and pains taken with them, do take their oaths, that the

prisoner at the bar did afflict them: And here I think it very observable, that often, when the afflicted do mean and intend only the appearance and shape of such an one, (say G. Proctor), yet they positively swear that G. Proctor did afflict them; and they have been allowed so to do; as though there was no real difference between G. Proctor and the shape of G. Proctor. This, methinks, may readily prove a stumbling block to the jury, lead them into a very fundamental error, and occasion innocent blood, yea the innocentest blood imaginable, to be in great danger. Whom it belongs unto, to be eyes unto the blind, and to remove such stumbling blocks, I know full well; and yet you, and every one else, do know as well as I who do not.

2. The confessors do declare what they know of the said prisoner; and some of the confessors are allowed to give their oaths; a thing which I believe was never heard of in this world; that such as confess themselves to be witches, to have renounced God and Christ, and all that is sacred, should yet be allowed and ordered to swear by the name of the great God! This indeed seemeth to me to be a gross taking of God's name in vain. I know the S. G. do say, that there is hope that the said confessors have repented: I shall only say, that if they have repented, it is well for themselves; but if they have not, it is very ill for you know who. But then,

3. Whoever can be an evidence against the prisoner at the bar is ordered to come into court; and here it scarce ever fails but that evidences, of one nature and another, are brought in, though, I think, all of them altogether alien to the matter of indictment; for they none of them do respect witchcraft upon the bodies of the afflicted, which is the alone matter of charge in the indictment.

4. They are searched by a jury; and as to some of them, the jury brought in, that on such or such a place there was a preternatural excrescence. And I wonder what person there is, whether man or woman, of whom it cannot be said but that, in some part of their body or other, there is a preternatural excrescence. The term is a very general and inclusive term.

Some of the S. G. are very forward to censure and condemn the poor prisoner at the bar, because he sheds no tears; but such betray great ignorance in the nature of passion, and as great heedlessness as to common passages of a man's life. Some there are who never shed tears; others there are that ordinarily shed tears upon light occasions, and yet for their lives cannot shed a tear when the deepest sorrow is upon their hearts; and who is there that knows not these things? Who knows not that an ecstacy of joy will sometimes fetch tears, when as the quite contrary passion will shut them close up? Why then should any be so silly and foolish as to take an argument from this appearance? But this is by the by. In short, the prisoner at the bar is indicted for sorcery and witchcraft acted upon the bodies of the afflicted. Now, for the proof of this, I reckon that the only pertinent evidences brought in are the evidences of the said afflicted.

. . . I cannot but admire that the justices, whom I think to be well-meaning men, should so far give ear to the devil, as merely upon his authority to issue out their warrants, and apprehend people. Liberty was evermore accounted the great privilege of an Englishman; but certainly, if the devil will be heard against us, and his testimony taken, to the seizing and apprehending of us, our liberty vanishes, and we are fools if we boast of our liberty. Now, that the justices have thus far given ear to the devil, I think may be mathematically demonstrated to any man of common sense: And for the demonstration and proof hereof, I desire, only, that these two things may be duly considered, viz.

1. That several persons have been apprehended purely upon the complaints of these afflicted, to whom the afflicted were perfect strangers, and had not the least knowledge of imaginable, before they were apprehended.

2. That the afflicted do own and assert, and the justices do grant, that the devil does inform and tell the afflicted the names of those persons that are thus unknown unto them. Now these two things being duly considered, I think it will appear evident to any one, that the devil's information is the fundamental testimony that is gone upon in the apprehending of the aforesaid people.

If I believe such or such an assertion as comes immediately from the minister of God in the pulpit, because it is the word of the ever-living God, I build my faith on God's testimony: and if I practise upon it, this my practice is properly built on the word of God: even so in the case before us.

If I believe the afflicted persons as informed by the devil, and act thereupon, this my act may properly be said to be grounded upon the testimony or information of the devil. And now, if things are thus,

I think it ought to be for a lamentation to you and me, and all such as would be accounted good christians. . . .

What will be the issue of these troubles, God only knows; I am afraid that ages will not wear off that reproach and those stains which these things will leave behind them upon our land. I pray God pity us, humble us, forgive us, and appear mercifully for us in this our mount of distress: herewith I conclude, and subscribe myself,

Reverend sir, your real friend and humble servant,

T. B.

II THE NATURE OF PURITANISM: THEOLOGY AND GOVERNMENT

FIGURE 2. Portrait of John Winthrop. (Courtesy, American Antiquarian Society)

Perry Miller

THE PURITAN WAY OF LIFE

Perry Miller (1905–1963) devoted his scholarly career at Harvard University to a sympathetic study of the ideas expressed in the writings of the leaders, both civil and church, in Massachusetts Bay and Connecticut. The selections here are drawn from some of his comprehensive writings on the religious, political, and social convictions of these leaders. Although criticized by later scholars as portraying too intellectualized, static, and American-centered a society, he often offers hints at variance with his own generalizations, tending to concede to criticisms developed by later writers.

Miller believes that New England society and its political structure rested on a uniform set of religious ideas. Though admittedly these ideas formed the basis for theocratic rule and religious orthodoxy, he considers that the vast majority of New Englanders consented to this oligarchy because of their dedication to a common ideal.

In the first excerpts that follow, the general characteristics of American Puritanism as Miller understands them are sketched, with particular attention to the relations between state and society.

A second selection deals with the crucial but rather technical subject of the covenant of grace, the "federal theology" that Miller saw as the heart of Puritan belief.

The Puritan in His Age

Puritanism may perhaps best be described as that point of view, that philosophy of life, that code of values, which was carried to New England by the first settlers in the early seventeenth century. Beginning thus, it has become one of the continuous factors in American life and American thought. Any inventory of the elements that have gone into the making of the "American mind" would have to commence with Puritanism. It is, indeed, only one among many: if we should attempt to enumerate these traditions, we should certainly have to mention such philosophies, such "isms," as the rational liberalism of Jeffersonian democracy, the Hamiltonian conception of conservatism and government, the Southern theory of racial aristocracy, the Transcendentalism of nineteenth-century New England, and what is generally spoken of as frontier individualism. Among

From *The Puritans: A Sourcebook of Their Writings*, ed. Perry Miller and Thomas H. Johnson (New York: Harper and Row, 1938). Reprinted by permission of the publisher.

these factors Puritanism has been perhaps the most conspicuous, the most sustained, and the most fecund. Its role in American thought has been almost the dominant one, for the descendants of Puritans have carried at least some habits of the Puritan mind into a variety of pursuits, have spread across the country, and in many fields of activity have played a leading part. The force of Puritanism, furthermore, has been accentuated because it was the first of these traditions to be fully articulated, and because it has inspired certain traits which have persisted long after the vanishing of the original creed. Without some understanding of Puritanism, it may safely be said, there is no understanding of America.

Yet important as Puritanism has undoubtedly been in shaping the nation, it is more easily described than defined. It figures frequently in controversy of the last decade, very seldom twice with exactly the same connotation. Particularly of recent years has it become a hazardous feat to run down its meaning. In the mood of revolt against the ideals of previous generations which has swept over our period, Puritanism has become a shining target for many sorts of marksmen. Confusion becomes worse confounded if we attempt to correlate modern usages with anything that can be proved pertinent to the original Puritans themselves. To seek no further, it was the habit of proponents for the repeal of the Eighteenth Amendment during the 1920s to dub Prohibitionists "Puritans," and cartoonists made the nation familiar with an image of the Puritan: a gaunt, lank-haired killjoy, wearing a black steeple hat and compounding for sins he was inclined to by damning those to which he had no mind. Yet any acquaintance with the Puritans of the seventeenth century will reveal at once, not only that they did not wear such hats, but also that they attired themselves in all the hues of the rainbow, and furthermore that in their daily life they imbibed what seem to us prodigious quantities of alcoholic beverages, with never the slightest inkling that they were doing anything sinful. True, they opposed drinking to excess, and ministers preached lengthy sermons condemning intoxication, but at such pious ceremonies as the ordination of new ministers the bill for rum, wine, and beer consumed by the congregation was often staggering. Increase Mather himself—who in popular imagination is apt to figure along with his son Cotton as the arch-embodiment of the Puritan—said in one of his sermons:

Drink is in itself a good creature of God, and to be received with thankfulness, but the abuse of drink is from Satan; the wine is from God, but the Drunkard is from the Devil.

Or again, the Puritan has acquired the reputation of having been blind to all aesthetic enjoyment and starved of beauty; yet the architecture of the Puritan age grows in the esteem of critics and the household objects of Puritan manufacture, pewter and furniture, achieve prohibitive prices by their appeal to discriminating collectors. Examples of such discrepancies between the modern usage of the word and the historical fact could be multiplied indefinitely. It is not the purpose of this volume to engage in controversy, nor does it intend particularly to defend the Puritan against the bewildering variety of critics who on every side today find him an object of scorn or pity. In his life he neither asked nor gave mercy to his foes; he demanded only that conflicts be joined on real and explicit issues. By examining his own words it may become possible to establish, for better or for worse, the meaning of Puritanism as the Puritan himself believed and practiced it.

Just as soon as we endeavor to free ourselves from prevailing conceptions or misconceptions, and to ascertain the historical facts about seventeenth-century New Englanders, we become aware that we face still another difficulty: not only must we extricate ourselves from interpretations that have been read into Puritanism by the twentieth century, but still more from those that have been attached to it by the eighteenth and nineteenth. The Puritan philosophy, brought to New England highly elaborated and codified, remained a fairly rigid orthodoxy during the seventeenth century. In the next age, however, it proved to be anything but static; by the middle of the eighteenth century there had proceeded from it two distinct schools of thought, almost unalterably opposed to each other. Certain elements were carried into the creeds and practices of the evangelical religious revivals, but others were perpetuated by the rationalists and the forerunners of Unitarianism. Consequently our conception of Puritanism is all too apt to be colored by subsequent happenings; we read ideas into the seventeenth century which belong to the eighteenth, and the real nature of Puritanism can hardly be discovered at all, because Puritanism itself became two distinct and contending things to two sorts of men. The most prevalent error arising from this fact has been the identification of Puritanism with evangelicalism in many accounts, though in histories written by Unitarian scholars the original doctrine has been almost as much distorted in the opposite direction.

Among the evangelicals the original doctrines were transformed or twisted into the new versions of Protestantism that spawned in the Great Awakening of the 1740s, in the succeeding revivals along the frontier and through the back country, in the centrifugal speculations of enraptured prophets and rabid sects in the nineteenth century. All these movements retained something of the theology or revived something of the intensity of spirit, but at the same time they threw aside so much of authentic Puritanism that there can be no doubt the founding fathers would vigorously have repudiated such progeny. They would have had no use, for instance, for the camp meeting and the revivalist orgy; "hitting the sawdust trail" would have been an action exceedingly distasteful to the most ardent among them. What we know as "fundamentalism" would have been completely antipathetic to them, for they never for one moment dreamed that the truth of scripture was to be maintained in spite of or against the evidences of reason, science, and learning. The sects that have arisen out of Puritanism have most strikingly betrayed their rebellion against the true spirit of their source by their attack upon the ideal of a learned ministry; Puritans considered religion a very complex, subtle, and highly intellectualized affair, and they trained their experts in theology with all the care we would lavish upon preparing men to be engineers or chemists. For the same reasons, Puritans would object strenuously to almost all recent attempts to "humanize" religion, to smooth over hard doctrines, to introduce sweetness and light at the cost of hardheaded realism and invincible logic. From their point of view, to bring Christ down to earth in such a fashion as is implied in statements we sometimes encounter—that He was the "first humanitarian" or that He would certainly endorse this or that political party—would seem to them frightful blasphemy. Puritanism was not only a religious creed, it was a philosophy and a metaphysic; it was an organization of man's whole life, emotional and intellectual, to a degree which has not been sustained by any denomination stemming from it. Yet because such creeds have sprung from Puritanism, the Puritans are frequently praised or blamed for qualities which never belonged to them or for ideas which originated only among their successors and which they themselves would have disowned.

On the other hand, if the line of development from Puritanism tends in one direction to frontier revivalism and evangelicalism, another line leads as directly to a more philosophical, critical, and even skeptical point of view. Unitarianism is as much the child of Puritanism as Methodism. And if the one accretion has colored or distorted our conception of the original doctrine, the other has done so no less. Descendants of the Puritans who revolted against what they considered the tyranny and cruelty of Puritan theology, who substituted taste and reason for dogma and authority and found the emotional fervor of the evangelicals so much sound and fury, have been prone to idealize their ancestors into their own image. A few decades ago it had become very much the mode to praise the Puritans for virtues which they did not possess and which they would not have considered virtues at all. In the pages of liberal historians, and above all in the speeches of Fourth of July orators, the Puritans have been hymned as the pioneers of religious liberty, though nothing was ever farther from their designs; they have been hailed as the forerunners of democracy, though if they were, it was quite beside their intention; they have been invoked in justification for an economic philosophy of free competition and laissez-faire, though they themselves believed in government regulation of business, the fixing of just prices, and the curtailing of individual profits in the interests of the welfare of the whole.

The moral of these reflections may very well be that it is dangerous to read history backwards, to interpret something that was by what it ultimately became, particularly when it became several things. . . .

The Puritans were not a bashful race, they could speak out and did; in their own words they have painted their own portraits, their majestic strength and their dignity, their humanity and solidity, more accurately than any admirer has been able to do; and also they have betrayed the motes and beams in their own eyes more clearly than any enemy has been able to point them out.

The Spirit of the Age

Puritanism began as an agitation within the Church of England
in the latter half of the sixteenth century. It was a movement for
reform of that institution, and at the time no more constituted a
distinct sect or denomination than the advocates of an amendment
to the Constitution of the United States constitute a separate nation. In the 1530s the Church of England broke with the Pope of
Rome. By the beginning of Elizabeth's reign it had proceeded a
certain distance in this revolt, had become Protestant, had dises-
tablished the monasteries and corrected many abuses. Puritanism
was the belief that the reform should be continued, that more
abuses remained to be corrected, that practices still survived from
the days of Popery which should be renounced, that the Church
of England should be restored to the "purity" of the first-century
Church as established by Christ Himself. In the 1560s, when the
advocates of purification first acquired the name of Puritans, no
one, not even the most radical, knew exactly how far the process
was to go or just what the ultimate goal would be; down to the
days of Cromwell there was never any agreement on this point,
and in the end this failure of unanimity proved the undoing of
English Puritanism. Many Puritans desired only that certain ceremonies be abolished or changed. Others wanted ministers to preach
more sermons, make up their own prayers on the inspiration of
the moment rather than read set forms out of a book. Others went
further and proposed a revision of the whole form of ecclesiastical
government. But whatever the shade or complexion of their Puritanism, Puritans were those who wanted to continue a movement
which was already under way. Their opponents, whom we shall
speak of as the Anglicans—though only for the sake of conve-
nience, because there was at that time not the remotest thought
on either side of an ultimate separation into distinct churches, and
Puritans insisted they were as stoutly loyal to the established institution as any men in England—the Anglicans were those who
felt that with the enthronement of Elizabeth and with the "Elizabethan Settlement" of the Church, things had gone far enough. They
wanted to call a halt, just where they were, and stabilize at that
point.

Thus the issue between the two views, though large enough, still involved only a limited number of questions. On everything except matters upon which the Puritans wanted further reformation, there was essential agreement. The Puritans who settled New England were among the more radical—though by no means the most radical that the movement produced—and even before their migration in 1630 had gone to the lengths of formulating a concrete platform of church organization which they wished to see instituted in England in place of the episcopal system. Joining battle on this front gave a sufficiently extended line and provided a vast number of salients to fight over; the gulf between the belief of these Puritans and the majority in the Church of England grew so wide that at last there was no bridging it at all. But notwithstanding the depth of this divergence, the fact still remains that only certain specific questions were raised. If we take a comprehensive survey of the whole body of Puritan thought and belief as it existed in 1630 or 1640, if we make an exhaustive enumeration of ideas held by New England Puritans, we shall find that the vast majority of them were precisely those of their opponents. In other words, Puritanism was a movement toward certain ends within the culture and state of England in the late sixteenth and early seventeenth centuries; it centered about a number of concrete problems and advocated a particular program. Outside of that, it was part and parcel of the times, and its culture was simply the culture of England at that moment. It is necessary to belabor the point, because most accounts of Puritanism, emphasizing the controversial tenets, attribute everything that Puritans said or did to the fact that they were Puritans; their attitudes toward all sorts of things are pounced upon and exhibited as peculiarities of their sect, when as a matter of fact they were normal attitudes for the time. Of course, the Puritans acquired their special quality and their essential individuality from their stand on the points actually at issue, and our final conception of Puritanism must give these concerns all due importance. Yet if first of all we wish to take Puritan culture as a whole, we shall find, let us say, that about 90 percent of the intellectual life, scientific knowledge, morality, manners and customs, notions and prejudices, was that of all Englishmen. The other 10 percent, the relatively small number of ideas upon which there was dispute, made all the difference between the Puritan and his fellow-Englishmen, made for him so much difference that he pulled up stakes in England, which he loved, and migrated to a wilderness rather than submit them to apparent defeat. Nevertheless, when we come to trace developments and influences on subsequent American history and thought, we shall find that the starting point of many ideas and practices is as apt to be found among the 90 percent as among the 10. The task of defining Puritanism and giving an account of its culture resolves itself, therefore, into isolating first of all the larger features which were not particularly or necessarily Puritan at all, the elements in the life and society which were products of the time and place, of the background of English life and society rather than of the individual belief or peculiar creed of Puritanism.

Many of the major interests and preoccupations of the New England Puritans belong to this list. They were just as patriotic as Englishmen who remained at home. They hated Spain like poison, and France only a little less. In their eyes, as in those of Anglicans, the most important issue in the Western world was the struggle between Catholicism and Protestantism. They were not unique or extreme in thinking that religion was the primary and all-engrossing business of man, or that all human thought and action should tend to the glory of God. . . .

In its major aspects the religious creed of Puritanism was neither peculiar to the Puritans nor different from that of the Anglicans. Both were essentially Protestant; both asserted that men were saved by their faith, not by their deeds. The two sides could agree on the general statement that Christians are bound to believe nothing but what the Gospel teaches, that all traditions of men "contrary to the Word of God" are to be renounced and abhorred. They both believed that the marks of a true church were profession of the creed, use of Christ's sacraments, preaching of the word—Anglican sermons being as long and often as dull as the Puritan—and the union of men in profession and practice under regularly constituted pastors. The Puritans always said that they could subscribe the doctrinal articles of the Church of England; even at the height of the controversy, even after they had left England rather than put up with what they considered its abominations, they always took care to insist that the Church of England was a "true" church, not Anti-Christ as was the Church of Rome, that it contained many saints, and that men might find salvation within it. Throughout the seventeenth century they read Anglican authors, quoted them in their sermons, and even reprinted some of them in Boston.

The vast substratum of agreement which actually underlay the disagreement between Puritans and Anglicans is explained by the fact that they were both the heirs of the Middle Ages. They still believed that all knowledge was one, that life was unified, that science, economics, political theory, aesthetic standards, rhetoric and art, all were organized in a hierarchical scale of values that tended upward to the end-all and be-all of creation, the glory of God. They both insisted that all human activity be regulated by that purpose. Consequently, even while fighting bitterly against each other, the Puritans and Anglicans stood shoulder to shoulder against what they called "enthusiasm." The leaders of the Puritan movement were trained at the universities, they were men of learning and scholars; no less than the Anglicans did they demand that religion be interpreted by study and logical exposition; they were both resolute against all pretences to immediate revelation, against all ignorant men who claimed to receive personal instructions from God. They agreed on the essential Christian contention that though God may govern the world, He is not the world itself, and that though He instills His grace into men, He does not deify them or unite them to Himself in one personality. He converses with men only through His revealed word, the Bible. His will is to be studied in the operation of His providence as exhibited in the workings of the natural world, but He delivers no new commands or special revelations to the inward consciousness of men. The larger unanimity of the Puritans and the Anglicans reveals itself whenever either of them was called upon to confront enthusiasm, . . . [as in] Governor John Winthrop's account of the so-called Antinomian affair, the crisis produced in the little colony by the teachings of Mistress Anne Hutchinson in 1636 and 1637. Beneath the theological jargon in which the opinions of this lady appear we can see the substance of her contention, which was that she was in direct communication with the God-head, and that she therefore was prepared to follow the promptings of the voice within against all the precepts of the Bible, the churches, reason, or the government of Massachusetts Bay. Winthrop relates how the magistrates and the ministers defended the community against this perversion of the doctrine of regeneration, but the tenor of his condemnation would have been duplicated practically word for word had Anne Hutchinson broached her theories in an Anglican community. The Anglicans fell in completely with the Puritans when both of them were confronted in the 1650s by the Quakers. All New England leaders saw in the Quaker doctrine of an inner light, accessible to all men and giving a perfect communication from God to their inmost spirits, just another form of Anne Hutchinson's blasphemy. John Norton declared that the "light of nature" itself taught us that "madmen acting according to their frantick passions are to be restrained with chaines, when they can not be restrained otherwise." About the same time George Hickes, Dean of Worcester, was advocating that Quakers be treated likewise in England, and he ended a sermon upon them by calling them "Imposters, or enthusiasts, and Blasphemers of the Holy Ghoast." Enthusiasts, whether Antinomian or Quaker, were proposing doctrines that threatened the unity of life by subduing the reason and the intellect to the passions and the emotions. Whatever their differences, Puritans and Anglicans were struggling to maintain a complete harmony of reason and faith, science and religion, earthly dominion and the government of God. When we immerse ourselves in the actual struggle, the difference between the Puritan and the Anglican may seem to us immense; but when we take the vantage point of subsequent history, and survey religious thought as a whole over the last three centuries, the two come very close together on essentials. Against all forms of chaotic emotionalism, against all over-simplifications of theology, learning, philosophy, and science, against all materialism, positivism or mechanism, both were endeavoring to uphold a symmetrical union of heart and head without impairment of either. By the beginning or middle of the next century their successors, both in England and America, found themselves no longer capable of sustaining this unity, and it has yet to be re-achieved today, if achieved again it ever can be. The greatness of the Puritans is not so much that they conquered a wilderness, or that they carried a religion into it, but that they carried a religion which, narrow and starved though it may have been in some respects, deficient in sensuous richness or brilliant color, was nevertheless indissolubly bound up with an ideal of culture and learning. In contrast to all other pioneers, they made no concessions to the forest, but in the midst of frontier conditions, in the very throes of clearing the land and erecting shelters, they maintained schools and a college, a standard of scholarship and of competent writing, a class of men devoted entirely to the life of the mind and of the soul. . . .

The wonder is that by and large the populace did yield their judgments to those who were supposed to know, respected learning and supported it, sat patiently during two- and three-hour sermons while ministers expounded the knottiest and most recondite of metaphysical texts. The testimony of visitors, travelers, and memoirs agrees that during the Puritan age in New England the common man, the farmer and merchant, was amazingly versed in systematic divinity. A gathering of yeomen and "hired help" around the kitchen fire of an evening produced long and unbelievably technical discussions of predestination, infant damnation, and the distinctions between faith and works. In the first half of the seventeenth century the people had not yet questioned the conception of religion as a difficult art in which the authority of the skilled dialectician should prevail over the inclinations of the merely devout. This ideal of subjection to qualified leadership was social as well as intellectual. Very few Englishmen had yet broached the notion that a lackey was as good as a lord, or that any Tom, Dick, or Harry, simply because he was a good, honest man, could understand the Sermon on the Mount as well as a Master of Arts from Oxford, Cambridge, or Harvard. Professor Morison has shown that the life of the college in New England was saved by the sacrifice of the yeomen farmers, who contributed their pecks of wheat, wrung from a stony soil, taken from their none too opulent stores, to support teaching fellows and to assist poor scholars at Harvard College, in order that they and their children might still sit under a literate ministry "when our present Ministers shall lie in the Dust."

. . . Though Protestantism can be viewed as a "liberation" of the common man, it was far from being a complete emancipation of the individual. It freed him from many intellectual restraints that had been imposed by the Church, but it did not give him full liberty to think anything he pleased; socially it freed him from many exactions, but it did not permit him to abandon his traditional subjection to his social and ecclesiastical superiors. The original settlers of New England carried this Protestantism intact from Europe to America. Except for the small band that was driven into exile with Anne

Hutchinson, and one or two other groups of visionaries who also were hustled across the borders into Rhode Island, the rank and file did follow their leaders, meekly and reverently. . . . The New England "theocracy" was simply a Protestant version of the European social ideal, and except for its Protestantism was thoroughly medieval in character.

*   *   *

Estimations

The Puritan attitude toward the Bible, to the extent that it was a preservation of intellectual values within the dogmatism, may elicit our hearty approbation. But when we come to the content of the dogma, to what the Puritan insisted the Bible did teach, and to what he expected the regenerate man to find reasonable, in short, when we come to Puritan theology, many persons encounter an insuperable stumbling block to an unqualified approval of Puritan thinking. Not only does the conventional picture of the Puritan creed seem exceedingly unattractive to twentieth-century taste, but the idea of theology in any form is almost equally objectionable. In most secondary accounts Puritans are called Calvinists, and then and there discussion of their intellectual life ceases. Dr. Holmes's "One-Hoss Shay" is deemed a sufficient description.

It is true, the Puritans were Calvinists, if we mean that they more or less agreed with the great theologian of Geneva. They held, that is, that men had fallen into a state of sin, that in order to be saved they must receive from God a special infusion of grace, that God gives the grace to some and not to others out of His own sovereign pleasure, and that therefore from the beginning of time certain souls were "predestined" to heaven and the others sentenced to damnation. But if the New Englanders were Calvinists, it was because they happened to agree with Calvin; they approved his doctrine not because he taught it, but because it seemed inescapably indicated when they studied scripture or observed the actions of men. The sinfulness of the average man was a fact that could be empirically verified, and in itself demonstrated that he needed divine grace in order to be lifted above himself; the men who did receive what they thought was an influx of grace learned by experience that only in such an ecstasy of illumination did truth become thoroughly evident and completely understandable. Obviously the experience was given to relatively few men; therefore God, who is outside time and who is omniscient, must have known from the beginning of time who would and who would not achieve it. This is the law of life; some men are born rich and some poor, some intelligent and some stupid, some are lucky and others unfortunate, some are happy and some melancholy, some are saved and some are not. There is no reason but that God so ordained it.

> The Lord to shew the soveraign freedom of his pleasure, that he may do with his own what he wil, and yet do wrong to none, he denyes pardon and acceptance to those who seek it with some importunity and earnestness . . . and yet bestowes mercy and makes known himself unto some who never sought him.

Puritan theology, therefore, is simply a statement in dogmatic guise of a philosophy of life, wherein it is held on the one hand that men must act by reason and abide by justice, and strive for an inward communication with the force that controls the world, but on the other hand that they must not expect that force always to be cribbed and confined by their conceptions of what is reasonable and just. There is an eternal obligation upon men to be equitable, fair, and good, but who can say that any such morality is also binding on the universe? There are certain amenities which men must observe in their dealings with men, but who can say that they must also be respected by the tiger, by the raging storm, by the lightning, or by the cancer? It is only when the theology of "predestination" is seen in these less technical terms that its vitality as a living faith and its strength as a sustaining philosophy become comprehensible.

But the theology of New England was not simply Calvinism, it was not a mere reduplication of the dogmas of the *Institutes*. What New Englanders believed was an outgrowth, as we have seen, of their background, which was humanistic and English, and it was conditioned by their particular controversy with the Church of England. Simon-pure Calvinism is a much more dogmatic, antirational creed than that of the Congregational parsons in Massachusetts. The emigrants went to New England to prove that a state and a church erected on the principles for which they were agitating in England would be blessed by God and prosper. The source of the New England ideology is not Calvin, but England, or more accurately, the Bible as it was read in England, not in Geneva.

Though, of course, the controversy in England was a political, social, and economic one, it was also the intellectual dispute we have outlined. We might summarize it at this point by saying that in order to harmonize reason, and scripture, the Anglican endeavored to reduce the doctrines imposed by scripture to the barest minimum; the Puritan extended scripture to cover the whole of existence and then set himself to prove the content of all scripture essentially reasonable. Only with this definition of origins and tendencies in mind can we read Puritan theology aright. In order to demonstrate that the content of scripture was comprehensible to reason, the Puritan theorists worked out a substantial addition to the theology of Calvinism which in New England was quite as important as the original doctrine. This addition or elaboration of the Calvinist doctrine is generally called the "Covenant theology" or the "federal theology." There is no necessity here for examining it in detail. It was a special way of reading scripture so that the books assembled in the Bible could all be seen to make sense in the same way. The doctrine held that after the fall of man, God voluntarily condescended to treat with man as with an equal and to draw up a covenant or contract with His creature in which He laid down the terms and conditions of salvation, and pledged Himself to abide by them. The covenant did not alter the fact that those only are saved upon whom God sheds His grace, but it made very clear and reasonable how and why certain men are selected, and prescribed the conditions under which they might reach a fair assurance of their own standing. Above all, in the covenant God pledged Himself not to run athwart human conceptions of right and justice. . . .

There was nothing lukewarm, halfhearted, or flabby about the Puritan; whatever he did, he did with zest and gusto. In that sense we might say that though his life was full of anguish of spirit, he nevertheless enjoyed it hugely. Existence for him was completely dramatic, every minute was charged with meaning. And when we come to an end of this roll call of characteristics, the one which yet remains the most difficult to evoke was his peculiar balance of zeal and enthusiasm with control and wariness. In his inner life he was overwhelmingly preoccupied with achieving a union with the divine; in his external life he was predominantly concerned with self-restraint. . . . No wonder the Puritan has been something of a puzzlement and a trial to the Gentiles. He was a visionary who never forgot that two plus two equals four; he was a soldier of Jehovah who never came out on the losing side of a bargain. He was a radical and a revolutionary, but not an anarchist; when he got into power he ruled with an iron hand, and also according to a fundamental law. He was a practical idealist with a strong dash of cynicism; he came to New England to found the perfect society and the kingdom of the elect— and never expected it to be perfect, but only the best that fallible men could make. His creed was the revealed word of God and his life was the rule of moderation; his beliefs were handed down from on high and his conduct was regulated by expediency. He was a doctrinaire and an opportunist. Truth for him had been written down once and for all in a definitive, immutable, complete volume, and the covers closed to any further additions; thereupon he devoted all the energies he could spare from more immediate tasks to scholarship and interpretation. He lived in the world according to the principles that must govern this world, with an ever-present sense that they were only for the time being and that his true home was elsewhere. . . .

*   *   *

There was a strong element of individualism in the Puritan creed; every man had to work out his own salvation, each soul had to face his maker alone. But at the same time, the Puritan philosophy demanded that in society all men, at least all regenerate men, be marshaled into one united array. The lone horseman, the single trapper, the solitary hunter was not a figure of the Puritan frontier; Puritans moved in groups and towns, settled in whole communities, and maintained firm government over all units. Neither was the individualistic business man, the shopkeeper who seized every opportunity to enlarge his profits, the speculator who contrived to gain wealth at the expense of his fellows, neither were these typical figures of the original Puritan society. . . . Puritan opinion was at the opposite pole from Jefferson's feeling that the best government governs as little as possible. The theorists of New England thought of society as a unit, bound together by inviolable ties; they thought of it not as an aggregation of individuals but as an organism, functioning for a definite purpose, with all parts subordinate to the whole, all members contributing a definite share, every person occupying a particular status. "Society in all sorts of humane affaires is better than Solitariness," said John Cotton. The society of early New England was decidedly "regimented." Puritans did not think the state was merely an umpire, standing on the side lines of a contest, limited to checking egregious fouls, but otherwise allowing men free play according to their abilities and the breaks of the game. They would have expected the rule of "laissez-faire" to result in a reign of rapine and horror. The state to them was an active instrument of leadership, discipline, and, wherever necessary, of coercion; it legislated over any or all aspects of human behavior, it not merely regulated misconduct but undertook to inspire and direct all conduct. The commanders were not to trim their policies by the desires of the people, but to drive ahead upon the predetermined course; the people were all to turn out as they were ordered, and together they were to crowd sail to the full capacity of the vessel. The officers were above the common men, as the quarter-deck is above the forecastle. There was no idea of the equality of all men. There was no questioning that men who would not serve the purposes of the society should be whipped into line. The objectives were clear and unmistakable; any one's disinclination to dedicate himself to them was obviously so much recalcitrancy and depravity. The government of Massachusetts, and of Connecticut as well, was a dictatorship, and never pretended to be anything else; it was a dictatorship, not of a single tyrant, or of an economic class, or of a political faction, but of the holy and regenerate. Those who did not hold with the ideals entertained by the righteous, or who believed God had preached other principles, or who desired that in religious belief, morality, and ecclesiastical preferences all men should be left at liberty to do as they wished—such persons had every liberty, as Nathaniel Ward said, to stay away from New England. If they did come, they were expected to keep their opinions to themselves; if they discussed them in public or attempted to act upon them, they were exiled; if they persisted in returning, they were cast out again; if they still came back, as did four Quakers, they were hanged on Boston Common. And from the Puritan point of view, it was good riddance.

These views of the nature and function of the state were not peculiar to the Puritans of New England; they were the heritage of the past, the ideals, if not always the actuality, of the previous centuries. That government was established by God in order to save depraved men from their own depravity had been orthodox Christian teaching for centuries; that men should be arranged in serried ranks, inferiors obeying superiors, was the essence of feudalism; that men should live a social life, that profit-making should be restrained within the limits of the "just price," that the welfare of the whole took precedence over any individual advantage, was the doctrine of the medieval church, and of the Church of England in the early seventeenth century. Furthermore, in addition to these general principles, there were two or three more doctrines in the New England philosophy which also were common to the age and the background. All the world at that moment believed with them that the church was to be maintained and protected by the civil authority, and a certain part of the world was contending that government was limited by fundamental law and that it took its origin from the consent of the people.

Every respectable state in the Western world assumed that it could allow only one church to exist within its borders, that every citizen should be compelled to attend it and conform to its requirements, and that all inhabitants should pay taxes for its support. When the Puritans came to New England the idea had not yet dawned that a government could safely permit several creeds to exist side by side within the confines of a single nation. They had not been fighting in England for any milk-and-water toleration, and had they been offered such religious freedom as dissenters now enjoy in Great Britain they would have scorned to accept such terms. Only a hypocrite, a person who did not really believe what he professed, would be content to practice his religion under such conditions. The Puritans were assured that they alone knew the exact truth, as it was contained in the written word of God, and they were fighting to enthrone it in England and to extirpate utterly and mercilessly all other pretended versions of Christianity. When they could not succeed at home, they came to America, where they could establish a society in which the one and only truth should reign forever. There is nothing so idle as to praise the Puritans for being in any sense conscious or deliberate pioneers of religious liberty—unless, indeed, it is still more idle to berate them because in America they persecuted dissenters from their beliefs after they themselves had undergone persecution for differing with the bishops. To allow no dissent from the truth was exactly the reason they had come to America. They maintained here precisely what they had maintained in England, and if they exiled, fined, jailed, whipped, or hanged those who disagreed with them in New England, they would have done the same thing in England could they have secured the power. It is almost pathetic to trace the puzzlement of New England leaders at the end of the seventeenth century, when the idea of toleration was becoming more and more respectable in European thought. They could hardly understand what was happening in the world, and they could not for a long time be persuaded that they had any reason to be ashamed of their record of so many Quakers whipped, blasphemers punished by the amputation of ears, Antinomians exiled, Anabaptists fined, or witches executed. By all the lights which had prevailed in Europe at the time the Puritans had left, these were achievements to which any government could point with pride. In 1681 a congregation of Anabaptists, who led a stormy and precarious existence for several years in Charlestown, published an attack upon the government of Massachusetts Bay; they justified themselves by appealing to the example of the first settlers, claiming that like themselves the founders had been nonconformists and had fled to New England to establish a refuge for persecuted consciences. When Samuel Willard, minister of the Third Church in Boston, read this, he could hardly believe his eyes; he hastened to assure the authors that they did not know what they were talking about:

> *I perceive they are mistaken in the design of our first Planters, whose business was not Toleration; but were professed Enemies of it, and could leave the World professing they died no Libertines. Their business was to settle, and (as much as in them lay) secure Religion to Posterity, according to that way which they believed was of God.*

The two other ideas which we have noted as being derived from the background of the age, rule by fundamental law and social compact, were the special tenets of English Puritanism. For three decades before the settlement of Massachusetts the Puritan party in England had been working hand in glove with the Parliament against the King. The absolutist Stuarts were allied with the bishops, and the

Puritan agitator and the Parliamentary leader made common cause against them both. As a result of this combination, the Puritan theorists had taken over the essentials of the Parliamentary conception of society, the contention that the power of the ruler should be exercised in accordance with established fundamental law, and that the government should owe its existence to a compact of the governed. Because these ideas were strategically invaluable in England, they became ingrained in the Puritan consciousness; they were carried to New England and were preached from every pulpit in the land.

The Puritans did not see any conflict between them and their religious intentions. In New England the fundamental law was the Bible. The magistrates were to have full power to rule men for the specific purposes to which the society was dedicated; but they as well as their subordinates were tied to the specific purposes, and could not go beyond the prescribed limits. The Bible was clear and definite on the form of the church, on the code of punishments for crimes, on the general purposes of social existence; its specifications were binding on all, magistrates, ministers, and citizens. Consequently, the Puritans did not find it difficult to conclude that in those matters upon which the Bible left men free to follow their own discretion, the society itself should establish basic rules. The New England leaders and the people frequently disagreed as to what these rules were, or as to how detailed they should be made, but neither side ever doubted that the community must abide by whatever laws had been enacted, either by God or by the state. The government of New England was, as we have said, a dictatorship, but the dictators were not absolute and irresponsible. John Cotton was the clerical spokesman for the Massachusetts rulers, but he stoutly demanded "that all power that is on earth be limited."

The belief that government originated in the consent of the governed was equally congenial to the Puritan creed. The theology is often enough described as deterministic, because it held that men were predestined to heaven or hell; but we are always in danger of forgetting that the life of the Puritan was completely voluntaristic. The natural man was indeed bound in slavery to sin and unable to make exertions toward his own salvation; but the man into whose soul grace had been infused was liberated from that bondage and made free to undertake the responsibilities and obligations of virtue and decency. The holy society was erected upon the belief that the

right sort of men could of their own free will and choice carry through
the creation and administration of the right sort of community. The
churches of New England were made up of "saints," who came into
the church because they wanted membership, not because they were
born in it, or were forced into it, or joined because of policy and con-
vention. Though every resident was obliged to attend and to pay
taxes for the support of the churches, no one became an actual
member who did not signify his strong desire to be one. The saints
were expected to act positively because they had in them a spirit of
God that made them capable of every exertion. No doubt the Puritans maintained that government originated in the consent of the
people because that theory was an implement for chastening the
absolutism of the Stuarts; but they maintained it also because they
did not believe that any society, civil or ecclesiastical, into which
men did not enter of themselves was worthy of the name.

Perry Miller

THE MARROW OF PURITAN DIVINITY

Setting forth from the nature of God as defined by the covenant,
these theologians enjoyed clear sailing to the haven of assurance.
The covenant of grace defines the conditions by which Heaven is
obtained, and he who fulfills the conditions has an incontestable title
to glorification, exactly as he who pays the advertised price owns
his freehold. God may continue to choose the elect in the impene-
trable fastness of His will, but according to the covenant He has
agreed to give the individual descernible grounds for His decision;
He is bound to bestow salvation only upon those who achieve the
qualifications, and, conversely, those who acquire the qualifications
are absolutely certain of their salvation:

Reprinted by permission of the publishers from pp. 71–74 of Perry Miller, "The Mar-
row of Puritan Divinity," in *Errand Into the Wilderness* (Cambridge, Mass.: The
Belknap Press of Harvard University Press, copyright 1956 by the President and
Fellows of Harvard College).

if thou beleeue, it is certaine then, thou art within the Couenant. . . . If thou canst finde this now, that thou art able to take Iesus Christ, to take him as a Lord and Sauiour, thou art able to beleeue all the Couenant of Grace, thou art by that put into the Couenant.

And to be really in the covenant is to be through with all doubts and misgivings: "If ever thou are in covenant with *God,* and hast this seale in thy soule, that there is a change wrought in thee by the covenant, then thy election is sure." The union with God is not torturing uncertainty, it is not a ravishing of the surprised soul by irresistible grace, unexpected and undeserved; it is a definite legal status, based on a *quid pro quo,* an "if I believe" necessitating a "you have to save me." God's will is originally free to pick and choose in any fashion, but once the covenant is drawn up, He no longer acts without a reason, He does not appear to man as a brutal or capricious tyrant. He is bound by certain commitments; He is compelled to play the game of salvation according to ascertained rules.

God comes and sayes; For my owne sake will I do thus and thus unto you in an absolute promise; *here is a ground for the faith of adherence to cleave unto. . . . There be also conditionall promises,* (He that believeth shall be saved) *by meanes of which (we having the experience and feeling of such grace in our selves) we grow to an assurance that we are of those that he will shew that free grace upon.*

The contract between God and man, once entered into, signed by both parties and sealed, as it were, in the presence of witnesses, is ever afterwards binding. This exceedingly legal basis furnishes the guarantee, not only for the assurance of the saints, but even for their perseverance. In the covenant, says Hooker, the soul "is inseparably knit to Christ"; though you falter in action and fall short of holiness, if you have once become a member of the covenant, the covenant "doth remain sure and firm," said John Cotton. "If we be hemm'd in within this Covenant, we cannot break out."

Thus bound by His own commitment, God must live up to His word. If you do your part, He must, willy-nilly, do His. As Bulkeley says, "He hath passed over those things by covenant, and he cannot be a covenant breaker"; hence, "we might have the more strong consolation, assuring ourselves of the fulfilling of his gracious promise towards us." Pursuing this logic, these men broached one of their most daring ideas: if a man can prove that he has faith, he has then done his part and can hold God to account, hale Him into court and force Him to give what has become the man's just and legal due: "You may sue him of his own bond written and sealed, and he cannot deny it."

> when faith hath once gotten a promise, be sure that thou keepe thy hold, pleade hard with the Lord, and tell him it is a part of his Couenant, and it is impossible that he should deny thee . . . when thou art on a sure ground, take no denyall, though the Lord may defer long, yet he will doe it, he cannot chuse; for it is a part of his Couenant.

We do not surrender ourselves to God without getting something in return: "we require this back againe of God, that as we give up our selves a sacrifice to him, so that the Lord Jesus Christ might be imputed unto us." If we are in the covenant, "we are then out of danger, wee need not to fear." Considering what the background of Protestant thought had been, what ruthless determination had been postulated behind the predestinating Divinity, one might well feel that Preston comments upon this conception of salvation with an understatement that is almost comic: "This is a very comfortable doctrine, if it be well considered."

The covenant theory admitted into the official theology many ideas that bade fair to undermine it entirely, and this idea, that man can by fulfilling terms extort salvation from God, might well seem the most incongruous. But at the moment the authors were confident that they had skillfully incorporated the new device into the old orthodoxy. Their account does not deny that God and God alone elects or rejects according to His mere pleasure; the grace which enables us to fulfill the covenant still comes from above, and only God knows whether we have it or not. But in practical life the dogmatic rigors of absolute predestination are materially softened. A juridical relationship is slyly substituted for the divine decree. Men cannot trace the private thought of God, but since God has agreed to manifest what He thinks concerning certain persons in an explicit bond, the individual has a way of knowing that much of the divine determination: "Now we can never know the things which are given unto us of God, but by knowing of the covenant which conveys all the blessings which God doth impart unto his people." Stating the theory of predestination within this frame shifts the point of view from that maintained by Calvin. We no longer contemplate the decrees in the abstract, as though they were relentlessly grinding cosmic forces, crushing or exalting souls without regard for virtue or excellence; instead we are free to concentrate our attention upon what immediately concerns us. We do not have to ask whether God be ours; we need ask only whether we be God's. Sibbes presented this reversal in emphasis most clearly, though it can be found consciously recognized in the works of all the covenant theologians. A man has no grounds, he says, to trouble himself about God's election as it exists in God's own mind. "It is not my duty to look to God's secret counsel, but to his open offer, invitation, and command, and thereupon to adventure my soul." To commence from the unfathomable election in the mind of God and endeavor then to discover if it pertains to oneself is the wrong procedure; one should begin with oneself, one's own response to God's proffered covenant, and argue from the degree of one's success in fulfilling it the fact of one's being chosen.

> Some are much troubled, because they proceed by a false method and order in judging their estates. They will begin with election, which is the highest step of the ladder; whereas they should begin from a work of grace wrought within their hearts. . . . Otherwise it is as great folly as in removing of a pile of wood, to begin at the lowest first, and so, besides the needless trouble, to be in danger to have the rest to fall upon our heads.

In fact, Sibbes carried this argument so far that he can actually tell men to reach out for the covenant, to promise to abide by it, to take it upon themselves, before they have had any recognizable experience of regeneration. If they can suceed, they can very probably secure faith, not only by prayer and fasting, but by demanding that God reward them according to His bond.

> The way, therefore, will be to put this into the condition of your promise now, and prayer after. Lord, I have promised this; but thou knowest I cannot perform the promise I have made, and the condition thou requirest, of myself. But in the covenant of grace, thou hast said that thou wilt make good the condition . . . If we come with sincere hearts, and with resolution to please God, we may look for all the promises of God. All that he hath promised he is ready to perform, if we in faith can allege the promise.

The covenant made it possible to argue that while God elects whom

He pleases, He is pleased to elect those who catch Him in His plighted word, and that it is up to fallen man to do so. The subtle casuistry of this dialectic is altogether obvious. Yet the spectacle of these men struggling in the coils of their doctrine, desperately striving on the one hand to maintain the subordination of humanity to God without unduly abasing human values, and on the other hand to vaunt the powers of the human intellect without losing the sense of divine transcendence, vividly recreates what might be called the central problem of the seventeenth century as it was confronted by the Puritan mind.

David D. Hall
UNDERSTANDING THE PURITANS

Where Miller portrayed a particularly American Puritanism, ordered and authoritarian, David D. Hall (b. 1936) of Boston University points up the paradoxical opposites that made up a changing rather than static ideal. He relates American Puritanism to a broader spectrum of Reformed religious belief both in Europe and America, and isolates the dominant theological point, the concern for redemption, the search for a conversion experience, that he believes made Puritan society flexible. Hall thinks that Puritanism may be understood only if described within a specific time period while accounting for the political, economic, and social adaptations that Puritanism made to conform to changing experiences in America.

"How does one define Puritanism?" This question, the first sentence of Alan Simpson's *Puritanism in Old and New England,* is one to which the answers in recent years have grown increasingly complex and contradictory. Thirty years ago there was no doubt about the answer; the scholarship of Morison and Haller, and towering over both, the massive symmetry of Perry Miller's *The New England Mind,* gave compelling definition to the subject. But climates of opinion change, and with them the historian's angle of perception. What Perry Miller had to say now has the ring of the 1930s, for the period in which he wrote saw the old myth that the Puritan hated life still strong upon us. If Miller's great achievement was to free us from that myth, the question remains as to the proper understanding of Puritanism. To describe the differences of opinion between Miller and his critics is one purpose of this essay. But its deeper task is to identify the problems that every student of the Puritans must inevitably confront, the problems of interpretation and methodology that always seem to turn up in dealing with this subject.

Abraham Lincoln once said that slavery was "somehow" the cause of the Civil War. Historians of Puritanism know likewise that the history of the movement was somehow related to the contemporary culture and social structure. Puritanism had social sources and social consequences; were historians to define precisely which groups supported (and dissented from) the Puritan program, as well as the movement's consequences for the broader culture, they would move closer to an understanding of its nature. One of their tasks, then, is to determine how Puritanism was socially functional.

A second problem arises out of the close relationship between Puritanism and two other religious movements, the Reformed tradition and Pietism. Heir of the first and parent of the second, Puritanism at the onset of its history depended for ideas on Reformed Protestantism, and at the close faded into Pietism. John Eusden has suggested that Puritanism may be understood as an "evangelical Calvinism," a term that links it both to the sixteenth-century world of Calvin and to the eighteenth-century world of the Pietists. If Eusden's suggestion is correct, historians must also be able to distinguish between Puritanism and these other movements. At the same time their task is to fix the time span within which Puritanism played out its course; to give dates to a movement is, perforce, to make a statement about its origins and legacy. A periodization of Puritanism and an inventory of its distinctive (or shared) religious ideas are two sides of the same problem: to mark off the historical and intellectual boundaries of the movement.

A third problem is to construct a definition that includes the range of Puritan types. Here I agree with Alan Simpson, who insists on viewing the broad spectrum from presbyterians to Quakers as one continuous whole. He is right in criticizing historians who legitimize too narrow a slice of this spectrum, and he is right also in asking if there is not something fundamental in the nature of Puritanism that made it dynamic and expansive. The history of the movement offers innumerable examples of the Puritan as a man in motion, a man possessed by a peculiar restlessness, a man who may attack the idea of a gathered church while still a minister in England, yet form such a group within his English parish and publicly defend the practice once he reached America. These inconsistencies, and more besides, mark the career of John Cotton, and the life histories of countless other Puritans were fashioned in the same erratic manner.

We need a definition of Puritanism which takes account of this restlessness, and if dissatisfaction with the scholarship of the 1930s is on the rise, the reason is largely its failure to meet such a test. It fails this test in one obvious way. Together with the denominational historians, Perry Miller assumed that denominational categories could be imposed upon Puritan conceptions of the church. But can we call the New England Puritans "congregationalists" with a capital C when the actual working-out of their church order was so confused and contradictory? Or can we call Thomas Cartwright a "presbyterian" with a capital P when his conception of the church involved recognizably "congregational" elements? More recent studies, in recognition of these ambiguities, have moved away from the categories of denominational history, substituting in their place an emphasis upon the "continuity of experience" which united all Puritans. The result may be a certain loss of clarity, but the new scholarship at least has the virtue of restoring the dynamic quality of Puritanism to the center of any definition.

The scholarship of the 1930s minimized the restlessness within Puritanism because of another assumption. In Perry Miller's view, "Puritanism was not only a religious creed, it was a philosophy and a metaphysic; it was an organization of man's whole life, emotional and intellectual." The structure of *The New England Mind* imposed a coherence upon Puritanism which Miller described as the reconciliation of "piety" and "intellect." To define the movement in these terms was explicitly to rule out any spiritualists as un-Puritan; it was to cut off the spectrum short of the Quakers and Antinomians. Here again, recent scholarship points toward a more inclusive definition. In place of the intellectual commitments Miller saw as crucial, Alan Simpson would put the terms "experience" and "thrust," intending by them a particular type of religious experience which unleashed the zeal of the Puritan saint. The value of these terms must not obscure their weaknesses; though they permit the Quakers to reenter the fold as authentic Puritans, their meaning seems inherently subjective, and they may act to exclude the array of distinctions that Miller so successfully identified as woven into the texture of Puritanism.

An adequate definition of the Puritan movement must therefore seek to unite the experiential dimension with the formal structure of the Puritan intellect. It must locate the movement within a particular time period, and with reference to the Reformed tradition and Pietism. It must identify the bond between the social sources of the movement and its history, between its rhetoric and its social consequences.

As for the second category of difference, there is general agreement among many historians that Puritanism has a different theological outlook from Calvinism. Comparison of the Puritans with John Calvin easily turns up some divergences: Calvin retained a sense of the real presence in his understanding of the Lord's Supper, while most Puritans followed Zwingli in adopting a memorialist view; Calvin's doctrine of assurance excluded the evidence of "works," evidence which many Puritans thought legitimate. In broader terms, Thomas Torrance has contrasted Calvin's Christocentric focus to the anthropocentric orientation of the Puritans. And Perry Miller declared that the New England Puritans fashioned the covenant theology in order to escape from the rigors of "strict Calvinism."

No idea of Miller's has gained greater currency, or been more widely attacked. Counter-interpretations of the covenant theology have generally succeeded in establishing two points. One is that the covenantal idiom figured in the Reformed tradition long before it appeared among the Puritans whom Miller cited. Certain of these studies suggest, in other words, that the Puritans in resorting to the idiom were not particularly novel or illegitimate by Reformed standards. The second point is that the idea of a covenant, though apparently implying a voluntary, contractual relationship between God and man, was not intended by the Puritans as a means of bringing God more within man's reach, but rather to accomplish other ends— to provide a rationale for the sacraments, or a basis for their doctrine of assurance.

In spite of all this scholarship we still lack a clear understanding of the covenant theology, and on the larger question of the theological differences between Calvin and the Puritans the confusion is just as great. The time has come, I believe, to reconsider the terms of the question, for we seem to be dealing with a question *mal posée,* so posed as to lead to answers which are never satisfactory. The essential error has been to postulate a "strict" orthodoxy, a "pure" Calvinism, defined in terms of John Calvin and the *Institutes of the Christian Religion.* Once the name of Calvin becomes synonymous with "orthodoxy," certain deadly consequences ensue: the concept presumes a static system of ideas, so that change of any kind—any variation, no matter how slight—is taken as evidence of declining rigor and faith. Perry Miller fell into this trap, and so have many others. But we have been warned against it by the post-Millerian scholarship on the covenant theology: on the one hand this scholarship suggests that the strict orthodoxy of the pure Calvin must not be interpreted so narrowly as to exclude the idiom of the covenant, and on the other, that the Puritans who invoked the idiom did not thereby fall from the heights of orthodoxy. These warnings must be extended. In particular, the differences between Puritans and continental Reformed theology must not be measured solely in terms of Calvin. Reformed theology was a system of thought elaborated and defended in varying ways by many persons in the sixteenth century. Several of these Reformed theologians—Beza, Piscator, Zanchy, Bullinger, Pareus—figure more often than Calvin in the religious thought of seventeenth century New England. To overlook these intermediary figures, in any case, is to risk overlooking the complexities of the Reformed tradition, and consequently the materials for proving the continuity between this tradition and the Puritans. In fact, once these Calvinists, and not Calvin, are brought into the comparison, the continuities far outweigh the differences. . . .

The political situation of the Puritans had one further consequence. Resentful of the Church's imperfection, yet believing that schism was a sin, Puritans found themselves caught in a dilemma from which flowed much of their restlessness. The same dilemma was a cause of the fragmentation of the movement into sects, a process that began in the late sixteenth century with the emergence of the separatists. By one set of Reformed standards the separatists were perfectly legitimate in demanding freedom for the church to cleanse itself; by another they were schismatics who carried their legalism too far. The emergence of the separatists is thus a perfect measure of how the English situation acted to confuse the meaning and application of Reformed ideas.

It is in this context, moreover, that denominational categories become inadequate; too abstract and rigid, they sever the Puritan sects from their dynamic and fluid relationship with the Reformed tradition. Denominational categories conceal the fact that all Puritans, whether "presbyterian" or "congregationalist" or some other group, held four propositions in common: the revitalization of the laymen's role, including greater privileges in the government of the church; the purification of church membership; the assignment of the power of the keys to each parish or congregation; and the separation of church and state so as to give the church effective responsibility for discipline. Many historians would add a fifth proposition to this list: the assertion that the nature of the church must conform to the will of God. But the Biblicism of the Puritans is less important in explaining their ecclesiology than the emphasis they placed upon the Holy Spirit. The essential impulse within the movement was to relate the church to the intervention of the Spirit, to understand the community of the saints as a type of the kingdom. In this they were not unique. Calvin himself looked upon the church in two ways, as an institution ordained by God to exist upon earth, and as the realm of the Spirit, a realm in which "the original order of creation" had been restored. Inheriting both views, the Puritans were driven to identify the first with the Church of England, and so to emphasize the second. But the issue of keeping the two in balance was inherent within the Reformed tradition.

There is another reason for discarding denominational categories. Puritanism began as a movement within the Church of England at the time of the Elizabethan religious settlement of 1559. From that time until the accession of William II, most Puritans thought of themselves as members of the Church, not as founders of new churches. It was only when the religious settlement under William denied the legitimacy of this claim that the connections between English Puritans and the Church were finally severed. On this side of the Atlantic, the new charter of 1691 and the events associated with it mark a similar end to the affiliation. Thereafter, any colonist who claimed membership or ministerial orders within the Church would have to renounce his current status and formally rejoin the mother body.

The historic association of Puritanism with the Church of England is a means of giving dates to the movement, a periodization which other evidence sustains. The decade of the 1690s saw Reformed scholasticism giving way under the impact of the Enlightenment, leaving eighteenth-century Reformed theologians to work out a new alliance between philosophy and religion. On the whole, however, Pietists were content to abandon philosophy and science, just as they abandoned the theocratic vision of a holy commonwealth which inspired Calvin and the Puritans. What passed from Puritanism to Pietism was the assertion that religion fundamentally involved the affective self, the heart, rather than the reason.

An adequate definition of Puritanism must incorporate this periodization of the movement, and go on from there to recognize the essential continuity between Calvinists and Puritans. An adequate definition must allow for the adaptation of Reformed ideas to England, a process that eventually resulted in the splintering of the movement into many sects. Despite this splintering, an adequate definition must recognize the wholeness of Puritan history. What gave substance to the movement was a certain inventory of ideas— the separation of grace and nature, an understanding of God and man as active forces, an eschatology. And what linked the Puritan program for reform of the church to Puritan descriptions of the spiritual life was the common motif of renewal. Edmund S. Morgan has seen the Puritan as caught in the dilemma of remaining pure while living in the world. Such a posture was forced upon the Puritan by the dynamic relationship between this world and the next. He knew himself to be at mid-point between these worlds, and his striving for self-discipline, his endless self-scrutiny, was directed toward the end of winning freedom from the world and entrance to the kingdom. . . .

The millennarian fervor which runs through Puritanism may provide the best clue to the social function of the movement. Puritanism, it seems, furnished certain Englishmen with a new identity as members of a special group. All English Protestants believed that the history of the Christian church revealed God's favoring providence toward England. And Christian history also taught that God's people must fight a cruel and bloody war against Anti-Christ and all his minions. The Puritans were able to appropriate this rhetoric and apply it to their cause for two reasons: they were most outspoken in attacking Catholicism, and their outgroup status lent itself to a sense of persecution. The identity of the Puritan as saint in covenant with God was reinforced by the idea that history was moving rapidly toward the coming of the kingdom. The prophetic stance of the Puritan teachers grew out of an historical perspective which saw the task of reformation as increasingly urgent, lest the final day prove a day of judgment. Those who responded to this preaching, those Englishmen who in life style withdrew from the "world" and set their hearts upon the kingdom, established a new identity for themselves as the Lord's free people.

From this identity flowed the Puritan understanding of the church as a voluntary, gathered congregation. From it came also the Puritan theory of community, the vision of a social order (to quote John Winthrop) "knit together" in a "bond of love." The immigration to New England can equally be counted as a consequence of this millennarianism. In the late 1620s events in England and abroad convinced many Puritans that the final day was close at hand. New England loomed before them both as refuge and as paradise, the wilderness which they could make into the kingdom. Not only did the chiliastic zeal of certain Puritans precipitate their immigration; it also inspired the congregationalism that emerged in New England in the 1630s—the strict limits on church membership, the more democratic church structure.

Whether the colonists were exceptional in their chiliasm is not clear. In their general vision of the kingdom, and in their activist drive, they stood as one with the entire Puritan movement, sharing in a historical consciousness that originated with Calvin and Bucer. Any understanding of Puritanism in America must ignore artificial boundaries and distinctions and build instead upon the continuities that linked England and America. On this matter of continuities, American scholarship has far to go in working out the relationships between institutional forms, and even ideas.

Does this mean there is nothing distinctive about American Puritanism, nothing American historians can study without going back to Perkins or Calvin? There is not as much as many would assert, but there is something. We can speak of the Americanizing of Puritan ideas just as historians of the Revolutionary period speak of the Americanizing of Whig ideas. The analogy is nearly exact; the colonists imported the radical Whig ideology from abroad, and we can only understand what they are saying by reference to the English sources. Yet there is a difference, for although the ideas seem the same on both sides of the Atlantic, the pattern of culture in America had departed from the English model in ways that affected the meaning and consequences of these ideas. So also in the seventeenth century, the Reformed tradition took on a new significance in the "free air of a new world." Here Puritanism became the majority point of view, and preachers who had whetted their fiery preaching on targets that the Church of England had to offer underwent an agonizing adjustment to a new life style. Here the ideal of a gathered church had strange consequences, and here the alliance between church and state gave the "New England Way" its notoriety. The future of Puritan studies in America, a future that seems without limit, lies in articulating these differences, as well as the continuities, between Old World and New.

Clifford K. Shipton
AUTHORITY AND THE GROWTH OF INDIVIDUALISM

Disagreeing with both the early critics of the Puritans and with the interpretations of Perry Miller and his followers, Clifford K. Shipton (b. 1902), distinguished former director of the American Antiquarian Society, finds the locus of authority in the Massachusetts Bay Colony decentralized, with individual towns and individual congregations wielding power based on a consensus of the local populace. The colonial authorities never attempted, in his view, to regulate in matters involving freedom of conscience, only acting when overt deeds rather than thoughts threatened the colony, as even a modern state will. So Shipton sees in Massachusetts a shift from the medieval stress on the good of the state to a concern for the individual, with revolutionary implications looking towards democracy.

We of the western world generally agree that the purpose of life is the realization of a set of values which in their political form we call democracy, by which we mean that they rest authority in the people. The course of the evolution of these principles is clearly marked from the Magna Carta, through the Massachusetts Civil Code of 1648, to the Bill of Rights in the federal Constitution. The century and a half during which the colony and province of Massachusetts Bay were trying to adjust law and authority in order to realize these principles are critical ones in this long period of their evolution. But what when on in these years has been quite generally misunderstood by historians, particularly by those who have not realized that in the period and the group with which we are concerned, religious and civil life were an integrated whole. Religious values were not segregated out and discriminated against as they are today when members of the Massachusetts legislature demand of anyone who would testify on social problems, "Do you take your stand on moral grounds," and deny him a hearing if he pleads guilty. The Puritan's preoccupation with moral values made him keenly aware that he should keep an eye out for the fallen sparrow, and should temper the law to the shorn lamb, or to the debtor. This is why Massachusetts

From Clifford K. Shipton, "The Locus of Authority in Colonial Massachusetts" in George Athan Billias, ed., *Law and Authority in Colonial America* (Barre, Mass.: Barre Publishers, 1965). Used by permission.

passed the first statute forbidding cruelty to animals, and, for their day, the most liberal laws for the protection of debtors. With the concern for the physical well-being of the individual went a certain amount of respect for his opinions.

The last generation of writers on colonial New England were cynical of the Puritan professions, and saw the Bay Colony as a self-centered autocracy devoted to the perpetuation of a particular theological orthodoxy. According to this interpretation, the significance of the evolution of law, authority, and democracy in Massachusetts was in the liberation of the colony from a theocracy by the extension of the franchise. One would have thought that this thesis had been entirely disproved by the research of this generation, but the recent publication of Emery Battis' excellent biography of Anne Hutchinson contains the following utterly irrelevant conclusion to describe the situation in the Bay Colony after Mrs. Hutchinson's exile: "the established church was the sole repository of religious truth, with full scope to determine who had erred against that truth in matters of doctrine and morals." Nonsense. There never was an established church in Massachusetts, there was no agreed-upon body of dogma, and serious moral deviation was punished by the state, not by the church.

In spite of the integration of civil and religious life in the seventeenth century, the government of Massachusetts never was a theocracy in any normal sense of the term. There was no unitary church, and many of the normal functions of the established churches in Europe were here transferred to the state. This was true at the local level as well. For most of the settlers, the accustomed instrument of local government had been the oligarchic Church of England parish; in New England its functions passed to the town, and were exercised by the inhabitants in open town meeting. Today, the established churches in England, Scandinavia, and the Latin countries exercise authority in what were purely civil fields in colonial Massachusetts. The Bay Colony never had an established church which could have exercised these civil powers; it had only individual and independent churches. The law required that every town maintain a minister and a schoolmaster, both of its own selection; but beyond that point the colony and province exercised no authority. Taxation of nonmembers of the church by the town to support the ministers was defended on the same ground as taxation of childless people to support the schools. Many towns were cited by the General Court for failing to maintain a school, but I cannot recollect a case in which a town was taken to task for failing to maintain a minister, though many did for years on end. The town, acting with the concurrence of an ecclesiastical council of its own choosing, formed the local church, which possessed no funds or property, and was independent of all other churches and of any outside authority. The town did not legally participate in the call of subsequent ministers until 1692, but inasmuch as the minister's contract was with the town, he was never called by the church without previous assurance of the concurrence of the town. Since all inhabitants, regardless of denominational preference, participated in these transactions, the minister's theological views had to be acceptable to the majority. Quakers, Baptists, and Presbyterians were vocal in these town and parish meetings, with the result that the minister's theological difficulties were usually with the civil body rather than with the church.

Unlike the Scottish presbyteries, the Massachusetts associations of ministers exercised no authority over the individual churches or their members. Their powers, like those of the occasional synods, were purely advisory. Their consent was not required for either the ordination or the dismissal of a minister, these functions being exercised by ad hoc councils chosen jointly by town and church with an eye to getting their own decisions ratified quietly. Ordaining councils heard any opponents of a call, and never proceeded to settle a minister who was opposed by a majority or even a large minority of the inhabitants of a town, knowing that he would be denied adequate financial support. Technically, the consent of such a council, chosen jointly by the disputants, was necessary for the dismissal of a minister. But even where the minister was clearly in the right, all that the council could do to protect him was to arbitrate the best possible terms of separation for him; for the town could refuse to pay the settlement and could go on calling other councils until it obtained a decision which it considered suitable. Where there was recourse to the courts, and it was frequent, the decision was almost always on the terms of the financial contract; rarely was cognizance taken of theological questions which might have been the reason for the dismissal.

It has been argued, however, that although there was no legal authority for a theocracy in Massachusetts, one existed because of the influence of the clergy. This is amply disproved by the legislative history of the colony, and by the contrasts between the suggestions of the synods and the subsequent legislation by the General Court. The tradition that a Black Regiment of the clergy led the American Revolution in New England has little substance. Many individual Congregational ministers were neutral or Tory, and ministerial associations usually avoided even expressions of opinion on political matters. Robert E. Brown in his *Middle-Class Democracy and the Revolution in Massachusetts 1691–1780* exaggerates the political influence of the clergy, as when he mistakenly makes the Reverend Charles Chauncy a member of the upper house of legislature. Brown was unaware of the existence of an absolutely fundamental principle of separation of church and state in Massachusetts, which forbade the election of clergymen to the General Court in colony or province time. So clearly understood was this principle that the clergy were not to participate in government that when the province asked a missionary to the Eastern Indians to negotiate a treaty, a wise old Roman Catholic chief pointed out to the minister the fact that his profession disqualified him from any such participation in government.

The clergyman was excluded from office in the civil government in the Bay Colony, but the meanest inhabitant was invited to participate in the legislative process. From the first, Massachusetts law provided that "Every man whether inhabitant or Forreiner, free or not free" had the right "to come to any publique Court, Council or Town Meeting" and there either by speech or writing to initiate and advocate action. The radical nature of this system is apparent when one realizes that through most of the world today legislation can be introduced only by the executive or by the ministry.

The great majority of the early settlers in the Bay Colony had held their English property not in what we would call fee simple, but by some type of feudal tenure or grant, and all of them had lived under local governments which were self-perpetuating oligarchies. In the Southern colonies, the English practice of local government by a self-perpetuating oligarchy of vestrymen remained. In New England, a few of the first town meetings had oligarchic tendencies, but within a decade the legislative and executive processes had passed into the hands of the body of inhabitants. In Massachusetts, the settler owned his land in fee simple, voted the taxes upon it in town meeting, and disposed of it at will. Liberty 12 of the Massachusetts Code of 1648 had guaranteed to everyone the right of a voice in town meeting, and, as Thomas Hutchinson later put it, "anything in the semblance of a man" was permitted to vote in spite of property qualifications established by law. In consequence, all of the functions of the English parish vestries, borough councils, and similar local bodies, passed into the hands of the body of inhabitants, who thus had control of most of the matters which affected their daily lives. The only cases I have found where votes have been challenged on the ground of voting by unqualified individuals have occurred when the minority has included the church members and more substantial people, while the majority has consisted of Baptists, Quakers, and small farmers, some of whom pretty obviously could not have met the property qualifications established by law. In no case which I have seen did the court which heard the appeal base its decision on the legal qualifications of the voters. So far as one can determine from the colonial record, the situation in town meeting was then precisely what it is today, when the chairman of the finance committee tries in vain to get the moderator to exclude unqualified persons from voting. The colonial statutes in regard to voting qualifications had little to do with actual practice, and give no substantial evidence as to the degree of democracy prevailing. Far better evidence, but quite impossible to evaluate, are such pictures as Governor Winthrop laboring in the fields with his servants, and Governor Endicott taking his turn in the saw pit.

One of the best criteria of the degree of democracy in any state is the amount of protection afforded by its laws to the individual; protection against the state itself, against other individuals, and against economic adversity. In this regard, the Massachusetts Code of 1648 was centuries ahead of the greater part of the world. The compilers, whetting their consciences to discover the will of God, selecting wisely, innovating when necessary, drew a document which is a milestone in the history of individual liberty. Their successors, a century and a half later, put forth the essence of these principles at the price of Massachusetts' ratification of the federal Constitution, and they became the substance of the Bill of Rights.

Guarantees of freedom of the person and of property of the type afforded by the Massachusetts Code of 1648 are, we of western tradition believe, essential to a life worth living. Even more important, however, is freedom of the mind. It is the attitude toward this freedom which is the critical difference between the East and West today. Indeed, it has been a problem in every civilized society. To the Massachusetts Puritans of 1630, the whole good of man, which was the end of society, required freedom for every man to live according to his conscience. What, then, was the actual place of this most crucial freedom, the freedom of the mind, in the legal system and in the society, of the colony and province of Massachusetts Bay? This is a point on which historians are still confused, and which even Perry Miller and George L. Haskins did not think through. The statement of the Cambridge Platform of 1648 is this:

> *Idolatry, Blasphemy, Heresy, venting corrupt & pernicious opinions, that destroy the foundations, open contempt of the word preached, prophanation of the Lords day, disturbing the peaceable administration of the worship & holy things of God, the like, are to be restrayned & punished by civil authority.*

Today every state will use the civil authority against those who disturb "the peaceable administration & Exercise of the worship" of God, or of the doctrines of Karl Marx; and every state has certain ground rules beyond which lie blasphemy and heresy, or intolerable indecency. Becoming a citizen of a state has always involved joining in a compact and accepting the local ground rules. North Americans who today live in other parts of the world may not like the local ground rules, but they must recognize the fact that the world respects the right of every state to make its own rules and to enforce them against those who have accepted its citizenship.

The Massachusetts Code of 1648 states explicitly that all who settle in the colony are assumed "totally to submit to this government." Massachusetts authorities, like those of any other state, used the civil power against individuals who "vented corrupt and vicious opinions" which tended to "destroy the foundations" of the City upon a Hill. Liberty of mind was limited to matters of "faith and conscience." This was the reason, however mistaken as a matter of policy, for the civil action taken against Roger Williams, Anne Hutchinson, and the Quakers. These Antinomians held that authority was vested in the conscience of the individual, not in the state, the church, nor in the consensus of the people. While accepting this principle, the Bay authorities believed that the venting of the views which Mrs. Hutchinson held was a danger sufficient to require the disarming of her followers. Note that the authorities did not claim jurisdiction over the beliefs of the Antinomians, but only over the promulgation of them.

The Bay government never sought out intellectual deviates. The great majority of Antinomians, Baptists, and Quakers in the Bay Colony lived in good relations with their neighbors who adhered to the majority view, and even Cotton Mather welcomed such dissenters at the Communion Table of his church. By contrast, the Book of Common Prayer of the Church of England forbade such unconfirmed persons to approach the Communion Table, and Blackstone declared that by the laws of the kingdom, all dissenters were criminals.

The New England respect for freedom of conscience eventually carried over into the political field. In the American Revolution, New England Tories suffered less than the losing side in perhaps any other civil war. There were no purges, no executions, and no lynchings. The right of Tories to their opinion was respected so long as they were not a menace to the state. Our yearning for freedom of the mind is not satisfied with mere tolerance; we insist that our beliefs must be accorded the dignity of reasonable truth. When the suggestions of the Cambridge Synod were incorporated into the legal code as adopted by the colony in the same year, they were qualified by a provision that "No human power [is] Lord over the Faith and Conscience of men, and therefore may not constrain them to believe or profess against their Consciences." That this was fundamental to the thinking of New England Puritans is indicated by the corresponding clause in the New Haven laws of 1656, asserting that "no Creature be Lord, or have any power over the faith and consciences of men, nor constreyn them to believe or profess, against their consciences."

After this doctrine had been tried in the fires of controversy with the New Haven Quakers for a century, William Livingston in *The Independent Reflector* for August 2, 1753, rephrased the Puritan principle thus: "The civil Power hath no jurisdiction over the [religious] Sentiments or Opinions of the subject, till such Opinions break out into Actions prejudicial to the Community, and then it is not the Opinion but the Action that is the Object of our Punishment." It has been recently asserted that this principle of freedom of thought was first expressed as state policy in the Virginia statutes of January 16, 1786, but it may well be that this is another case where the Virginians were deliberately drawing on Puritan documents.

What were the heresies which could not be vented without danger to the Bay community? In 1646 the General Court enumerated a number of theological errors the promulgation of which should be punished by banishment. All of these, it pointed out, were recognized as dangerous errors in most contemporary societies; the Puritans were not peculiar in dreading them. Neither the General Court, nor any ecclesiastical body in Massachusetts attempted to define heresy in any way other than by pointing out European consensus. Since there was no theological code in the Bay Colony, it is not surprising that there was no civil trial for heresy in colony or province. Of the literally hundreds of ecclesiastical councils before which ministers were charged with, among other things, theological deviations, there was only one which was clearly a heresy trial, and in that the foolish young defendant was out of bounds by most standards.

Modern historians are fond of using the word "orthodoxy" in connection with the Puritans, although the latter rarely employed the word themselves. Haskins uses the term "Puritan Orthodoxy" without defining it, and other historians use it with the terms "Baptist Orthodoxy" and "Quaker Orthodoxy" as if these were clearly stated theological positions. If by "Puritan Orthodoxy" you mean loyalty to the community, the term has cohesion, but once you try to prod its theological implications, you are in trouble. The fact is that orthodoxy was incompatible with the Puritan faith in reason. Orthodoxy is static. The Reverend John Robinson's parting words to the Pilgrims leaving Leyden included an admonition not to close their minds, as the Lutherans and Calvinists had done, to the progress of the knowledge of the nature of God. The minority in the Westminster Assembly of Divines took this same attitude, and they represented the Independent element which provided the leadership for the settlement of Massachusetts. Oliver Cromwell was probably the only head of state ever to beseech his followers to believe that they might be mistaken. The Puritans, recognizing that they were the children of an intellectual reformation resulting from individual examination of orthodoxy, thought of themselves as in a current sweeping toward a better knowledge of God, a knowledge to be reached by learning and study, not by the unpredictable personal revelations of the Antinomians.

To map the theological beliefs of a few Puritan theologians and to call the result "Puritan Orthodoxy" is to ignore one of the chief tenets of that community. The favorite Biblical text of the New England ministers was that which enjoins us to call no man father; and the improvement which they made of it was to point out that they, the clergy, had no authority to enjoin upon laymen any particular interpretation of doctrine. Even some of the most conservative of the Massachusetts ministers, themselves completely Calvinistic in doctrine, told the members of their congregations that the layman's chief duty toward God was to arrive at an understanding of Him by an examination of the validity of every tenet of Christian doctrine. The Calvinistic and Lutheran churches of Europe required that their members accept certain thological dogmas, but in Massachusetts the primary requirement for church membership was an individual experience of God's Grace, described by the individual in his own words.

This emphasis on freedom of the mind was then unique, and today is far from universal. Most of the early settlers of Massachusetts had been members of Church of England parishes, which were by definition agencies of an external power which dictated doctrine and practice, and discouraged criticism of it. Today the Roman Catholic Church denies liberty of conscience in matters of orthodoxy and morals, and the Protestant Episcopal Church requires its members to accept its doctrines and discipline. The colonial New England churches, like the Church of England, required the consent of the individual members to their moral discipline, but each offender was heard by his peers in open church meeting, instead of being tried by the clergy according to a fixed external standard. Instead of an established Congregational Church with power to enforce conformity in doctrine and morals, we have only individual churches which could punish what they determined to be heresy or sin only by denying the sinners fellowship until they repented. Actually, they rarely excommunicated anyone for heresy. The General Court submitted the Platform of 1648 to the local churches for their approval, but no ratification was called for, for it would not have been binding. The General Court printed the result of the Boston Synod of 1662, and "commended" it "unto the churches and people." In 1680 it ordered the Savoy Confession printed "for the benefit of the churches," but its use was optional. In 1708 Connecticut "commended" the Saybrook Platform to the churches.

Puritan orthodoxy, then, was a consensus of the views of the whole community, most members of which did not feel that they were authorized to cast stones at any man who held other theological opinions. Let's see how this worked out in practice. The one significant employment of the term "orthodoxy" in Massachusetts law was that requiring every town to maintain a learned and orthodox minister. Under this law, a few towns or parishes called Baptist ministers and used the power of civil taxation to support them, but there never was a case, so far as I can find, in which the town's choice of a minister was challenged in the courts on the basis of his orthodoxy.

After a town had chosen a minister, a group of neighboring churches was invited to send lay and clerical delegates to ordain him. In eighteenth-century ordinations there were frequently minority protests to the effect that the candidate was not sound on certain points of Calvinistic theology, but in few if any cases was a candidate rejected on primarily theological grounds. The council sometimes advised a candidate to decline a call because his theological views would cause trouble in that particular town, but I cannot remember the record of a case in which he was denied ordination because the council disagreed with his theology. The general custom was for the council to ask the candidate to state his religious convictions in his own words, although there were some ministers who would never permit a council of which they were members to require any theological statements. If the candidate said that he agreed with the Westminster Assembly of Divines, his orthodoxy was questioned no further; but candidates were never required to subscribe to the Westminster Catechism, or to accept any creed, or any other prearranged theological formulation. The minister who delivered the charge to the candidate commonly took the opportunity to disclaim any authority over his beliefs, or teachings.

The candidate would accept the covenant of the church over which he was ordained, but this document usually contained no theology, being a general statement of pious intent which any good man of the present generation could accept. Among the Massachusetts churches, the confession of faith was a late and limited development. When, in the Calvinistic reaction of the eighteenth century, some of the churches adopted detailed theological covenants, they also, commonly, adopted simple and untheological "forms of admission" so that people with "tender consciences" would not be excluded from communion. Some of these churches thus had a kind of theological "Half Way Covenant" which permitted Arminians and Unitarians to be members of Calvinistic town churches. In any case, the covenant or confession of faith was not dictated by any external authority, but was arrived at by mutual consent of its members and was subject to frequent revision. No Puritan church used any of the creeds in its services, much less required the acceptance of them as proof of orthodoxy. The creeds were, the ministers said, worthy of respect as the beliefs of pious men, but they were formulated by men, and therefore no other man could be required to accept them. Ministers who were Calvinists held to their beliefs because to them they seemed logically sound, not because they were received from authority. Revelation was confined strictly to the Bible, and if a colleague could find no proof of the Trinity in it, this personal idiosyncrasy did not disqualify his as a minister in good standing.

Since there was no Congregational Church, but only individual churches, each with a doctrine arrived at by a consensus of the opinions of the inhabitants of town or parish, there could be no Congregational orthodoxy except of the vaguest and most general sort. There was no clear-cut theological difference between Congregationalists, Baptists, and Episcopalians. So far as the Baptists were concerned, the Congregationalists admitted that they were right as to baptism. The dread which the early Puritans had of Baptist Antinomianism had proved unfounded, and their chief criticism of that denomination was the lack of college-educated clergy among them. The Baptists tended to attack the Congregational ministers as not being sound Calvinists, but some of their own ministers were overt Arminians. The Baptist churches were congregational in polity, each with its own consensus of theological beliefs, so a Baptist orthodoxy would be as hard to find as a Congregational one.

The Puritans made the Thirty-Nine Articles the shibboleth which divided Dissenter from Anglican, but their objection was not to the theological content of the Articles but the fact that they were a limitation on freedom of conscience. The liberal bishops were as

Arminian as Charles Chauncy could wish, while the American converts to the Church of England tended to be as Calvinistic as any New-Light whose noisy conduct they deplored. The American converts to Anglicanism to a large degree represented a reaction against the democratic theological polity of the Congregationalists. One of the reasons for the founding of King's College was to have an institution in which the students were not, as at Harvard and Yale, encouraged to get intellectual exercise by playing battledore and shuttlecock with the axioms of Christian dogma. Thus the difference between Anglican and Congregationalist was not in theology, but in the locus of authority.

Massachusetts in her first century and a half was an ideal proving ground for the principles on which our democratic way of life rests. Fortunate choice of settlers, happy isolation which afforded freedom to experiment, a basic philosophical faith in the reason of the common man, and freedom from the shackles of orthodoxy, make this a critical period in the growth of the democratic doctrine which we today regard as fundamental. The critical moment of the American Revolution came in the first decade of settlement, when the individual settlers took into their own hands and managed, through democratic town and church machinery, all of the matters of property, civil government, and religion which could be handled at that level. They made what was perhaps the most remarkable effort in the history of civilization to establish a society in which authority rested, in so far as possible, on the conscience of the individual. The rest of the colonial period in New England is the story of the adjustments in law and authority which that revolution made necessary.

Darrett B. Rutman

THE MIRROR OF PURITAN AUTHORITY

Perry Miller admitted that about 90 percent of New England's make-up was typically seventeenth-century English and only about 10 percent discretely Puritan. Darrett B. Rutman (b. 1929), professor of history at the University of New Hampshire, is interested in determining what was that 10 percent that was Puritan.

One of the sharpest critics of the Harvard school, he rejects their pre-occupation with ideas. Rutman uses, instead, a wide range of materials anticipating the quantifiers and, like them, concentrating on particular towns.

In the essay below he finds that in Boston, and probably in other New England towns, people lived life in all its variety and in so doing built a modern society. His study, like Shipton's, reveals no oligarchy of leaders imposing a medieval orthodoxy, no monolithic "Puritan" state. Churches, town governments, and institutions exhibited division and diversity from first to last. The Puritan dream, to Rutman, bears little relation to New England realities.

"Puritanism" is a time-honored word in American history. On the highest level of scholarship it signifies a concept dear to historians who have made a life's work defining the New England "mind" and its role in the evolution of a peculiar American "mind." On the lowest level it is one of many catchwords and slogans which serve to half-educate our youth, a capsule description to distinguish the New England colonies from those to the south and explain the course of New England's institutional and political development. On either level, the historians' "Puritanism" would seem to be their own creation, a stereotype which, as any intimate view of a "Puritan" community will show, has little to do with reality in New England.

The stereotype has arisen as the result of a tendency among historians of early New England, and particularly the intellectual historians who have dominated the field in the last generation, to limit themselves to the study of the writings of the articulate few, on the assumption that the public professions of the ministers and magistrates constitute a true mirror of the New England mind. The historian seeking to understand a New England concept of

From Darrett B. Rutman, "The Mirror of Puritan Authority," in George Athan Billias, ed., *Law and Authority in Colonial America* (Barre, Mass.: Barre Publishers, 1965). Used by permission.

authority, for example, has familiarized himself with the literature of England and Europe relative to the nature of man in society. He has scanned the works of such lay leaders of early New England as John Winthrop, noting his "little speech" on liberty of July 1645 and his earlier "A Modell of Christian Charity": "God Almightie in his most holy and wise providence hath soe disposed of the Condicion of mankinde, as in all times some must be rich some poore, some highe and eminent in power and dignitie; others meane and in subjeccion." He has thumbed through the ministerial writings to find Thomas Hooker: "However it is true, [that] the rule bindes such to the duties of their places and relations, yet it is certain, it requires that they should *first freely ingage* themselves in such covenants, and *then* be carefull to fullfill such duties." Or perhaps he has dipped into the pages of John Cotton: "It is evident by the light of nature, that all civill Relations are founded in Covenant. For, to passe by naturall Relations between Parents and Children, and Violent Relations, between Conquerors and Captives; there is no other way given whereby a people . . . can be united or combined into one visible body, to stand by mutuall Relations, fellow-members of the same body, but onely by mutuall Covenant; as appeareth between husband and wife in the family, Magistrates and subjects in the Commonwealth, fellow Citizens in the same Citie."

On occasion, the historian has turned also to the law, noting that it is replete with examples of the intrusion of authority into every aspect of New England life: "Taking into consideration the great neglect of many parents and masters in training up their children in learning, and labor, and other implyments which may be proffitable to the common wealth," it is ordered that the selectmen of every town "shall henceforth stand charged with the care of the redresse of this evill"; "forasmuch as in these countryes, where the churches of Christ are seated, the prosperity of the civil state is much advanced and blessed of God" and the ministers' preaching of the word "is of generall and common behoofe to all sorts of people, as being the ordinary meanes to subdue the harts of hearers not onely to the faith, and obedience to the Lord Jesus, but also to civill obedience, and allegiance unto magistracy" it is ordered that "every person shall duely resort and attend" to church services; it is ordered that "hereafter, noe dwelling howse shalbe builte above halfe a myle from the meeteing howse."

From such sources modern historians have drawn a picture of a highly cohesive and ordered social structure in which authority was omnipresent—the authority of the father in the family, of the minister in the church, of the magistrate in town and commonwealth. Both the cohesiveness of society and the authority were God-ordained, for man from the moment of Adam's fall was a degenerate being who required the oversight of his fellows in order to avoid the worst of sins. (*"In multitude of counsellers is safetie,"* Cotton was fond of saying.) Within the family, the father's authority was a natural concomitant to parenthood. But for the rest, man chose for himself. He submitted himself to the oversight of a congregation and through it a presbytery of ministers and elders, and to the civil authority of a king or prince or magistrate. Having submitted, however, he was bound by a godly duty to "faithe patience, obedience." Thus the ministers wrote that the congregations were obliged to "yeeld obedience to their Overseers, in whatsoever they see and hear by them commanded to them from the Lord"; the magistrates that "we have our authority from God, in way of an ordinance, such as hath the image of God eminently stamped upon it, the contempt and violation whereof hath been vindicated with examples of divine vengeance." To further the interests of the community as a whole, the individual's personal aspirations were to be sublimated. "Goe forth, everyman that goeth, with a publicke spirit, looking not on your owne things onely, but also on the things of others," Cotton commanded the settlers who sailed with Winthrop in 1630. And Winthrop echoed him: "Wee must be knitt together in this worke as one man." Magistrates and ministers, too, were committed ɔ the welfare of the entire community. The ministry was to guide th community in the way of God's truth. The civil authorities were to ʼreserve the community in its liberty to do "that only which is goɔd, just, and honest." The "ultimate and supreme" goal of both was that "the common Good of the Society, State or Kingdom" be preserved and *"God in all things . . . glorified."*

The current view of New England Puritanism, of which this view of New England authority is but a part, rests upon two major implicit assumptions. The first is that there is such a thing as "Puritanism" —a term impossible perhaps to define, but capable nevertheless of being described—and that the acme of Puritan ideals is to be found in New England during the years 1630–1650. After that date, it is

asserted, degeneration set in and there was a gradual falling away
from the Puritan ideal. George L. Haskins, the outstanding writer on
law and authority in early Massachusetts, reflects this assumption
when he writes that "the initial decades of the Bay Colony's existence
were the formative years" when, "under the pervasive influence of
Puritan doctrine," government, law, ecclesiastical polity, and social
structure were fully shaped; "the early social and political structure
was to endure for several decades, but it gradually crumbled as
primitive zeals began to wane and the religious aspects of life were
subordinated to commercial interests."

Haskins owes an unacknowledged debt to Cotton Mather and
other New England Jeremiahs, for the notion of Puritan quintessence
and decline goes back to Mather's day. Sitting down to pen his
Magnalia Christi Americana at the end of the seventeenth century,
Mather was convinced that the years in which he was living were
degenerate ones, that the years preceding his—the founding years
—had constituted a golden age of which he was one of the few pure
survivors. By telling the story of the past and its leaders he hoped to
call his own time to the dutiful obedience to God's will (in both
religious and social matters) which had previously prevailed. Mather's
motive was succinctly set forth in the introduction to his sketches of
the lives of the early ministers: "Reader, behold these *examples;*
admire and follow what thou dost behold *exemplary* in them. They are
offered unto the publick, with the intention . . . that *patterns* may
have upon us the force which *precepts* have not."

This first assumption, though old, has proved of great pragmatic
value to the modern historian. Having established that the first
decades of New England were the acme of Puritanism, the historian
can then turn around and describe Puritanism in terms of what he
has found in New England during those early years. Hence, he can
avoid the problem of defining Puritanism, a task which Samuel Eliot
Morison once found distasteful but necessary. The historian can also
evade the issue of separating those facets of New England thought
and character which were uniquely Puritan from those which merely
reflected the way of life in England. Moreover, by accepting Mather's
progression from golden age to degeneration, the historian can
conceptualize Puritanism by drawing upon a vast quantity of material
without worrying whether his sources are being used out of context
as regards time, place, or persons. If Puritanism can "best be

described as that point of view, that philosophy of life, that code of values, which was carried to New England by the first settlers in the early seventeenth century" and became "one of the continuous factors in American life and thought," as a leading anthology by Perry Miller and Thomas H. Johnson asserts, then certainly (the historian reasons) one can postulate a unique and unchanging Puritan ideal of society in terms of the letters and tracts emanating from New England during the first two decades of settlement, and, with increasing caution in view of the degeneration, from the whole of the seventeenth century. The same anthology contains selections from Winthrop's 1630 "Modell of Christian Charity" through John Wise's 1717 *Vindication of the Government of New-England Churches* to exemplify a Puritan theory of state and society, and concludes that:

> *the most obvious lesson of the selections printed herein is that . . . the theorists of New England thought of society as a unit, bound together by inviolable ties; they thought of it not as an aggregation of individuals but as an organism, functioning for a definite purpose, with all parts subordinate to the whole, all members contributing a definite share, every person occupying a particular status . . . . The society of early New England was decidedly 'regimented.' Puritans did not think the state was merely an umpire, standing on the side lines of a contest, limited to checking egregious fouls, but otherwise allowing men free play according to their abilities and the breaks of the game . . . . The state to them was an active instrument of leadership, discipline, and, wherever necessary, of coercion . . . . The commanders were not to trim their policies by the desires of the people, but to drive ahead upon the predetermined course . . . . There was no questioning that men who would not serve the purposes of the society should be whipped into line. The objectives were clear and unmistakable; any one's disinclination to dedicate himself to them was obviously so much recalcitrancy and depravity.*

The second major assumption is that one is free to ignore the "if" in Winthrop's "little speech" on liberty: "If you stand for your natural corrupt liberties, and will do what is good in your own eyes, you will not endure the least weight of authority, but will murmur, and oppose, and be always striving to shake off that yoke." Winthrop, had of course, no call to speak of those who "stand" for natural liberties unless there were individuals who took such a point of view. Similarly, one assumes oneself free to ignore the nature of the law—that law reflects not merely the assumptions of society, but the antithesis of those assumptions. The law calling upon town selectmen to insure the proper upbringing of children when their parents were neglecting to educate them to serve the community indicates not only that children were expected to receive such an education, but implies strongly that some children were *not* being prepared in the prescribed manner. The law requiring settlers to build their houses within a half-mile of the agencies of social control—church and magistrates— not only echoes the ideal of a cohesive society, but the fact that some persons were perfectly willing to break with the ideal and scatter across the rich New England countryside. One indication that the law (and the ideal it reflected) was being disregarded is a 1639 letter written by the Plymouth congregation to Boston's First Church "concerning the holding of Farmes of which there is noe lesse frequent use with your selves then with us . . . by means of [which] a mans famylie is Divided so in busie tymes they cannot (except upon the Lord's day) all of them joyne with him in famylie duties." The repeal of the Massachusetts law in 1640 on the grounds that it was unenforceable is still further substantiation.

The assumption is not without its rationalization. If the historian accepts as a matter of faith that, as Richard Schlatter writes, "it was the Puritan leaders who shaped the culture of New England, whatever the rank and file may have wanted"—an extension of the notion of a Puritan oligarchy from the political to the social milieu—then it is easy to explain away those who disregarded the law or who stood for "natural corrupt liberties." Once again, Mather has provided the modern historian with a ready-made answer. To him incidents of social and religious dissent were merely the "continual *temptation* of the devil" which were, at least in the early years, overcome by the pure in heart.

That an ideal arrangement of society was visualized by some of the first comers to New England and that they contemplated realizing the ideal in the New World is patently obvious. One need only glance at Winthrop's "Modell of Christian Charity" to see it. But was the ideal uniquely Puritan? The thought that men, like the diverse parts of nature, ideally stood in ordered symmetry is to be found in Shakespeare's *Troilus and Cressida*:

> *The heavens themselves, the planets and this centre,*
> *Observe degree, priority and place.*
> *. . . . O, when degree is shaked,*
> *Which is the ladder of all high designs,*

> *The enterprise is sick! How could communities . . .*
> *Prerogative of age, crowns, sceptres, laurels,*
> *But by degree, stand in authentic place?*

The notion of men entering society by compact or covenant and thereby binding themselves to authority was a pervading theme in Western thought, although particularly relevant for the religious polemicists of the sixteenth and seventeenth centuries. One finds it, for example, in the *Vindiciae Contra Tyrannos* of the French Protestants and in Richard Hooker's *Ecclesiastical Polity.* In Hooker's work, too, is found the idea of the divine nature of authority once established by man: "God creating mankind did endue it naturally with full power to guide itselv, in what kind of societies soever it should choose to live," yet those on whom power "is bestowed even at men's discretion, they likewise do hold it by divine right" for "albeit God do neither appoint the thing nor assign the person; nevertheless when men have established both, who doth doubt that sundry duties and offices depending thereupon are prescribed in the word of God"; therefore, "we by the law of God stand bound meekly to acknowledge them for God's lieutenants."

More importantly, was the ideal—so often expressed by the articulate few and commented upon by the intellectual historians—ever a reality in New England? Certainly conditions in America were not conducive to it. The very ideal contained a flaw, for while in England the social and religious covenant was an abstract principle to be toyed with by logicians, in New England it was, in town and church, transformed into practice. How does one convince the generality that the forms and personnel of authority are within its province, but that once established they are in God's domain and are to be honored as such? What spokesman for New England orthodoxy could surpass Ireland's Cuchulinn in battling the waves of the sea? Moreover, the transition from old to New England constituted a break in the social fabric familiar to the individual. In an English borough or village the individual located himself according to well-established social and political relationships, but these were no more. Family ties in New England during the early years were relatively few. Ties to the traditional elements of authority—vestrymen, churchwardens, manor stewards, borough councillors, justices-of-the-peace—had disappeared, to be created anew in the New England town, it is true, but such new relationships lacked the sanctity of long familiarity. And even when new ties existed, there was little stability in the New Englander's place in the social and political order. What mattered the regular assertion that God had ordained some to ride and some to walk when those who walked one day could, by virtue of the absence of traditional leaders, the presence of New World opportunities, and the application of their own diligence, ride another?

Such musings give a hint of the answer as to whether the ideal was ever a reality in New England. For more than a hint, however, one must turn to the New Englander's own habitat, his town. For many historians such research necessitates a shift to an entirely different set of sources. It means leaving behind published sermons, tracts, and laws and turning instead to town and church records. It calls for an end to the relatively comfortable perusal of the writings of a few and undertaking the drudgery of culling local records to identify the persons in a given town—their backgrounds, landholdings, economic activities, social and economic affiliations, and politics. Research of such nature is time-consuming, but the rewards are rich.

One such study is that of Sudbury, Massachusetts, undertaken by Sumner Chilton Powell. Sudbury was a small interior town devoted to the raising of cattle. It was not directly affected by the turn to trade and commerce in the 1640s as were some other communities. Moreover, its population was relatively homogeneous during the period with which Powell dealt. One might expect, therefore, that all the generalizations respecting Puritan attitudes would be reflected in the activities of Sudbury's people. But Powell's story is far from that. The founders were acquisitive English yeomen, little touched by any formal Puritan movement in England. During the town's first years, its people were devoted to building and cultivating the land, using the "open-field" or common agricultural method which most of them had known in England. In the early 1650s, however, they felt the pinch of too little land and solicited the General Court for an additional tract. The subsequent enlargement opened Pandora's box. One segment of the town demanded a shift to closed agriculture—large tracts individually operated—and a division by which "every man shall enjoy a like quantity of land"; another resisted. This issue became entangled with a second, the desire of some to build a new meeting house. Matters were complicated still further by a third issue, the desire of the older settlers to limit the number of cattle allowed on the town meadow. The heated debates that followed involved every person in the town, including minister Edmund Brown. Town meetings became "exciting and well-attended"; tempers flared. In the end, the town split, one faction moving away to found Marlborough, Massachusetts.

The debates divided the town into warring factions, Peter Noyes and Edmund Goodnow representing the first settlers and heads of families, John Ruddock and John How leading the younger men of the town, and minister Brown acting largely in his own interest. At one point Goodnow declared that, "be it right or wrong, we will have [our way] . . . if we can have it no other way, we will have it by club law." At another point, How threatened secession by the young men: "If you oppresse the poore, they will cry out; and if you persecute us in one city, wee must fly to another." Pastor Brown called a meeting "to see to the constraining of youth from the profanation of the Lord's day in time of public service" and turned the session into a political harangue; subsequently the minister appeared at a town meeting to cry out he would "put it to a Vote, before I would be nosed by them." Townsmen refused to attend Sabbath lectures and services for fear of being "ensnared" by their political opponents. One party visited the minister "to desire him not to meddle" and Ruddock bluntly told his pastor that, "setting aside your office, I regard you no more than another man." The Reverend Mr. Brown ultimately attempted to have the dispute submitted to a council of elders drawn from neighboring churches, but the various factions refused on the grounds that "it was a civil difference." Where in this debate is there any indication that the New Englanders "thought of society as a unit, bound together by inviolable ties . . . all parts subordinate to the whole . . . every person occupying a particular status"?

In Boston, too, much the same story is to be found: actions quite contrary to attitudes so often generalized upon. In 1634, the generality—again, a relatively homogeneous populace—challenged the town's leadership by demanding an immediate division of all available land on an equal basis. The response of the leadership was to some extent based on attitudes made classic by historians. Winthrop, thinking in terms of the community, argued against the allocation of more land than an individual could use, partly out of his desire "to

prevent the neglect of trades, and other more necessary employ-
ments" and "partly that there might be place to receive such as
should come after." To him, it would be "very prejudicial" if newcomers "should be forced to go far off for land, while others had
much, and could make no use of it, more than to please their eye
with it." But the townsmen would have none of it. Land was too much
a way to personal gain.

The issue reached a climax in December when a committee of
seven was elected to divide the town lands. Winthrop "and other of
the chief men" failed of election. The townsmen feared "that the
richer men would give the poorer sort no great proportions of land"
and chose "one of the elders and a deacon, and the rest of the in-
ferior sort." All the advocates of an ordered society were brought
to bear to overturn the election. Winthrop spoke of his grief "that
Boston should be the first who should shake off their magistrates,"
and the Reverend Mr. Cotton of "the Lord's order among the Israel-
ites" by which "all such businesses" were "committed to the elders."
"It had been nearer the rule," Cotton argued, "to have chosen some
of each sort." The generality gave way for the moment and agreed to
a new election. Subsequently a more proper committee was chosen
"to devide and dispose" of the land "leaving such portions in Common for the use of newe Commers, and the further benefitt of the
towne, as in theire best discretions they shall thinke fitt."

The battle, however, was by no means over. The pursuit of
individual gain continued to prompt political activity. The prevailing
economic view (and one not uniquely Puritan) was that all phases of
the economy were subject to government regulation. Town governments in Massachusetts had the authority to regulate land distribution, land usage, and the laying out of streets; in Boston, the town
government established embryonic building codes and licensed inns
and wharves. Given this actual exercise of power over the various
avenues of opportunity, it was to one's advantage to participate in
public affairs.

Land, for a time, continued to be the principal issue. The town had
a limited area into which it could expand. By the second decade it
had become difficult to find plots for newcomers or additional acreage for older settlers. In 1641, popular pressure forced the selectmen
to review the larger grants made in the 1630s, but this action served
little purpose. Even where surveys indicated that a Winthrop, Oliver

or Cotton held more land than had been allocated, the selectmen took no remedial action. During the following year, the selectmen—in order to obtain more room on Boston's tiny peninsula for house lots—resurrected an earlier order denying the inhabitants permanent possession of their lots in the Boston fields. The result was an angry town meeting in which the order was repealed "for peace sake, and for avoyding of confusion in the Towne."

Boston's turn to trade in the 1640s brought about a change. Opportunities for personal aggrandizement in land were gradually replaced by the better chances for advancement in commerce and allied crafts such as coopering, leatherworking, and shipbuilding. For the artisan, participation in local government was equally as important as it had been for those persons interested in land. The leatherworker or butcher, subject to the selectmen under local regulations regarding the cleanliness of his establishment, or even his very right to carry on his trade within the town, of necessity participated in the town meetings to elect the men who could, in a moment, curtail or end his business activities. The retailer, subject to the inspection of clerks of the market operating under commonwealth law, was quick to make known his choice for such officials. Almost everyone engaged in any kind of economic activity—the laws limiting the electorate notwithstanding—sought to vote for the deputies to the General Court and the assistants inasmuch as these men wrote the commonwealth ordinances governing economic activity.

On the inter-town level in Massachusetts, too, the desire for personal aggrandizement played havoc with the ideal of an orderly and cohesive society. Town rivalries arose; boundary disputes raged interminably between communities, the prize being a rich meadow or copse. Craftsmen in one town were jealous of those in another. Shoemakers outside Boston, for example, objected to shoemakers within that town organizing a company and seeking exclusive privileges regarding shoes sold in the Boston market. Do not allow "our Brethren of Boston" to "have power put into their hands to hinder a free trade," they wrote to the General Court. "Keeping out Country shoomakers from Coming into the Market," they continued, "wil weaken the hands of the Country shoomakers from using their trade, or occasion them to Remove to boston which wilbe hurtful to Other townes." Merchants and tradesmen in the northern towns—Ipswich, Salem, Newbury—bitterly resented the fact that "Boston, being the

chiefest place of resort of Shipping, carries away all the Trade."
They reacted in a series of political moves aimed at reducing Boston's central position in the commonwealth. An effort was made to
move the seat of government from Boston; an attempt got underway
to change the basis of representation in the House of Deputies to
Boston's disadvantage; and an alliance was formed between northern
towns and country towns to create a bloc within the House to oppose
those towns immediately around Boston harbor.

The political activity in and among the towns suggests that the
people of Massachusetts Bay, and one can extrapolate to include
the other New England colonies, were not acting within the concept
of authority and cohesive, ordered society which modern historians
have so carefully delineated and pronounced to be characteristic of
Puritanism and Puritan New England. Society was not something to
which the people of the Bay commonwealth invariably subordinated
their own interests. Indeed, the abstract concept of "society" seems
to have held little meaning for a generality intent upon individual
pursuits. Nor was authority a pervasive thing, obliging the individual
through family, church, and state to sublimate his personal aspirations to the interests of the community as a whole. The "state" in
Sudbury—in the form of either town or commonwealth government—
could provide no other solution to the town's disputes than to permit
the community to divide. The church—the Reverend Mr. Brown
personally and the elders of the neighboring churches invited in by
Brown—was unable to interpose its authority to settle matters. Family fidelity failed to check the personal aspirations of the "landless
young sons" who followed Ruddock and How.

The people of Massachusetts, it would appear, were coming to
view the elements of authority as being divided rather than united.
In particular, they viewed the church and state as distinct entities
with well-defined (and to a large extent mutually exclusive) areas
of operation. In Sudbury, for example, Pastor Brown's intervention
in a civil affair led to his being asked not to "meddle." In Boston, the
calling of the Synod of 1646–1648 by the commonwealth government
roused strong opposition from those who lashed out against the in-
terjection of "civil authority" in church business. The conflict so
begun would eventuate in a full scale assault upon the imposition of
ministerial authority within the church and of synodical authority
among churches—further evidence that the historians' concept of

authority and cohesiveness bears little resemblance to New England reality. The historians might cite as evidence of the concept the Cambridge *Platform* which emanated from the Synod and pronounced ministerial and synodical authority to be part of the New England Way, but the deathbed utterances of the Reverend John Wilson are more to the point. Wilson cited as "those sins amongst us, which provoked the displeasure of God" the rising up of the people *"against their Ministers . . . when indeed they do but Rule for Christ,"* and *"the making light of, and not subjecting to the Authority of* Synods, *without which the Churches cannot long subsist."*

The same dichotomy between church and state which one finds in the towns may be seen on the commonwealth level. The historians have noted all too often those laws passed by civil authorities to further the views of the church and those cases where the ministry advised the magistrates on civil matters. But they have paid far too little attention to the arduous efforts made to define the respective spheres of church and state. As John Cotton wrote in 1640, "the government of the Church is as the Kingdome of Christ is, not of this world, but spirituall and heavenly . . . . The power of the keyes is far distant from the power of the sword." To him church and state in Massachusetts were involved in the same task, "the Establishment of pure Religion, in doctrine, worship, and [church] government, according to the word of God: As also the reformation of all corruptions in any of these." Hence the ministers, in whose care the word of God was placed, could logically press for "sweet and wholsom" laws and "civil punishments upon the willfull opposers and disturbers" of the church. But for the things of this world—"the disposing of mens goods or lands, lives or liberties, tributes, customes, worldly honors, and inheritances"—"in these the Church submitteth, and refereth it self to the civill state."

For the most part, too, historians in the past few years have tended to overlook those cases where there was a clash between magistrates and ministers. In 1639, the General Court decided that too frequent and overly long church meetings were detrimental to the community and asked the elders "to consider about the length and frequency of church assemblies." The ministers promptly denounced the magistrates. The request "cast a blemish upon the elders," they said, one "which would remain to posterity, that they should need to be regulated by the civil magistrates." The over-anxious intervention of an elder in a matter before the Assistants in 1643, on the other hand, drove one magistrate to exasperation. "Do you think to come with your eldership here to carry matters?" he shouted. On another occasion, when the elders of Essex County went beyond the bounds that Winthrop considered proper in espousing the cause of the northern towns against Boston—for when town argued with town the elders tended to identify with their communities—the governor lashed out. They "had done no good offices in this matter, through their misapprehensions both of the intentions of the magistrates, and also of the matters themselves, being affairs of state, which did not belong to their calling."

In the division of authority that was taking place, it would seem that the church was freely conceded the power of opening and closing the doors of heaven. To whatever extent the individual sought heaven, he honored the authority of the church in moral and theological matters. But the keys to personal aggrandizement in this world were lodged with the state, and the generality was coming to look upon the state in a peculiarly modern way. In one sense the state was the servant of the individual, obligated to foster his welfare and prosperity. At the same time, it was to protect him from the aspirations of others—acting, so to speak, as an umpire for society, exercising authority in such a way as to avoid collisions between members of the community who were following their individual yet concentric orbits. One can perceive such a view of society, however obliquely, in the political theory of the later New Englanders. For indeed, their writings on this matter are not all of a piece. There is a subtle difference between a Winthrop or Cotton for whom the goal of society was the pleasing of God; a Samuel Willard to whom a happy, contented people was most pleasing to God; and a John Wise to whom "the Happiness of the People, is the End of its [the state's] Being; or main Business to be attended and done."

The view of society discernible in the New England community is quite different from that expounded by intellectual historians who have turned to the writings of the articulate few—and little else—as their mirror of New England's mind. Are we to discard their mirror and the "Puritan" concepts which they have seen in it? The purpose of intellectual history is to delineate the ideological framework within which a people acted. If the actions of the people under consideration do not fall within the framework created, it follows that the framework is invalid. It is not that simple, of course. In the case of New England, the intellectual framework erected over the past years has been firmly based upon the writings of the leading laymen and clergy in the society. We must accept such works as a valid expression of their ideals, even though their ideals might not apply to the people as a whole.

But what are we to describe as "Puritan," the ideals of the articulate few which, relative to society and authority, were neither unique nor pervasive, or the actuality of the man in the street—more accurately, the man in the village lane—which does not fit the ideals? The very fact that such a question can be asked would seem to imply that the description of New England in terms of Puritanism, or of Puritanism in terms of New England, is erroneous. Certainly, the concept of a Puritan golden age, followed by decline, disappears. Mather's degeneration is, in large part, nothing more than the insistence by the generality upon a relationship between the individual and society rather different from that held to by the leaders. And the golden age, as Mather himself admitted, was marked by continual controversies which "made neighbours that should have been like sheep, to 'bite and devour one another' " and inspired "unaccountable party-making," a symptom of that different relationship.

The historian must, of course, address himself to the problem of New England's intellectuals. Isolated from reality as they were, they clung for almost half a century to ideals which grew more outdated with the passing of each day, and then gradually and subtly accommodated their ideals to the realities of the situation facing them. But their accommodation and the forces in society that caused them to make changes represent a much more important aspect of history than the mere description of "Puritanism." And the historian must dispense with the easy generalization that such leaders "shaped" New England's culture regardless of what "the rank and file may have wanted." He must seek instead to understand the rank and file, their motivations, aspirations, and achievements. For in the last analysis which is more vital, an ideological "Puritanism" divorced from reality which has received so much attention over the years, or the reality which has received so little attention but which was in essence laying down the basis for two-and-a-half centuries of American history ahead?

III NEW ENGLAND SOCIETY

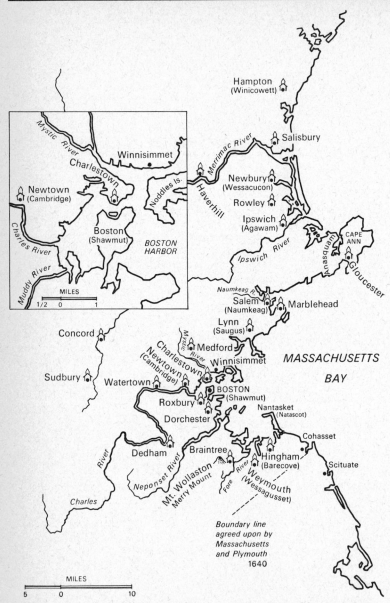

FIGURE 3. Towns discussed in the readings may be located on this map, except for Andover, which is southwest of Haverhill. After a map drawn under the supervision of Robert E. Moody. Reproduced by permission of Charles Scribner's Sons from *Atlas of American History* by James Truslow Adams. Copyright 1943 Charles Scribner's Sons, renewal copyright © 1971.

Sumner Chilton Powell
PURITAN VILLAGE

In a Pulitzer Prize-winning account of the colonial village of Sudbury Sumner Chilton Powell (b. 1924) provided a model for modern writers of local history. Puritan Village was written in 1963 before the more recent emphasis on the concepts of the behavioral sciences but Powell's evidence tends to support some of the findings of the quantifiers even though he fits them into a more traditional interpretation of Puritanism. Taking account of varying English influences on the Sudbury villagers, he is especially concerned to show the changes they made in adapting their society to New World conditions. In the selection reprinted here on the search for stability through transition and change he finds perspective on the analogous problem faced by our own times.

The historical debate on "the origin" of a type of social and political structure called "the New England town" is probably not over, but the question itself may be superficial today. We can now realize that there were multiple origins and many distinct early towns, and that all of these towns and their relationships need careful examination.

If the question of the origin seems superficial, the investigation of the change, transition, and stability of English local institutions across the Atlantic Ocean in the seventeenth century is not. The members of these groups came from quite diverse social and political locales in England, with definite sets of attitudes and drives, usually expressed in religious terms—but not always. England itself contained a large variety of local institutions. As a skilled archivist and local historian has said, "No place is 'representative' of English local government in seventeenth-century England. The evidence one finds tells us what local government was like in one distinct village, or parish, or town or borough, no more, no less."

Apparently those men and women who emigrated to New England and formed new groups were inventive, as were some who settled in southern areas. Certainly they had the unique challenge of a "town grant," which could be defined more or less as the inhabitants wished.

They made a staggering number of changes. How many men

today, founding a "godly plantation" on the moon or on any habitable planet, would make as many significant alterations in religion, in social organization, in local government, and in attitude and values generally? Consider what might be called the constructive dissent in the first generation of Sudbury men. What were the selectmen there actually doing? They were constructing a community of free townsmen. This seems to have been their principal ideal, and their loyalty to the town even transcended their professions of religious faith. They had been trained in a variety of local institutions in England. They knew how to function as jurymen, vestrymen, borough councilors, or parish officers. But they must have wanted more, for they constructed an entirely new type of town.

Even the minister succumbed to the charged atmosphere. When his leadership over the youth was threatened by John Ruddock, when his sermons did not prevent "prophanation of the Lord's Day," he appeared in town meetings and prosecuted his cause "with violence." "Put it to vote!" shouted Edmund Brown. He could not believe that the new political entity would abandon him. But it did—at least for a while. John Ruddock and his group, facing severe restrictions, wanted to construct a new town.

Examine the solemn meetings in Sudbury in January 1655. Note how completely absent the traditional legal sanctions are. The selectmen did not bolster themselves with citations of Elizabethan laws, English customs, or warrants from local justices of the peace. As far as one can tell from reading the Sudbury orders, the selectmen assumed that once the General Court had made the initial town grant, they were the principal source of power in their area, subject only to the approval of the townsmen. It was very significant that when the General Court sent out an investigating committee in 1656, not only was there resentment in Sudbury, but also there is no indication that the townsmen followed the recommendations on the sizing of the commons.

There seems to have been deep meaning to the phrase in the Sudbury Town Book, *free townsman*. Since it is never fully defined, it may have implied a status more like that of borough freeman than that of freeman written in the orders of the General Court. In Sudbury at any rate, such a man knew he could dissent and that he would be heard.

To quote the town clerk, "John Ruddock, being then present, did, by his vote, dissent from the act." At that point Ruddock was the leader of a minority group. But did he, full of frustration and ill-will, call his youth to arms and resort to violence? He did not. Finding his ambitions blocked in the Musketaquid valley, he proceeded to construct another community. Once again, he rebuilt human institutions in the face of necessity.

Ruddock developed his constructive faith in relation to the area about him and with the full permission and support of the Massachusetts government. When he dissented in 1655, Ruddock hoped that another land area would be available to him and to his petitioners. He could have swallowed his pride and remained in Sudbury. He could have moved across the river and settled on the plots which the selectmen offered him. But he did neither. Whether tacitly or explicitly, he made a series of daring assumptions, involving predictions about his own leadership, his group, the General Court, the Indians, and the opposition party in Sudbury. With his confidence fortified by the grant of town land from the General Court, he then proceeded to express his ideals and his will.

Each step demanded both logic and leadership. Ruddock had to "view" the area to assure his group that it would be productive and satisfying to them. He then recognized the rights of the Indians, although there is no evidence that he tried to communicate with them to see whether they understood his purpose. Had he tried to do this sincerely, he might have made the unhappy discovery that the English concept of the individual, exploitative ownership of soil was causing apprehensions among the original natives.

Next, Ruddock needed to display confidence in his woodsmen and farmers, and to develop this into a reciprocal relationship. Not only did he have to prove that crops could be raised, but he had to show that a market for them could be found and a road built for their transportation. In addition, he had to hope that even though he might be considered immoral, some minister would forgive him and join his new group. This took many years, as the new town later learned.

Above all, Ruddock had to display a type of idealism that could transcend his previous failures. He probably had to achieve a remarkable synthesis of the new awareness of the ideals of his young followers and his own ability to assist his men in fulfilling them. In short, to be able to establish a community that would function "forever" in the same spot where the leaders planted it, Ruddock must have had a complex mind and a profound faith which he could communicate to others.

Later generations use the term "New England town," and thereby assume the established set of relationships and attitudes which New Englanders have known for decades. Today we think we know what a "town" is. But to the first settlers, the term "town" must have meant a life of uncertainty, balanced by a faith in social order and stability.

To emigrate from accustomed social institutions and relationships to a set of unfamiliar communities in the way in which Noyes and Ruddock shifted from England to Sudbury, and the latter from Sudbury to Marlborough, meant a startling transformation. The townsmen had to change or abandon almost every formal institution which they had taken for granted.

The Sudbury Town Book, read in the context of close examination of English local records of the period, actually describes this set of reforms. The first clerk, Hugh Griffin, began using a new vocabulary as he recorded the orders made by his selectmen and his free townsmen.

Gone were the courts-baron, courts-leet, vestries, out-hundred courts, courts of election, courts of record, courts of the borough, courts of orders and decrees, courts of investigation, courts of ordination, and views of frankpledge. In their place came meetings of men to order town affairs, or later, selectmen's meetings and town meetings, with a few references to the General Court and the county court.

Gone were the seneschal, bailiff, jurymen, virgate, yardland, reversion, messuage, tenement, toft, croft, heriot, close, fealty to the lord, admission, hayward, annual rent, copyholders, coliarholders, and freeholders. In their stead came selectmen, grants of land, freemen, and free townsmen.

The medieval church calendar was completely abandoned in the first generation. Whereas the Hampshire farmers had started the year in England with Lady Day (March 25) and ended it with Plow Monday, which was the first Monday after Epiphany (January 6), the entire calendar in early Sudbury was reduced to a numerical sequence of months, monotonous in their prosaic designations, starting with "the first month" or March. The second generation in both Sudbury and

Marlborough returned to the old calendar. The men of Marlborough had a town meeting on December 25, 1663. They were using the day not for the ancient ceremony they had celebrated since childhood, but for a new kind of ritual—the formation of a godly community.

Gone also were the rector, curate, sexton, ringers, glebe land, terrier, tithe, parish perambulation, churchwardens, sidemen, questmen, overseers of the poor, and all the many familiar objects of church "furniture," from the cross to the goblet. The town clerk of Sudbury spoke of pastor, deacon, meetinghouse, town perambulation, and a town "rate" to pay the pastor and to repair or rebuild the meetinghouse.

Into the dark mists had disappeared articles of visitation, Book of Common Prayer, presentments, commissary, archdeacon, church courts, purgation, certificate of penance, and holy days. Hugh Griffin had no substitution for these. As far as local historians can tell, the first Sudbury "church" did not even keep a separate book. Only the visit of the "Reverend Elders" tried to impose an external church discipline on Sudbury, and Griffin did not even record their presence in the Town Book.

Abolished too were the quarter sessions, justices of the peace, knights of the shire, king's sheriff, house of correction, Marshalsea payments, king's bench, assizes, Privy Council, and Parliament. The King and Queen were never mentioned. In their places were governor, magistrates, General Court, and town deputy.

Sudbury was no longer an ancient borough and had no mayor, bailiff, collector of rents of the assizes, chamberlain, chief constable, sergeants at mace, coroner, burgess, aldermen, market overseers, ale tasters, or master of the grammar school. No one met in the Town House or aspired to build paneled rooms for the "select fraternity" who governed the town. There were only selectmen, marshal, clerk, and various townsmen doing various specific jobs, as assigned by the town meeting.

Hugh Griffin did not have to note any maimed soldiers, travelers from Ireland, Dunkirkers, or soldiers from Bohemia. Someone had tried to dignify the resident Indian chiefs by giving them the names Jethro and Cato, but it seems there were few visitors during the first generation, and few people "warned out."

Life in Sudbury was indeed a "new" England. No wonder men like Samuel Gordon and Thomas Morton were amazed and alarmed as they inspected other towns. What held these communities together and gave them stability? What welded relationships and created loyalties and mutual respect?

Bold leaders, the tacit and sometimes actual approval by the General Court, concern for every inhabitant, and a deep faith were sufficient for the first generation of Sudbury townsmen. One can argue that three institutions gave a structure and a harmony to the community: the open-field system of farming, the town meeting, and the town church. Sudbury continued "general and particular" fields until 1694, and Professor Ault has clearly shown how this joint administration of agriculture led to a kind of local democratic government. The Sudbury town meeting considered a wide variety of social problems, from the granting, renting, taxation, and sale of land to bastardy and the mental health of its citizens. When one reads the Town Book closely, one is impressed that the selectmen were aware of the precise "condition" of every inhabitant and quick to note any "dangerous" or "suspicious" person amongst the group. Any unusual occurrence which caused a problem seems to have been brought before the town, and the townsmen voted on the policy of warning out "maimed, defective, or suspicious persons," the problem of finding a smith and keeping the mill running, the correct height of field fences, an inventory of "all mens' estates," and the sickness of any citizen. They also considered the menace of hungry cows and marauding wolves, the correct placement of roads between communities, and any infringement of town meadow or town land, which seems to have been managed as a kind of corporate bank account, to be granted, rented, or called back at the will of the inhabitants and selectmen.

The Sudbury church seems to have been virtually indistinguishable from the town throughout the seventeenth century, but it must have given a sense of order and security until 1655, after which the church was "in a most deplorable state, from which it was long in recovering." Town meetings discussed the problem of finding a substitute when the Reverend Edmund Brown fell ill in 1678, hired his successor, the Reverend James Sherman, and set the conditions of his contract, drew up the design and levied taxes for the third meetinghouse 1686–1688, appealed to those citizens who were negligent in paying their share of Mr. Sherman's salary, and decided who could or could not build pews in the church in place of the normal "seats left open at both ends."

The first generation found that it could not abandon the traditional calendar, and from 1648 onward the pagan names of February, March, and the rest were introduced into the Town Book and have been used ever since. The second generation, however, returned to several deep-seated English institutions and customs. The farmers grew "English pasture" and sedge fences, the military company purchased a "flight of colors," men were elected tithingmen to collect the church tax, and town accounts began to appear in the Town Book, making some pages read like any English borough book, citing income and expenses.

The most significant institution which was reintroduced was the English common law. When Widow Loker refused to resign to the town the housing, ground, trees, and privileges which she had sold to the town, the selectmen turned to the county court at Cambridge and started a suit at law. Another entry indicates the relationship of Sudbury to the courts and to ultimate authority. "This day Sarjt. Barnard made report to the Town what success hee mett withall att the Quarter Sessions; and then did chuse a commity to meet with and treat the Jury that shall be appointed to state his Majesties hy way betweene our Town and Marlbrough and Indevor to the uttmost of thear power that it may bee layd out so as it may bee least prejudijuall to our Town."

Ten years before Barnard's report, Sudbury acknowledged that it was now part of the British empire, for the town, desiring to be rid of one D. Hedley, warned him out in "his Majesty's name." The King's tax started to be collected by the town constable by April 1693, and once again these town officers relied on the ultimate authority of the King. It is particularly interesting to read that the town voted a special tax of "eight pounds in money . . . for the sending and transporting of Thomas Blake to Old England." The absence of any references in the Sudbury Town Book to "his Majesty" during the famous governorship of Sir Edmund Andros, 1686–1690, clearly illustrates the spirit of insubordination of which the governor constantly complained while he was in Boston. Apparently Sudbury was willing to acknowledge the authority of the King, but on its own terms and at specific times.

Sudbury, like the other early New England towns, was a remarkable experiment in the formation and growth of a social community. Now that this town presents an explicit case study, further examination in group behavior can be made of the whole problem of the growth and stability of such communities, provided that accurate categories of investigation are formed. William Caudill suggests the concepts of the "stress" on various groups and the formation of "linked open systems" and feels that students should consider the Atlantic only as a highway between related communities. He advises that we try to define and discover "cultural pairs" of communities on both sides of the ocean and then ask why some citizens left, why some stayed, why some shuttled back and forth in the whole Atlantic system. Bernard Bailyn has clearly shown that the Boston merchants returned to the British trade system by the end of the seventeenth century, and certainly both the inhabitants and the free townsmen of Sudbury felt the compelling need of the authority of the King and common law by the second generation.

If, as it seems, we today are in a period of radical social upheaval and violent transformation of communities and entire national and international populations, much perspective can be gained from close examination of a somewhat analogous period in the seventeenth century. Above all, we should not lose the faith in our ability to create "godly, orderly communities," or our desire to rely on law and common consent, rather than on violence and the authority of a powerful central government. If we abandon our New England heritage, we do so at our peril. The Sudbury townsmen might not have been able to order their community "forever" as they hoped, but they set a remarkable example for all the generations which have followed them.

Darrett B. Rutman
WINTHROP'S BOSTON

Rutman, whose views of New England realities were represented in the previous section of the readings, here presents more specific evidence, based on his study of Boston, of the divisions that prevented realization of Winthrop's dream of unity.

As Rutman sees it, the Puritan state and church tended to an exclusiveness that increasingly ignored the real nature of town society which ultimately brought accommodations far from the medieval utopian ideal of the founders.

Aboard the *Arbella,* contemplating his "Citty upon a Hill," Winthrop had envisioned a truly united society. He had spoken of the human body as a single entity, each part accepting its role and quietly performing its proper function that the body itself might live and flourish. His ideal society was a similar entity, each individual accepting his place and quietly contributing to the welfare of the whole. In the New World, however, men argued over the rich land and the truth of God; Boston's developing land policy increasingly acknowledged the necessity of giving opportunity for fulfillment of personal aspirations; emerging orthodoxy reflected, in the ministerial attempt to limit contention, the contentious nature of man. And all the while artificial distinctions were arising between the inhabitants of Winthrop's "Citty," dividing the populace which Winthrop on the *Arbella* would have so firmly "knitt together."

Initially there were few prerequisites and no formal bars to admission to town or commonwealth, or to participation in public affairs. The moving force which had brought the first settlers together had been a small group in England—Winthrop, his brother-in-law Emmanuel Downing, Isaac Johnson, Sir Richard Saltonstall, Dudley, John Humphrey (like Johnson, a brother-in-law of the Earl of Lincoln), Increase Nowell, and others. Among friends, neighbors, acquaintances, they had circulated descriptions of New England and various arguments for the plantation; where necessary, they had specifically solicited the participation of persons whose occupations

From Darrett B. Rutman, *Winthrop's Boston, A Portrait of a Puritan Town, 1630–1649* (Chapel Hill, 1965). Used by permission of the publisher, University of North Carolina Press, and the Institute of Early American History and Culture.

were indispensable to the success of the settlement: ministers, carpenters, stonemasons, soldiers, a surgeon, a midwife. Winthrop, for one, had established a rough standard which prospective settlers had to meet, one involving no peculiar creed or belief, but simply "honest conviction" toward the godliness of the venture and faithfulness and diligence to one's work or "calling." He wanted none who would prove disruptive or obstinate, who would not accept his own "unitie bond, and waie of pietie, and devocion" to the enterprise. The screening process had continued in the New World, and, like the men of Plymouth, the Bay leaders had adopted in the first years the policy of accepting into the settlement "only of shuch as come to dwell, and inhabite, whether as servants or free men; and not sojourners which come but for a seasone." But they moved even farther in this direction. When the sixty passengers aboard the ship *Handmaid* arrived in New England in 1630 and expressed their desire "to plant" in the Bay area, the authorities "would not receive them," "having no testimony" as to their character and godliness.

Given this regular, though informal, screening and Winthrop's optimism—that he could effect his ideal community among those with him in the 1630 fleet—it is not surprising that there was no general exclusion from participation in public affairs (other than the usual exclusion of women and servants). To the contrary, Winthrop and his cohorts had thrown open the door to participation in commonwealth government almost as soon as they arrived, calling together the whole body of settlers in the first General Court of October 1630, and resolving issues "by the generall vote of the people, and erreccion of hands." Quite naturally, however, the leaders had attempted to retain their own paramount position by limiting the activity of the generality they were inviting into the government. Thus the Court ordered at this first meeting that the assistants, to be elected by the Court, "should have the power of makeing lawes and chuseing officers to execute the same" rather than the Court itself as specified in the charter.

Yet practicality decreed that the generality in its broadest sense could not be admitted precipitously to the public affairs of the commonwealth even in this limited fashion, just as they could not be admitted en masse and immediately to the church without putting it in danger of degeneration. The leaders had met the problem of the church by turning to a congregationalism which required assurances of godliness and character from the would-be member. They met the problem of participation in commonwealth affairs—or commonwealth citizenship—in the same way. In May 1631, at the second General Court, participation was made contingent upon admission to freemanship as defined in the charter, thus giving the leadership a device whereby it could be assured of the caliber of those joining in the government. At the same time, 116 men were admitted to freemanship, apparently on the basis of their earlier requests and their proven characters as judged by the leaders. For the most part the new freemen were relatively prominent and well-to-do, although not necessarily members of the church. Among the dozen-odd from Boston, for example, were William Colborne, Robert Harding, Samuel Cole, William Hudson, John Underhill, William Baulston, Edward Gibbons, the Reverend Mr. Blackston. (Such men as Winthrop and Coddington were already freemen by virtue of their prior investment in the company.) Provision was made by which others from among newcomers and those already in the commonwealth—by no means all of the adult males were included among the 116—could apply for and be admitted to freemanship and participation. But the test of character was to be made within the local congregations rather than by the government itself, the Court voting to insure the participation of none but "honest and good men" by providing "that for time to come noe man shalbe admitted to the freedome of this body pollitick, but such as are members of some of the churches within the lymitts of the same." In effect commonwealth citizenship was further defined in terms of the church. For the moment, too, participation remained limited to voting for officers—governor, deputy governor, assistants—in whose hands full power rested, for not until 1634 would the freemen, through a representative General Court, insert themselves into the legislative process.

The establishment of criteria for commonwealth citizenship did not affect Boston immediately. As a result of the gathering together of the first settlers through the personal solicitation of a small group, the rough screening, and a natural screening inherent in the necessity of traveling across a dangerous ocean to an unsettled and forbidding land, there was a homogeneity about the firstcomers to the town. It was imperfect, Winthrop aboard the *Arbella* having spoken of the settlers coming together from many miles apart. Yet of those persons aboard the ships of the Winthrop fleet who settled on

Shawmut in 1630 and whose origins are known (a total of 141) forty
were from villages immediately surrounding Winthrop's manor at
Groton out of a total of eighty-three from the East Anglian counties
of Suffolk and Essex, and the rest were scattered in origins among
ten counties, the city of London (fourteen), and the English community in the Netherlands (three). This first population was generally
young, the emigrants from the fleet including thirty-one childless
couples out of forty-eight family groups. Some among the settlers
were servants, eight persons (including single men and women and
even couples) being readily identifiable as such, though the number
was presumably greater. For the most part the emigrants had been
associated with agriculture and small household manufactures.

In view of this homogeneity—augmented during the early years
by the inclusiveness of the church and the synonymous nature of
town and church government—formal prerequisites for admission to
the town would have been superfluous and there is no indication
that they existed. The privileges and duties associated with residence
within the community were conferred across-the-board. All adult
males (servants excepted) participated and held office when called
upon; all shared in the distribution of land and grazed cattle on those
lands which the town held in common; over all was extended the
protection of the community in sickness or want; all contributed to
the support of the commonwealth, town, and church.

Servants constituted a separate group, but one integrated into
the early society. The term as used at the time was a broad one,
embracing voluntary servants working for wages ("hired servants"
or "labourers"), apprentices whose servitude was a form of education, and bound servants, largely those committing themselves to
so many years' service to cover the cost of their trip from England.
The hired laborer was only semantically a servant, however; technically free, he might be a "setled housekeeper" with a family and
permanent residence, hence a part of the free community. Bound
servants and apprentices (and henceforth the term servant will be
applied only to these) were assimilated into the society through the
church, which was open to them with regard both to attendance
and membership—between 1630 and 1640 the First Church was
to admit sixty-one men and women identified as servants—and
through their affiliation with particular families, partaking of the
protection and moral discipline of the head of the family much as

did women and children. Winthrop, for example, referred to his servants as "my family" in reporting their health and prosperity to his wife in 1630, while a law of 1631 provided that even the hired laborer, unless maintaining his own home and family, be engaged for no less than a year and incorporated into the family of his employer during that time. The individual serving his master well and truly during his term of service would ultimately merge into the homogeneous free society, obtaining land, a family, and the freedom of the town.

BOSTON'S FIRST TOWN-HOUSE
1657–1711

FIGURE 4. Boston's first Town House, 1657–1711. (Courtesy The Bostonian Society, Old State House)

However, the town was growing, the population becoming more complex; homogeneity was giving way to heterogeneity. The nature of the incoming settlers changed as the difficulties of the first settlement were overcome and relative stability appeared. Family groups became larger, and the presence of elderly persons within a family, if not common, was not unusual. In 1633 the Leveretts arrived —Thomas, his wife Anne, and three children. In 1634 the huge Hutchinson clan made its appearance in the town, as did the Heatons and the Freeborns—William, aged forty, his wife Mary, thirty-three, and two children, aged seven and two. The same year, Robert Wing of Lawford, Suffolk, aged sixty, arrived. The Tuttles—an aged mother of seventy, two sons, their wives, and a total of seven children—came in 1635, as did George and Alice Griggs, both forty-two, with their children, Thomas, fifteen, William, fourteen, Elizabeth, ten, Mary, six, and James, two. A greater variety of occupations was indicated. The Northamptonshire Tuttles were both "husbandmen," as were the Webbs, the Newcombs, the Meareses; but "mercer," "draper," "carpenter," "joiner," "tailor," "glover," "miller," "shoemaker," "tanner" were common occupational designations. Increasingly, the later emigrants were from the towns rather than the villages—Norwich, Boston, London.

The number of unattached men and women rose, increasing the number of hired laborers. Servants brought into the community to serve a limited number of years began completing their obligatory service in the third and fourth year of settlement, swelling the ranks of free laborers even more. Some could not wait to complete their terms and either bought their freedom or otherwise convinced their masters to dispense with their services—despite the laws forbidding the freeing of servants before-time. All the while, additional servants were arriving. Many were actively solicited from England, for the task of building in a wilderness was an enormous one and labor was always scarce. Those soliciting looked for servants of "good towardnes," yet those solicited were interested not in the venture, but in "what shal be the most of their employment there, whether dayrie, washing, etc. and what should be the Wages, and for how many yeers tyed"; once in the commonwealth they would seek only their freedom and a share of the New World. The number of children arriving without parents grew noticeably as the decade progressed, many of them apparently attached to families as servants at the time of their arrival. For example, Stephen Beckett, aged eleven, was attached to the Pepys family, which settled in the Reverend Mr. Blackston's old home after that gentleman departed for Rhode Island; Mary Fuller, Richard Smith, and Richard Ridley (aged fifteen, fourteen, and sixteen respectively) were attached to the Saunders family. But many of the children were gathered from the London streets and shipped over en masse to be put out to families already in the country, children such as Katherine, "one of the maids brought over on the countryes stocke" early in the second decade, for whose services John Winthrop paid five pounds.

The pressure of both numbers and complexity broke the unity of congregation and town. The early church was open to the newcomers, Cotton calling for personal reformation and conversion, and precipitating that enthusiastic religion which would culminate in the Hutchinsonian outburst. But not all came to hear him. By March 1635 there were enough absenting themselves from the churches everywhere on a Sabbath to warrant the attention of the General Court, and attendance was made mandatory upon pain of fine or imprisonment. To maintain a unity which was fast slipping away, town citizenship was made contingent upon membership in the church, as commonwealth citizenship had been earlier, the General Court in September 1635 placing conditions upon participation in town affairs for the first time by ordering that "none but freemen shall have any vote in any towne, in any accion of authority . . . as receaveing inhabitants, and layeing out of lotts." Before this act was passed, the general government had been proceeding upon the assumption that only freemen were involved in land distribution, and in December 1635 the town itself had resolved that none should receive town lands unless they were "likely to be received members of the Congregation." Bound servants were specifically excluded from receiving town land by an act of the General Court of 1636.

The net effect of these regulations, ideally carried out, would have been the maintenance of the earlier homogeneity. On the one hand, the church—and hence freemanship—was not yet a closed body, for, as has been suggested, the idea of conversion was strong. On the other hand, the belief that all free families of the town should share in the land was clearly indicated, "all the inhabitants" being directed on one occasion to plant in a given area and the acreage of every "able man" established. Consequently, since town practice held that all free inhabitants should receive land, specifying only that they be actual or obviously potential church members, and commonwealth law established church membership as a prerequisite to freemanship and participation in town affairs, then the implied hope

was that the whole body of male inhabitants exclusive of servants
would eventually be freemen, participating citizens of the town,
property holders, and church members.

But such an ideal was impossible to realize. The number of newcomers was far too great to be readily absorbed; the variety of
backgrounds, outlooks, desires, and personalities was too much to
be pressed into a common matrix, the newcomers ranging from the
intensely devout Anne Hutchinson and urbane, acquisitive William
Tyng, through shopkeepers, farmers, artisans, free laborers, and
servants, to Samuel Maverick's Negroes—he had three in 1638,
one claiming to have been "a Queen in her own Countrey."

The church was fundamental to the ideal, for its role was to mold
"honest and good men" that they might take their places in town
and commonwealth. Yet the church failed. Unable to cope with the
growing, variegated population, it came to accept a disparity between church and town, one indicated in the division of land to the
male inhabitants of 1635—that division ostensibly limited to those
who were or were likely to be members of the church—when one-
quarter of the recipients were nonmembers.

In part, the failure lay in the caliber of the newcomers themselves,
their decadence being deplored in letters passing among the leaders.
"Our Towne of late but somewhat too late have bene carefull on
whome they bestowe lotts," Nathaniel Ward of Ipswich wrote Winthrop Jr. in 1635, "being awakned therto by the confluence of many ill
and doubtfull persons, and by their behaviour since they came in
drinking and pilferinge . . . . We conceive the lesse of Satans kingdome we have in our Towne, the more of Gods presence and bless-
inge we may expect." In part it was the material opportunities of the
New World which were bringing men to think less of heaven, and
the land system which was dispersing them to pursue material gain.
The dispersal provoked the law of 1636 restricting men's habitations
to within a half-mile of the meeting house, a futile injunction, as
indicated by Plymouth's plaintive letter of 1639 soliciting advice on
how to counteract the dispersal of its people and by the repeal of
the law in 1640. The all-too-apparent materialism was evident to a
friend in England. "Many in your plantacions discover much pride, as
appeareth by the lettres we receave from them, wherein some of
them write over to us for lace . . . cuttworke coifes . . . deep stammell
dyes; and some of your owne men tell us that many with you goe

finely cladd," he complained; "if once Pride, Covetousnes, opposicion and contention etc. destroy the [power] of holiness among you . . . there will soone grow a strangenes betweene you and God."

But in part the failure of the church to encompass all men rested with the church itself—the traumatic schism of the late 1630s and its aftermath. The proud piety of the Hutchinsonians, their conceit in their personal knowledge of the saved and damned, kept those of lesser faith away from the church. (Like Roger Williams, the Hutchinsonians would have left Winthrop's "weake Christians" to their own fate and would not have stooped to help them.) At the same time, the conflict brought about a cessation of admittances, both sides being fearful that new members would espouse the cause of their enemies; between January 9, 1637, and December 29, 1638, not a single new member was admitted. Indeed, in the three-year period from January 1637 to December 1639, when more than 1,000 people poured into the town, the church added only 76 communicants, an increase canceled out by the withdrawal of the exiled Hutchinsonians. Close scrutiny of the extant town and church records has indicated 362 families resident in the town in 1639; 70 were represented in the church by both husband and wife, and 95 by either one or the other, but 197 families—over one-half the town—had no formal tie.

Even after the Hutchinsonians were downed, the effects lingered. The ready acceptance of new members was a thing of the past. "Be verye carefull in admission of members," Winthrop wrote to his son at Ipswich. "There be some of these newe opinions that will simulare and dissimulare beyond expectation, to gett into our churches: . . . I hope the sad experience of the effects of such spiritts in other churches wilbe caution enoughe to them and others, to beware and knowe men well ere they admitt them." In Boston, the would-be members were required to speak extensively of their *"knowledge* in the principles of religion, and of their *experience in the wayes of grace,* and of their *godly conversation* amongst men"; those found *"ignorant,* and *graceless,* or *scandalous"* were refused. How many applied and were rejected cannot be known, but there were some. "We have had much experience of it," the ministers wrote to England; "men of approved pietie in the judgement of some have been found too light not onely in the judgement of others, but even of their own consciences, when they have come to triall in offering themselves to be members of Churches." Certainly, too, many who might have otherwise sought membership were dissuaded by the piercing, grueling examinations which came to be a part of the formality of entering the church, the "high stiles for hypocrites" as Cotton called them. Thomas Lechford, early in the 1640s, was to observe that "here is required such confessions, and professions, both in private and public, both by men and women . . . that three parts of the people of the Country remaine out of the Church." The percentage was exaggerated, but the onerous nature of the procedure was not.

The church continued to grow through the 1640s, but the gap which had opened between it and the town did not close. From 1639 to 1642 many whose membership had been delayed by the Hutchinsonian controversy joined. Others, both newcomers and longtime residents of the commonwealth, joined. The religious force, so powerful on the seventeenth-century mind, drew some, for in that sacramental age it was difficult to accept exclusion from holy communion, and even those willing to accept the risk of hell for themselves undoubtedly hesitated before leaving their children in jeopardy for want of baptism. Ropemaker Alexander Baker and his wife Elizabeth, for example, arrived in town in 1635 but were not accepted into the church until a decade later, October 4, 1645; on the day following they brought their Boston-born children to be baptized, Alexander, Samuel, John, Joshua, and Hannah, the eldest almost ten years of age. And there were other considerations. Church membership was a necessary prerequisite to success in the community; until the latter years of the second decade no major officeholder or leading merchant residing permanently in the town remained outside, the single exception being merchant John Coggan, and even he was connected to the church through his wife, nephew, and daughter. The church drew its members from all walks and levels of life—merchants and coopers, farmers and laborers; even Negroes and Indians were not excluded. But only the upper class, the economic and political leaders, were so inclusively represented; those outside the church were most often of low status, the "unregenerates" being largely holders of minimal or no property and designated "laborer," "wheelwright," "housecarpenter."

The outsiders eventually constituted a considerable part of the town's population, however. Of 421 families identifiable as resident in 1645, 128 were represented in the church by neither husband nor wife, while of the 481 families of 1649, 156 were unrepresented. The figures can only be approximations, inasmuch as the records for the 1640s are scant and not every family left an imprint on what little has survived. Yet the nature of the extant material would indicate that error would lie only in an understatement of the number of families outside the church, for while the later church records contain the names of virtually all members, the town and land records by which the number of nonmember residents is ascertained are far less complete. Moreover, computation by families does not take cognizance of Boston's enlarged servant population, which was almost entirely excluded from church membership following the Hutchinsonian disturbances, the number of servants admitted declining precipitously from one-third of all those admitted in 1634 to less than one-tenth of those of 1639, from 62 of the 445 admittances during the first decade to 29 of the 345 of the second. By extrapolation, one can estimate that by the end of 1649 the 484 communicants of the First Church represented certainly no more than two-thirds of the town's families and less than one-half of the town's total adult male population.

Most serious for the future, however, was the failure of the children of church communicants to follow their parents into membership, particularly the children born in the Bay area and baptized in the First Church. Within certain families, notably those prominent in public affairs, the church quickly became traditional. Thus, Thomas and Anne Leverett, who joined the church on their arrival in 1633, were followed by their English-born son and daughter in 1639, and a second grown daughter in the 1640s. John and Margaret Winthrop, together with their children Mary, Stephen, and John Jr. joined in the 1630s, while another son, Adam, his wife, Stephen's wife Judith, and Sarah, the wife of Deane Winthrop, joined in the 1640s. Thomasine Scotto, a widow, joined in 1634; in 1639 her sons Joshua and Thomas joined and in the 1640s their wives Joan and Lydia were added. Of the Hutchinsons and Olivers there were twenty-four members enrolled during the two decades. Yet more frequently the opposite was the case, the grown sons and daughters remaining outside. Of forty-seven children (over sixteen years old) found living with their parents in 1639, but five were members; of thirty-two in 1645, only seven had joined; while of fifty-three in 1649,

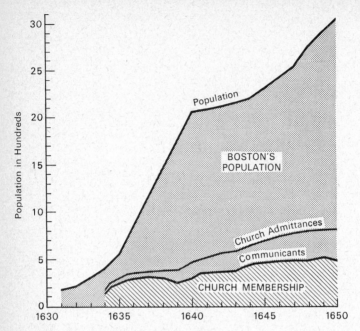

FIGURE 5. The Town and Church through 1649.

only six were communicants. Of children born in the commonwealth and baptized in the First Church, only one, Elizabeth Wilson, the daughter of Pastor John, sought and obtained full membership in Boston during the two decades under consideration.

In the face of the continuing discrepancy between church and town, the church turned inward. To the tendency toward formality and ministerial domination which followed the Hutchinsonian disturbance was added that toward "tribalism," so named by historian Edmund S. Morgan: the church's accenting itself and its own to the exclusion of outsiders. The notion of the church as an assemblage of visible saints—inherent in the confession of grace first introduced by Cotton—was increasingly stressed. At the same time the idea of a general conversion was lost, Cotton in 1641 teaching out of Revelation, "none could enter into the temple until, etc." and delivering the doctrine "that neither Jews nor any more of the Gentiles should be called until Antichrist were destroyed, viz. to a church estate, though here and there a proselyte." In essence, the church ceased to appeal for souls; it became simply a vehicle, traveling in a godly direction and filled with passengers whom God had put aboard.

The ministers from their pulpits still called upon all to live the good and pure life, while urging individual church members to reform their families, servants, and neighbors. But the purpose was not the salvation of the subjects of this zeal; rather, it was a Christian obligation, an act of devotion on the part of the believer. "When we undertake to be obedient to him," Cotton wrote, we undertake not only "in our owne names, and for our owne parts, but in the behalfe of every soule that belongs to us . . . our wives, and children, and servants, and kindred, and acquaintance, and all that are under our reach." The sinner might be brought to better conduct as a result, yet reformation did not bring salvation. Only God could grant that. "It is not in the power of men to ordaine or provide meanes or helps to such ends; but onely for him that can worke upon the Soule and Conscience." More and more intent upon divining those most probably saved through an increasingly sophisticated evaluation of the would-be members' conduct and confessions of grace and faith, the church did not call the reformed sinner to communion, but merely waited until God moved him to seek its comfort. "Wee have nothing to doe to bring them to the Church," Edward Winslow wrote in his *New-Englands Salamander.*

The nonmembers could, and probably in some measure did, attend services in the church, though regularity was undoubtedly lacking in the great majority and the number absent from any given service large. Indeed, it could not have been otherwise, for the single church building in the town could not possibly have held the town's populace, even discounting the young and old and those necessarily detained elsewhere. Even with the construction at the beginning of the second decade of a new meetinghouse—large for the time and place and boasting a balcony for the town's youngsters—it is difficult to envision its holding many more than the four to five hundred actual communicants of the years after 1643. Nevertheless, the law required the attendance of all, and the religious aura of the time prompted at least occasional attendance. . . .

Similarly, the purity of the church became all important. During the formative years, the status of baptized children was unclear. The way to God was open to them, "but whether they should . . . be admitted to all other privileges when they come to age," notably holy communion, "without any personall profession of Faith, or entring into Church Covenant, is another Question, of which by Reason of the Infancy of thse Churches, we have had no occasion yet to determine what to judge or practise one way or other." As the children grew and displayed their secular proclivities, however, and as the church institutionalized and turned inward, the question was answered. When agitation arose for a broadening of the church and a lessening of the gap between church and town by the automatic admission of baptized children to communion and active membership, Cotton was adamant in advocating that system by which "all the Infants of the Church-members bee baptised; yet none of them are received . . . unto Communion at the Lords Table, nor unto liberty of power in the Government of the Church, until they doe approve themselves both by publick Profession before the Church, and also by their Christian conversation, to take hold of the Covenant of their Fathers." By "this primitive practise," he argued, "there will bee no more feare of pestering Churches with a carnall Generation of members baptized in their Infancy." "Either the Lord in the faithfulnesse of his Covenant, will sanctifie the hearts of the baptized Infants to prepare them for his Table; or else hee will discover their hypocrisie and profaneness in the presence of his Church, before Men and Angels, and so prevent the pollution of the Lords Table, and corruption of the Discipline of the Church."

Turning inward, the church eschewed its social function. It no longer screened men for society; rather it was becoming an end in itself, a society within the total society. In the early years, it had been the guardian of public morals throughout the town, both directly by dealing with offenders in a church way, and indirectly by advising the magistrates and people of the proper course to be taken in public business. Church and town had to all intents and purposes been but two facets of the same society and a crime against one was a moral offense within the jurisdiction of the other. Disputes between town residents had been settled amicably by arbitration within the church, without recourse to law and courts. It was in this atmosphere that a general meeting of the town in 1635 ordered that "none of the members of this congregation or inhabitants among us shall sue one another at lawe before that Mr. Henry Vane and the twoe Elders Mr. Thomas Ollyver and Thomas Leveritt have had the hearing and

desyding of the cause if they cann"; that Cotton and his fellow ministers, at the behest of the magistrates, debated a written code for
the commonwealth and proceeded to frame one which envisioned the
towns of Massachusetts as the tribes of Israel reincarnate.

In subsequent years, the church still gave advice. But a fine line
was being drawn between sacral and secular: "The government of
the Church is as the Kingdome of Christ is, not of this world, but
spirituall and heavenly," Cotton wrote in 1640; "the power of the
keyes is far distant from the power of the sword." Church and state
in Massachusetts were set about the same task: "The Establishment
of pure Religion, in doctrine, worship, and government, according
to the word of God: As also the reformation of all corruptions in any
of these." Hence the ministers, in whose care the word of God was
placed, could and did press for "sweet and wholesom laws" and
"civil punishments upon the willfull opposers and disturbers" of the
church; an observer could laud "Moyses and Aaron . . . magistrate
and minister, in church and common[wealth]" walking "hand in
hand, discountenancing and punishinge sinne in whomsoever, and
standinge for the praise of them that doe well." But for the things
of this world—"the disposing of mens goods or lands, lives or liberties, tributes, customes, worldly honors, and inheritances"—"in these
the Church submitteth, and referreth it self to the civill state."

The church might meet the challenge of a rapidly growing and
heterogeneous population by maintaining artificial signs of conformity—conversion and church membership—and disregarding all
who failed to comply. So too, from the standpoint of political activity,
could the commonwealth, which attempted to adhere to church
membership as a prerequisite for freemanship despite the growing
disparity between the number of freemen and the number of adult
males. But the town of necessity had to establish a framework by
which it could deal with those who, newly arrived or newly freed
from obligatory service, demanded its rights and privileges while
refraining or being barred from church membership. Hence the town
gradually assumed to itself the right to judge the character of would-
be residents in line with that English tradition which refused to allow
a newcomer "to take up his dwelling in the vill, without the express
permission of the community."

As early as 1635 the town began screening newcomers, a town
ordinance of that year requiring the approval of the town's authori-

ties for any sale of land from an established settler to a "stranger."
In March 1636 the town empowered the newly created selectmen to
oversee "all Comers in unto us," the selectmen subsequently pre-
scribing that "noe Townesman shall entertaine any strangers into theire
houses for above 14 days, without leave" from them. At the same
time the pressure of an ever-growing population brought about the
abandonment of the fiction that linked land and church membership.
Commonwealth law recognized in 1635, as it had not in 1634, the
ownership of land by nonfreemen, while in 1636 the town gave up
the policy of granting land only to those who were, or would eventually become, church members, making it available to newcomers
and freed servants "upon the usual Condition of inoffensive Carryage." Similarly, the transfer of land from established settlers to
newcomers was being approved on the basis of the "inoffensive
Carryage" of the purchaser.

Just as the attempt to maintain a unity between town and church
had been futile, so too was the attempt to maintain a correlation
between town and property owners. The growing segment of the
population without land could not long be excluded. Herrick, for
example, still a renter, was admitted an inhabitant in January 1639;
laborer Henry Dawson, who was co-renter of Owen Roe's house, lot,
and three-acre garden for nine pounds a year, was admitted in January 1641. As the second decade advanced, as the town land dimin-
ished and less and less was available for distribution, as the town
became more and more a place for crafts and merchandising, the
link between land and town citizenship disappeared entirely. Men
were admitted "an inhabitant," "a townesman," or "to dwell in the
town"—and the three terms were used interchangeably—without
regard to house or holdings. Yet even though divorced from the land,
inhabitantship was still a special status, one formally conferred by
the selectmen in a specific act entered into the records after a due
consideration of the character and quality of the applicant. At times,
such consideration could take months; Edward Arnold, for example,
was "taken into Consideration" in January 1641 and finally admitted
in November.

Confusion marks the freemanship law on the town level. Despite
the fact that church and town were no longer synonymous, that a
distinct town citizenship was emerging, the general government continued to view the body politic in terms of church members and

freemen. The law of 1635 restricting the town electorate to freemen was followed by others. In September 1636 the General Court established representation on the basis of the number of freemen in the towns; the following month, the Court gave the freemen of the towns control over workmen's wages and bound all nonfreemen to their decisions. The "Body of Liberties" of 1641—the commonwealth's first code of laws—placed in the freemen's hands "full power" to choose deputies to the General Court and selectmen of the town and "make such by laws and constitutions as may concerne the wellfare of their Towne," the nonfreemen being bound to abide by their laws and decisions. . . .

And yet there was a clear and regular ignoring of the law. The Court itself, in 1636, empowered "the inhabitants" of the towns— not just the freemen—to demolish houses built without local permission; "the Townes . . . by orderly agreement amonge themselves" (no mention of freemen) were charged with the election of certain judicial officers in the "Body of Liberties." That code, again, implied that town meetings consisted only of freemen, one section stipulating that "if any man shall behave himselfe offensively at any Towne meeting, the rest of the freemen then present, shall have power to sentence him for his offence"; but in another section it recognized that any man, "Inhabitant or forreiner, free or not free," could attend any court, council, or town meeting and propose measures "in convenient time, due order, and respectful manner." Among the militiamen there was an outright expansion of the suffrage, the Court enfranchising both freemen and nonfreemen for the selection of trained-band officers in 1637. A general failure to maintain the division between free and nonfree within the town is shown in the Court's penalizing of townsmen for participating in illegal elections. Newbury's freemen were fined six pence apiece in 1636 "for chuseing and sending to this Court a deputy which was noe freeman"; Concord's freemen and "those that were not free, which had a hand in the undewe election of Mr Flint" were fined six shillings eight pence each in 1638; a general law of 1643 established a standard fine of ten pounds to be levied upon "any man that is not free, putting in any vote" and "the choyce of any officer." George Bowers of Cambridge, haled before the General Court "for putting in a vote on the day of election for Governor (he being no freeman)," readily acknowledged his guilt, but added that he had been voting "every yeare since he came into these parts."

Boston's town meeting throughout the period gives every indication of being an open body. Participation of nonfreemen was not at all uncommon, although the town records, by their nature, indicate only cases of officeholding. . . .

As it so often does, the law trailed the fact and it was not until 1647 that the commonwealth formally acknowledged the political activity of the town inhabitant (though the matter had been considered in 1644 and again in 1646). "Taking into consideration the useful . . . abilities of divers inhabitants amongst us, which are not freemen, which, if improved to publike use, the affaires of this common wealth may be the easier carried on end, in the severall townes," the Court declared that henceforth it would be lawful for the freemen of the towns "to make choyce of such inhabitants . . . to have their vote in the choyce of the select men for towne affaires, asseasment of rates, and other prudentials proper" and to hold certain town offices, including that of selectman although a majority of the selectmen had always to be freemen. The only restrictions were that those admitted to town suffrage must have taken the "oath of fidelity to this government," must have reached the age of twenty-four (reduced to twenty-one by the following year), and that they must not be under sentence "for any evil carriage against the government, or commonwealth, or churches." Participation in commonwealth elections, as distinct from town elections, was still limited in law to freemen, and nonfreemen continued to be barred from major offices. But the fine distinction drawn could not be held to; the town meeting—at which, until the 1650s, both town and commonwealth officers were chosen—retained its air of openness. A committee of the General Court protested in 1655 that everyone, including "scotch servants, Irish negers and persons under one and twenty years," was voting.

Participation in public affairs, the right to live and work in the town, and, until the mid-1640s, land and commonage—these were the privileges of the town, and they were shared alike by Boston's freemen and inhabitants, church members and nonmembers. But the freedom of the town did not, in law, include the freedom of the commonwealth. The general government, concerned with the purity of the state, clung steadfastly (if not always effectively) to a definition of commonwealth citizenship in terms of the church, attempting to enforce the laws which limited commonwealth suffrage and office to the freemen while encouraging the sometimes reluctant church members to seek the privilege of freemanship. Nor did the freedom of the town include the freedom of the church. Concerned with its internal purity and that of its visible saints, tending more and more to formality, the church and its Levitical guardians were a part of, but apart from, the total community. The result was a tripartite division of the town, some men being inhabitants, freemen, and church members; others being inhabitants and church members; still others being mere inhabitants. In these distinctions was a denial of that fundamental unity which Winthrop had spoken of aboard the *Arbella,* the one community to which all belonged "as members of the same body."

Philip J. Greven
FAMILY STRUCTURE IN ANDOVER

One of the scholars working with quantified sociological and demographic concepts is Philip J. Greven (b. 1935), author of the study of Andover, Massachusetts, Four Generations: Population, Land, and Family in Colonial Andover, Massachusetts, *(Ithaca, 1970). In the following selection from a preliminary article, Greven's data support the conclusion that in this town a patriarchal first generation controlled family, church, and town life. Andover appears isolated from outside influences and was stable and conservative. Greven and the others using similar methods mention "Puritanism" infrequently, finding in their search for understanding the history of the towns or the colony that they are better served by specific data rather than generalizations about such a concept. Greven concedes that Andover may not be typical of other towns. May that not support those who contend that New England showed great diversity?*

Surprisingly little is known at present about family life and family structure in the seventeenth-century American colonies. The gen-

From Philip J. Greven, "Family Structure in Seventeenth-Century Andover, Massachusetts" in *William and Mary Quarterly,* 3rd series, XXIII (1966): 234–256, used by permission. An expanded version of the article may be found in *Four Generations: Population, Land, and Family in Colonial Andover, Massachusetts* (Ithaca, N.Y.: Cornell University Press, 1970).

eralizations about colonial family life embedded in textbooks are seldom the result of studies of the extant source materials, which historians until recently have tended to ignore. Genealogists long have been using records preserved in county archives, town halls, churches, and graveyards as well as personal documents to compile detailed information on successive generations of early American families. In addition to the work of local genealogists, many communities possess probate records and deeds for the colonial period. A study of these last testaments and deeds together with the vital statistics of family genealogies can provide the answers to such questions as how many children people had, how long people lived, at what ages did they marry, how much control did fathers have over their children, and to what extent and under what conditions did children remain in their parents' community. The answers to such questions enable an historian to reconstruct to some extent the basic characteristics of family life for specific families in specific communities. This essay is a study of a single seventeenth-century New England town, Andover, Massachusetts, during the lifetimes of its first and second generations—the pioneers who carved the community out of the wilderness, and their children who settled upon the lands which their fathers had acquired. A consideration of their births, marriages, and deaths, together with the disposition of land and property within the town from one generation to the next reveals some of the most important aspects of family life and family structure in early Andover.

The development of a particular type of family structure in seventeenth-century Andover was dependent in part upon the economic development of the community during the same period. Andover, settled by a group of about eighteen men during the early 1640s and incorporated in 1646, was patterned at the outset after the English open field villages familiar to many of the early settlers. The inhabitants resided on house lots adjacent to each other in the village center, with their individual holdings of land being distributed in small plots within two large fields beyond the village center. House lots ranged in size from four to twenty acres, and subsequent divisions of land within the town were proportionate to the size of the house lots. By the early 1660s, about forty-two men had arrived to settle in Andover, of whom thirty-six became permanent residents. During the first decade and a half, four major divisions of the arable land in the town were granted. The first two divisions established two open fields, in which land was granted to the inhabitants on the basis of one acre of land for each acre of house lot. The third division, which provided four acres of land for each acre of house lot, evidently did not form another open field, but was scattered about the town. The fourth and final division of land during the seventeenth century occurred in 1662, and gave land to the householders at the rate of twenty acres for each acre of their house lots. Each householder thus obtained a minimum division allotment of about eighty acres and a maximum allotment of about four hundred acres. Cumulatively, these four successive divisions of town land, together with additional divisions of meadow and swampland, provided each of the inhabitants with at least one hundred acres of land for farming, and as much as six hundred acres. During the years following these substantial grants of land, many of the families in the town removed their habitations from the house lots in the town center onto their distant, and extensive, farm lands, thus altering the character of the community through the establishment of independent family farms and scattered residences. By the 1680s, more than half the families in Andover lived outside the original center of the town on their own ample farms. The transformation of the earlier open field village effectively recast the basis for family life within the community.

An examination of the number of children whose births are recorded in the Andover town records between 1651 and 1699 reveals a steady increase in the number of children being born throughout the period. (See Table 1.) Between 1651 and 1654, 28 births are recorded, followed by 32 between 1655 and 1659, 43 between 1660 and 1664, 44 between 1665 and 1669, 78 between 1670 and 1674, and 90 between 1675 and 1679. After 1680, the figures rise to more

TABLE 1

The Number of Sons and Daughters Living at the Age of 21 in Twenty-nine First-Generation Families

Sons	0	1	2	3	4	5	6	7	8	9	10
Families	1	2	7	1	6	6	3	3	0	0	0
Daughters	0	1	2	3	4	5	6	7	8	9	10
Families	0	2	7	6	11	2	0	0	0	1	0

than one hundred births every five years. The entire picture of population growth in Andover, however, cannot be formed from a study of the town records alone since these records do not reflect the pattern of generations within the town. Looked at from the point of view of the births of the children of the first generation of settlers who arrived in Andover between the first settlement in the mid-1640s and 1660, a very different picture emerges, hidden within the entries of the town records and genealogies. The majority of the second-generation children were born during the two decades of the 1650s and the 1660s. The births of 159 second-generation children were distributed in decades as follows: 10 were born during the 1630s, either in England or in the towns along the Massachusetts coast where their parents first settled; 28 were born during the 1640s; 49 were born during the 1650s; 43 were born during the 1660s; declining to 21 during the 1670s, and falling to only 8 during the 1680s. Because of this pattern of births, the second generation of Andover children, born largely during the 1650s and the 1660s, would mature during the late 1670s and the 1680s. Many of the developments of the second half of the seventeenth century in Andover, both within the town itself and within the families residing there, were the result of the problems posed by a maturing second generation.

From the records which remain, it is not possible to determine the size of the first-generation family with complete accuracy, since a number of children were undoubtedly stillborn, or died almost immediately after birth without ever being recorded in the town records. It is possible, however, to determine the number of children surviving childhood and adolescence with considerable accuracy, in part because of the greater likelihood of their names being recorded among the children born in the town, and in part because other records, such as church records, marriage records, tax lists, and wills, also note their presence. Evidence from all of these sources indicates that the families of Andover's first settlers were large, even without taking into account the numbers of children who may have been born but died unrecorded. An examination of the families of twenty-nine men who settled in Andover between 1645 and 1660 reveals that a total of 247 children are known to have been born to these particular families. Of these 247 children whose births may be ascertained, thirty-nine, or 15.7 percent, are known to have died before reaching the age of 21 years. A total of 208 children or 84.3 percent of the number of children known to be born thus reached the age of 21 years, having survived the hazards both of infancy and of adolescence. This suggests that the number of deaths among children and adolescents during the middle of the seventeenth century in Andover was lower than might have been expected.

In terms of their actual sizes, the twenty-nine first-generation families varied considerably, as one might expect. Eleven of these twenty-nine families had between 0 and 3 sons who survived to the age of 21 years; twelve families had either 4 or 5 sons surviving, and six families had either 6 or 7 sons living to be 21. Eighteen of these families thus had four or more sons to provide with land or a trade when they reached maturity and wished to marry, a fact of considerable significance in terms of the development of family life in Andover during the years prior to 1690. Fewer of these twenty-nine families had large numbers of daughters. Fifteen families had between 0 and 3 daughters who reached adulthood, eleven families had 4 daughters surviving, and three families had 5 or more daughters reaching the age of 21. In terms of the total number of their children born and surviving to the age of 21 or more, four of these twenty-nine first-generation families had between 2 and 4 children (13.8 percent), eleven families had between 5 and 7 children (37.9 percent), and fourteen families had between 8 and 11 children (48.3 percent). Well over half of the first-generation families thus had 6 or more children who are known to have survived adolescence and to have reached the age of 21. The average number of children known to have been born to these twenty-nine first-generation families was 8.5, with an average of 7.2 children in these families being known to have reached the age of 21 years. The size of the family, and particularly the number of sons who survived adolescence, was a matter of great importance in terms of the problems which would arise later over the settlement of the second generation upon land in Andover and the division of the estates of the first generation among their surviving children. The development of a particular type of family structure within Andover during the first two generations depended in part upon the number of children born and surviving in particular families.

Longevity was a second factor of considerable importance in

the development of the family in Andover. For the first forty years following the settlement of the town in 1645, relatively few deaths were recorded among the inhabitants of the town. Unlike Boston, which evidently suffered from smallpox epidemics throughout the seventeenth century, there is no evidence to suggest the presence of smallpox or other epidemical diseases in Andover prior to 1690. With relatively few people, many of whom by the 1670s were scattered about the town upon their own farms, Andover appears to have been a remarkably healthy community during its early years. Lacking virulent epidemics, the principal hazards to health and to life were birth, accidents, nonepidemical diseases, and Indians. Death, consequently, visited relatively few of Andover's inhabitants during the first four decades following its settlement. This is evident in the fact that the first generation of Andover's settlers was very long lived. Prior to 1680, only five of the original settlers who came to Andover before 1660 and established permanent residence there had died; in 1690, fifteen of the first settlers (more than half of the original group) were still alive, forty-five years after the establishment of their town. The age at death of thirty men who settled in Andover prior to 1660 can be determined with a relative degree of accuracy. Their average age at the time of their deaths was 71.8 years. Six of the thirty settlers died while in their fifties, 11 in their sixties, 3 in their seventies, 6 in their eighties, 3 in their nineties, and 1 at the advanced age of 106 years. The longevity of the first-generation fathers was to have great influence on the lives of their children, for the authority of the first generation was maintained far longer than would have been possible if death had struck them down at an early age. The second generation, in turn, was almost as long lived as the first generation had been. The average age of 138 second-generation men at the time of their deaths was 65.2 years, and the average age of sixty-six second-generation women at the time of their deaths was 64.0 years. (See Table 2.) Of the 138 second-generation men who reached the age of 21 years and whose lifespan is known, only twenty-five or 18.1 percent, died between the ages of 20 and 49. Forty-two (30.3 percent) of these 138 men died between the ages of 50 and 69; seventy-one (51.6 percent) died after reaching the age of 70. Twenty-five second-generation men died in their eighties, and four died in

TABLE 2
Second-Generation Ages at Death

	Males		Females	
Ages	Numbers	Percentages	Numbers	Percentages
20–29	10	7.3	4	6.1
30–39	9	6.5	4	6.1
40–49	6	4.3	6	9.1
50–59	16	11.5	10	15.2
60–69	26	18.8	13	19.7
70–79	42	30.4	16	24.2
80–89	25	18.1	8	12.1
90–99	4	3.1	5	7.5
Total	138	100.0%	66	100.0%

their nineties. Longevity was characteristic of men living in seventeenth-century Andover.

The age of marriage often provides significant clues to circumstances affecting family life and to patterns of family relationships which might otherwise remain elusive. Since marriages throughout the seventeenth century and the early part of the eighteenth century were rarely fortuitous, parental authority and concern, family interests, and economic considerations played into the decisions determining when particular men and women could and would marry for the first time. And during the seventeenth century in Andover, factors such as these frequently dictated delays of appreciable duration before young men, especially, might marry. The age of marriage both of men and of women in the second generation proved to be much higher than most historians hitherto have suspected.

Traditionally in America women have married younger than men, and this was generally true for the second generation in Andover. Although the assertion is sometimes made that daughters of colonial families frequently married while in their early teens, the average age of sixty-six second-generation daughters of Andover families at the time of their first marriage was 22.8 years. (See Table 3.) Only two girls are known to have married at 14 years, none at 15, and two more at 16. Four married at the age of 17, with a total of twenty-two of the sixty-six girls marrying before attaining the age of 21 years (33.3 percent). The largest percentage of women married be-

TABLE 3
Second-Generation Female Marriage Ages

Age	Numbers	Percentages	
Under 21	22	33.3	24 & under = 69.7%
21–24	24	36.4	25 & over = 30.3%
25–29	14	21.2	29 & under = 90.9%
30–34	4	6.1	30 & over = 9.1%
35–39	1	1.5	
40 & over	1	1.5	
			Average age = 22.8 years
Total	66	100.0%	

tween the ages of 21 and 24, with twenty-four or 36.4 percent being married during these years, making a total of 69.7 percent of the second-generation daughters married before reaching the age of 25. Between the ages of 25 and 29 years, fourteen women (21.2 percent) married, with six others marrying at the age of 30 or more (9.1 percent). Relatively few second-generation women thus married before the age of 17, and nearly 70 percent married before the age of 25. They were not as young in most instances as one might have expected if very early marriages had prevailed, but they were relatively young nonetheless.

The age of marriage for second-generation men reveals a very different picture, for instead of marrying young, as they so often are said to have done, they frequently married quite late. (See Table 4.) The average age for ninety-four second-generation sons

TABLE 4
Second-Generation Male Marriage Ages

Age	Numbers	Percentages	
Under 21	4	4.3	24 & under = 39.4%
21–24	33	35.1	25 & over = 60.6%
25–29	34	36.2	29 & under = 75.6%
30–34	16	17.2	30 & over = 24.4%
35–39	4	4.3	
40 & over	3	2.9	
			Average age = 27.1 years
Total	94	100.0%	

of Andover families at the time of their first marriages was 27.1 years. No son is known to have married before the age of 18, and only one actually married then. None of the ninety-four second-generation men whose marriage ages could be determined married at the age of 19, and only three married at the age of 20. The contrast with the marriages of the women of the same generation is evident, since only 4.3 percent of the men married before the age of 21 compared to 33.3 percent of the women. The majority of second-generation men married while in their twenties, with thirty-three of the ninety-four men marrying between the ages of 21 and 24 (35.1 percent), and thirty-four men marrying between the ages of 25 and 29 (36.2 percent). Nearly one quarter of the second-generation men married at the age of 30 or later, however, since twenty-three men or 24.4 percent delayed their marriages until after their thirtieth year. In sharp contrast with the women of this generation, an appreciable majority of the second-generation men married at the age of 25 or more, with 60.6 percent marrying after that age. This tendency to delay marriages by men until after the age of 25, with the average age being about 27 years, proved to be characteristic of male marriage ages in Andover throughout the seventeenth century.

Averages can sometimes obscure significant variations in patterns of behavior, and it is worth noting that in the second generation the age at which particular sons might marry depended in part upon which son was being married. Eldest sons tended to marry earlier than younger sons in many families, which suggests variations in their roles within their families, and differences in the attitudes of their fathers towards them compared to their younger brothers. For twenty-six eldest second-generation sons, the average age at their first marriage was 25.6 years. Second sons in the family often met with greater difficulties and married at an average age of 27.5 years, roughly two years later than their elder brothers. Youngest sons tended to marry later still, with the average of twenty-two youngest sons being 27.9 years. In their marriages as in their inheritances, eldest sons often proved to be favored by their families; and family interests and paternal wishes were major factors in deciding which son should marry and when. More often than not, a son's marriage depended upon the willingness of his father to allow it and the ability of his father to provide the means for the couple's economic independence. Until a second-generation son had been given the means to support a wife—which in Andover during the seventeenth century generally meant land—marriage was virtually impossible.

Marriage negotiations between the parents of couples proposing marriage and the frequent agreement by the father of a suitor to provide a house and land for the settlement of his son and new bride are familiar facts. But the significance of this seventeenth-century custom is much greater than is sometimes realized. It generally meant that the marriages of the second generation were dependent upon their fathers' willingness to let them leave their families and to establish themselves in separate households elsewhere. The late age at which so many sons married during this period indicates that the majority of first-generation parents were unwilling to see their sons married and settled in their own families until long after they had passed the age of 21. The usual age of adulthood, marked by marriage and the establishment of another family, was often 24 or later. Since 60 percent of the second-generation sons were 25 or over at the time of their marriage and nearly one quarter of them were 30 or over, one wonders what made the first generation so reluctant to part with its sons?

At least part of the answer seems to lie in the fact that Andover was largely a farming community during the seventeenth century, structured, by the time that the second generation was maturing, around the family farm which stood isolated from its neighbors and which functioned independently. The family farm required all the labor it could obtain from its own members, and the sons evidently were expected to assist their fathers on their family farms as long as their fathers felt that it was necessary for them to provide their labor. In return for this essential, but prolonged, contribution to their family's economic security, the sons must have been promised land by their fathers when they married, established their own families, and wished to begin their own farms. But this meant that the sons were fully dependent upon their fathers as long as they remained at home. Even if they wanted to leave, they still needed paternal assistance and money in order to purchase land elsewhere. The delayed marriages of second-generation men thus indicate their prolonged attachment to their families, and the continuation of paternal authority over second-generation sons until they had reached their mid-twenties, at least. In effect, it appears, the maturity of this generation was appreciably later than has been supected hitherto. The psychological consequences of this prolonged dependence of sons are difficult to assess, but they must have been significant.

Even more significant of the type of family relationships emerging with the maturing of the second generation than their late age of marriage is the fact that paternal authority over sons did not cease with marriage. In this community, at least, paternal authority was exercised by the first generation not only prior to their sons' marriages, while the second generation continued to reside under the same roof with their parents and to work on the family farm, and not only at the time of marriage, when fathers generally provided the economic means for their sons' establishment in separate households, but also *after* marriage, by the further step of the father's withholding legal control of the land from the sons who had settled upon it. The majority of first generation fathers continued to own the land which they settled their sons upon from the time the older men received it from the town to the day of their deaths. All of the first-generation fathers were willing to allow their sons to build houses upon their land, and to live apart from the paternal house after their marriage, but few were willing to permit their sons to become fully independent as long as they were still alive. By withholding deeds to the land which they had settled their sons upon, and which presumably would be theirs to inherit someday, the first generation successfully assured the continuity of their authority over their families long after their sons had become adults and had gained a nominal independence. Since the second generation, with a few exceptions, lacked clear legal titles to the land which they lived upon and farmed, they were prohibited from selling the land which their fathers had settled them upon, or from alienating the land in any other way without the consent of their fathers, who continued to own it. Being unable to sell the land which they expected to inherit, second-generation sons could not even depart from Andover without their fathers' consent, since few had sufficient capital of their own with which to purchase land for themselves outside of Andover. The family thus was held together not only by settling sons upon family land in Andover, but also by refusing to relinquish control of the land until long after the second generation had established its nominal independence following their marriages and the establishment of separate households. In a majority of cases, the dependence of the second-generation sons continued until the deaths of their fathers. And most of the first generation of settlers was very long lived.

The first generations' reluctance to hand over the control of their property to their second-generation sons is evident in their actions. Only three first-generation fathers divided their land among all of their sons before their deaths and gave them deeds of gift for their portions of the paternal estate. All three, however, waited until late in their lives to give their sons legal title to their portions of the family lands. Eleven first-generation fathers settled all of their sons upon their family estates in Andover, but gave a deed of gift for the land to only one of their sons; the rest of their sons had to await their fathers' deaths before inheriting the land which they had been settled upon. Ten of the settlers retained the title to all of their land until their deaths, handing over control to their sons only by means of their last wills and testaments. For the great majority of the second generation, inheritances constituted the principal means of transferring the ownership of land from one generation to the next. The use of partible inheritances in Andover is evident in the division of the estates of the first generation. Twenty-one of twenty-two first-generation families which had two or more sons divided all of their land among all of their surviving sons. Out of seventy-seven sons who were alive at the time their fathers either wrote their wills or gave them deeds to the land, seventy-two sons received some land from their fathers. Out of a total of sixty-six sons whose inheritances can be determined from their fathers' wills, sixty-one or 92.4 percent received land from their fathers' estates in Andover. Often the land bequeathed to them by will was already in their possession, but without legal conveyances having been given. Thus although the great majority of second-generation sons were settled upon their fathers' lands while their fathers were still alive, few actually owned the land which they lived upon until after their fathers' deaths. With their inheritances came ownership; and with ownership came independence. Many waited a long time.

The characteristic delays in the handing over of control of the land from the first to the second generation may be illustrated by the lives and actions of several Andover families. Like most of the men who wrested their farms and their community from the wilderness, William Ballard was reluctant to part with the control over his land. When Ballard died intestate in 1689, aged about 72 years, his three sons, Joseph, William, and John, agreed to divide their father's estate among themselves "as Equally as they could." They also agreed to give their elderly mother, Grace Ballard, a room in their father's house and to care for her as long as she remained a widow, thus adhering voluntarily to a common practice for the provision of the widow. The eldest son, Joseph, had married in 1665/6, almost certainly a rather young man, whereas his two brothers did not marry until the early 1680s, when their father was in his mid-sixties. William, Jr., must have been well over 30 by then, and John was 28. Both Joseph and William received as part of their division of their father's estate in Andover the land where their houses already stood, as well as more than 75 acres of land apiece. The youngest son, John, got all the housing, land, and meadow "his father lived upon except the land and meadow his father gave William Blunt upon the marriage with his daughter," which had taken place in 1668. It is unclear whether John lived with his wife and their four children in the same house as his parents, but there is a strong likelihood that this was the case in view of his assuming control of it after his father's death. His two older brothers had been given land to build upon by their father before his death, but no deeds of gift had been granted to them, thus preventing their full independence so long as he remained alive. Their family remained closely knit both by their establishment of residences near their paternal home on family land and by the prolonged control by William Ballard over the land he had received as one of the first settlers in Andover. It was a pattern repeated in many families.

There were variations, however, such as those exemplified by the Holt family, one of the most prominent in Andover during the seventeenth century. Nicholas Holt, originally a tanner by trade, had settled in Newbury, Massachusetts, for nearly a decade before joining the group of men planting the new town of Andover during the 1640s. Once established in the wilderness community, Holt ranked third among the householders, with an estate which eventually included at least 400 acres of land in Andover as a result of successive divisions of the common land. At some time prior to 1675, he removed his family from the village, where all the original house lots had been located, and built a dwelling house on his third division of land. Although a small portion of his land still lay to the north and west of the old village center, the greatest part of his estate lay in a reasonably compact farm south of his new house. Holt owned no land outside of Andover, and he acquired very little besides the original division grants from the town. It was upon this land that he eventually settled all his sons. In 1662, however, when Nicholas Holt received the fourth division grant of 300 acres from the town, his eldest son, Samuel, was 21 years old, and his three other sons were 18, 15, and 11. The fifth son was yet unborn. His four sons were thus still adolescents, and at ages at which they could provide the physical labor needed to cultivate the land already cleared about the house, and to clear and break up the land which their father had just received. The family probably provided most of the labor, since there is no evidence to indicate that servants or hired laborers were numerous in Andover at the time. With the exception of two daughters who married in the late 1650s, the Holt family remained together on their farm until 1669, when the two oldest sons and the eldest daughter married.

By 1669, when Holt's eldest son, Samuel, finally married at the age of 28, the only possible means of obtaining land to settle upon from the town was to purchase one of the twenty-acre lots which were offered for sale. House-lot grants with accommodation land had long since been abandoned by the town, and Samuel's marriage and independence therefore depended upon his father's willingness to provide him with sufficient land to build upon and to farm for himself. Evidently his father had proved unwilling for many years, but when Samuel did at last marry, he was allowed to build a house for himself and his wife upon his father's "Three-score Acres of upland," known otherwise as his third division. Soon afterwards, his second brother, Henry, married and also was given land to build upon in the third division. Neither Samuel nor Henry was given a deed to his land by their father at the time he settled upon it. Their marriages and their establishment of separate households left their three younger brothers still living with their aging father and stepmother. Five years passed before the next son married. James, the fourth of the five sons, married in 1675, at the age of 24, whereupon he, too, was provided with a part of his father's farm to build a house upon. The third son, Nicholas, Jr., continued to live with his father, waiting until 1680 to marry at the late age of 32. His willingness to delay even a token independence so long suggests that personal factors must have played an important part in his continued assistance to his father, who was then about 77 years old. John Holt, the youngest of the sons, married at the age of 21, shortly before his father's death.

For Nicholas Holt's four oldest sons, full economic independence was delayed for many years. Although all had withdrawn from their father's house and had established separate residences of their own, they nonetheless were settled upon their father's land not too far distant from their family homestead, and none had yet been given a legal title to the land where he lived. Until Nicholas Holt was willing to give his sons deeds of gift for the lands where he had allowed them to build and to farm, he retained all legal rights to his estate and could still dispose of it in any way he chose. Without his consent, therefore, none of his sons could sell or mortgage the land where he lived since none of them owned it. In the Holt family, paternal authority rested upon firm economic foundations, a situation characteristic of the majority of Andover families of this period and these two generations.

Eventually, Nicholas Holt decided to relinquish his control over his Andover property by giving to his sons, after many years, legal titles to the lands which they lived upon. In a deed of gift, dated February 14, 1680/1, he conveyed to his eldest son, Samuel, who had been married almost twelve years, one half of his third division land, "the Said land on which the said Samuels House now Stands," which had the land of his brother, Henry, adjoining on the west, as well as an additional 130 acres of upland from the fourth division of land, several parcels of meadow, and all privileges accompanying these grants of land. In return for this gift, Samuel, then forty years old, promised to pay his father for his maintenance so long as his "naturall life Shall Continue," the sum of twenty shillings a year. Ten months later, December 15, 1681, Nicholas Holt conveyed almost exactly the same amount of land to his second son, Henry, and also obligated him to pay twenty shillings yearly for his maintenance. Prior to this gift, Nicholas had given his fourth son, James, his portion, which consisted of one-third part of "my farme" including "the land where his house now stands," some upland, a third of the great meadow, and other small parcels. In return, James promised to pay his father three pounds a year for life (three times the sum his two elder brothers were to pay), and to pay his mother-in-law forty shillings a year when she should become a widow. The farm which James received was shared by his two other brothers, Nicholas and John, as well. Nicholas, in a deed of June 16, 1682, received "one third part of the farme where he now dwells," some meadow, and, most importantly, his father's own dwelling house, including the cellar, orchard, and barn, which constituted the principal homestead and house of Nicholas Holt, Sr. In "consideration of this my fathers gift . . . to me his sone," Nicholas, Junior, wrote, "I doe promise and engage to pay yearly" the sum of three pounds for his father's maintenance. Thus Nicholas, Junior, in return for his labors and sacrifices as a son who stayed with his father until the age of 32, received not only a share in the family farm equal to that of his two younger brothers, but in addition received the paternal house and homestead. The youngest of the five Holt sons, John, was the only one to receive his inheritance from his father by deed prior to his marriage. On June 19, 1685, Nicholas Holt, Sr., at the age of 83, gave his "Lovinge" son a parcel of land lying on the easterly side of "my now Dwelling house," some meadow, and fifteen acres of upland "as yett unlaid out." One month later, John married, having already built himself a house upon the land which his father promised to give him. Unlike his older brothers, John Holt thus gained his complete independence as an exceptionally young man. His brothers, however, still were not completely free from obligations to their father since each had agreed to the yearly payment of money to their father in return for full ownership of their farms. Not until Nicholas Holt's death at the end of January 1685/6 could his sons consider themselves fully independent of their aged father. He must have died content in the knowledge that all of his sons had been established on farms fashioned out of his own ample estate in Andover, all enjoying as a result of his patriarchal hand the rewards of his venture into the wilderness.

Some Andover families were less reluctant than Nicholas Holt to let their sons marry early and to establish separate households, although the control of the land in most instances still rested in the father's hands. The Lovejoy family, with seven sons, enabled the four oldest sons to marry at the ages of 22 and 23. John Lovejoy, Sr., who originally emigrated from England as a young indentured servant, acquired a seven-acre house lot after his settlement in

Andover during the mid-1640s, and eventually possessed an estate of over 200 acres in the town. At his death in 1690, at the age of 68, he left an estate worth a total of £327.11.6, with housing and land valued at £260.00.0, a substantial sum at the time. Although he himself had waited until the age of 29 to marry, his sons married earlier. His eldest son, John, Jr., married on March 23, 1677/8, aged 22, and built a house and began to raise crops on land which his father gave him for that purpose. He did not receive a deed of gift for his land, however; his inventory, taken in 1680 after his premature death, showed his major possessions to consist of "one house and a crope of corn" worth only twenty pounds. His entire estate, both real and personal, was valued at only £45.15.0, and was encumbered with £29.14.7 in debts. Three years later, on April 6, 1683, the land which he had farmed without owning was given to his three-year-old son by his father, John Lovejoy, Sr. In a deed of gift, the elder Lovejoy gave his grandson, as a token of the love and affection he felt for his deceased son, the land which John, Junior, had had, consisting of fifty acres of upland, a piece of meadow, and a small parcel of another meadow, all of which lay in Andover. Of the surviving Lovejoy sons only the second, William, received a deed of gift from the elder Lovejoy for the land which he had given them. The others had to await their inheritances to come into full possession of their land. In his will dated September 1, 1690, shortly before his death, Lovejoy distributed his estate among his five surviving sons: Christopher received thirty acres together with other unstated amounts of land, and Nathaniel received the land which his father had originally intended to give to his brother, Benjamin, who had been killed in 1689. Benjamin was 25 years old and unmarried at the time of his death, and left an estate worth only £1.02.8, his wages as a soldier. Without their father's land, sons were penniless. The youngest of the Lovejoy sons, Ebenezer, received his father's homestead, with the house and lands, in return for fulfilling his father's wish that his mother should "be made comfortable while she Continues in this world." His mother inherited the east end of the house, and elaborate provisions in the will ensured her comfort. With all the surviving sons settled upon their father's land in Andover, with the residence of the widow in the son's house, and with the fact that only one of the sons actually received a deed for his land during their father's lifetime, the Lovejoys also epitomized some of the principal characteristics of family life in seventeenth-century Andover.

Exceptions to the general pattern of prolonged paternal control over sons were rare. The actions taken by Edmund Faulkner to settle his eldest son in Andover are instructive precisely because they were so exceptional. The first sign that Faulkner was planning ahead for his son came with his purchase of a twenty-acre lot from the town at the annual town meeting of March 22, 1669/70. He was the only first-generation settler to purchase such a lot, all of the other purchasers being either second-generation sons or newcomers, and it was evident that he did not buy it for himself since he already had a six-acre house lot and more than one hundred acres of land in Andover. The town voted that "in case the said Edmond shall at any time put such to live upon it as the town shall approve, or have no just matter against them, he is to be admitted to be a townsman." The eldest of his two sons, Francis, was then a youth of about nineteen years. Five years later, January 4, 1674/5, Francis was admitted as a townsman of Andover "upon the account of the land he now enjoyeth," almost certainly his father's twenty acres. The following October, aged about 24, Francis married the minister's daughter. A year and a half later, in a deed dated February 1, 1676/7, Edmund Faulkner freely gave his eldest son "one halfe of my Living here at home" to be "Equally Divided between us both." Francis was to pay the town rates on his half, and was to have half the barn, half the orchard, and half the land about his father's house, and both he and his father were to divide the meadows. Significantly, Edmund added that "all my Sixscore acres over Shawshinne river I wholly give unto him," thus handing over, at the relatively young age of 52, most of his upland and half of the remainder of his estate to his eldest son. The control of most of his estate thereby was transferred legally and completely from the first to the second generation. Edmund's second and youngest son, John, was still unmarried at the time Francis received his gift, and waited until 1682 before marrying at the age of 28. Eventually he received some land by his father's will, but his inheritance was small compared to his brother's. Edmund Faulkner's eagerness to hand over the control of his estate to his eldest son is notable for its rarity and accentuates the fact that almost none of his friends and neighbors chose to do likewise. It is just possible that Faulkner, himself a younger son of an English gentry family, sought to preserve most of his Andover estate intact by giving it to his eldest son. If so, it would only emphasize his distinctiveness from his neighbors. For the great majority of the first-generation settlers in Andover, partible inheritances and delayed control by the first generation over the land were the rule. Faulkner was the exception which proved it.

Embedded in the reconstructions of particular family histories is a general pattern of family structure unlike any which are known or suspected to have existed either in England or its American colonies during the seventeenth century. It is evident that the family structure which developed during the lifetimes of the first two generations in Andover cannot be classified satisfactorily according to any of the more recent definitions applied to types of family life in the seventeenth century. It was not simply a "patrilineal group of extended kinship gathered into a single household," nor was it simply a "nuclear independent family, that is man, wife, and children living apart from relatives." The characteristic family structure which emerged in Andover with the maturing of the second generation during the 1670s and 1680s was a combination of both the classical extended family and the nuclear family. This distinctive form of family structure is best described as a *modified extended family*—defined as a kinship group of two or more generations living within a single community in which the dependence of the children upon their parents continues after the children have married and are living under a separate roof. This family structure is a *modified* extended family because all members of the family are not "gathered into a single household," but it is still an *extended* family because the newly created conjugal unit of husband and wife live in separate households in close proximity to their parents and siblings and continue to be economically dependent in some respects upon their parents. And because of the continuing dependence of the second generation upon their first-generation fathers, who continued to own most of the family land throughout the better part of their lives, the family in seventeenth-century Andover was *patriarchal* as well. The men who first settled the town long remained the dominant figures both in their families and their community. It was their decisions and their actions which produced the family characteristic of seventeenth-century Andover.

One of the most significant consequences of the development of

the modified extended family characteristic of Andover during this
period was the fact that remarkably few second-generation sons
moved away from their families and their community. More than four
fifths of the second-generation sons lived their entire lives in the
town which their fathers had wrested from the wilderness. The first
generation evidently was intent upon guaranteeing the future of the
community and of their families within it through the settlement of
all of their sons upon the lands originally granted to them by the
town. Since it was quite true that the second generation could not
expect to acquire as much land by staying in Andover as their fathers
had by undergoing the perils of founding a new town on the frontier,
it is quite possible that their reluctance to hand over the control
of the land to their sons when young is not only a reflection of their
patriarchalism, justified both by custom and by theology, but also of
the fact that they could not be sure that their sons would stay, given
a free choice. Through a series of delays, however, particularly
those involving marriages and economic independence, the second
generation continued to be closely tied to their paternal families. By
keeping their sons in positions of prolonged dependence, the first
generation successfully managed to keep them in Andover during
those years in which their youth and energy might have led them to
seek their fortunes elsewhere. Later generations achieved their independence earlier and moved more. It remains to be seen to what
extent the family life characteristic of seventeenth-century Andover
was the exception or the rule in the American colonies.

John J. Waters
HINGHAM, MASSACHUSETTS, 1631–1661

Another study of a New England town, by John J. Waters (b. 1937), employs the genealogical approach rather than the demographic. He traces the individuals and families who occupied positions of importance in Hingham. Like Powell's study of Sudbury and Greven's of Andover, the history of Hingham shows the attempt to replicate the English peasant community, a point also emphasized by Lockridge in the study of Dedham that follows this one.

After initial conflict between settlers from very different parts of England, a local elite arose based on class status, something Rutman did not find in Boston. This class oligarchy wielded power and united against the Massachusetts Bay authorities. Far from accepting the oligarchical control or orthodoxy of the Boston "Saints," Hingham professed independence both religious and political. It neither sought nor achieved a Puritan utopia such as Lockridge finds in Dedham.

Until fairly recently the study of early New England towns reflected the "germ theory" approach of nineteenth-century historical scholarship. Such distinguished historians as Herbert Baxter Adams, Edward Channing, and Charles McLean Andrews sought the origins of those "virile little commonwealths" in the teutonic woods, the Anglo-Saxon villages, or the towns of Elizabethan England. Contemporary historians, while using these studies for information, generally reject their quest for primeval archetypes. For the present-day student, settlement and immigration involve different kinds of questions. He wants to know why these immigrants came to New England. Were they established members of the English social structure or displaced yeomen looking for a second chance? How did these "planters," coming as they did from different parts of England, with different attitudes on politics and religion, and with diverse customs, adjust to each other? How did the institutions they brought with them change in the New World?

The detailed investigations of Andover and Sudbury by Philip Greven and Sumner Chilton Powell give two partial answers to these questions; this study of Hingham offers a third analysis. Greven in

From John J. Waters, "Hingham, Massachusetts, 1631–1661: An East Anglian Oligarchy in the New World." Published by permission of The Journal of Social History, Vol. I (Summer 1968). © 1968 The Journal of Social History.

his essay on Andover points out that its first settlers conceived of their town as a "replica of an English village . . . in which all of the inhabitants dwelt side by side and tilled their lands in small plots adjacent to those of their neighbors in the general fields." Within a generation, however, this community-centered ideal had been transformed by the sheer abundance of available land into an individually oriented farming area. Sumner Chilton Powell, by focusing his attention on the English backgrounds of Sudbury's settlers, sees a diversity of farming and leadership patterns tempered by the American experience. Sudbury's first generation found its aims and ideals opposed by the new. Both Andover and Sudbury underwent real change within the lives of their founders. They show marked contrast to the much more conservative town of Hingham which successfully preserved many features of traditional English life in the Massachusetts wilderness.

The internal life of Bear Cove, or what became Hingham Plantation, was dominated for its first generation by a rivalry between its first settlers from the English "West Country," who arrived between 1631 and 1634, and the subsequent immigrants from East Anglia who came between 1633 and 1640. These two groups are broadly representative of almost 40 percent of the "Great Emigration." Their contrasting values led to ethnic, political, and theological conflicts. These differences illuminate Hingham's constitutional challenges to both the political and religious norms of John Winthrop's Massachusetts. Its 1645 militia dispute involved a direct attack upon the role of the "Assistants" in that Puritan Commonwealth, while its support of Dr. Child's *Petition* showed its opposition to the "Congregational" religious policy. Hingham's East Anglians took their values from their experiences in old Hingham. They came with an established ruling class and a church policy that was clearly Presbyterian. Once in Bear Cove they had to fight first the West Countrymen and then the Massachusetts authorities before their East Anglian pattern could triumph. This is one of the reasons why the new Hingham resisted change and insisted upon the retention of traditional ways. Yet within a generation the rivalry of West Countrymen and East Anglian ceased to be important. It was replaced by class interest. West Countrymen and East Anglian had joined together in an upper class oligarchy intent upon perpetuation of its way of life.

The original "planters" of Bear Cove came from England's West

Country. Their land differed in both soil and husbandry from East Anglia. In Devon and Dorset tilling the land stood for a way of life yet to be changed by the loom. Those towns that faced the sea, such as Plymouth, Weymouth, and Barnstaple, combined the working of both the sea and land. In the ancient city of Glastonbury in Somerset, the people took the new Puritan ethos lightly. They raised the May pole, evoking with it merriment and the primitive rites of spring. Pretty girls cast their spells, drunkards crowded its streets, and the barber plied his trade on the Sabbath. The 1620 episcopal visitation of St. John the Baptist Church found it without the "booke of sermons and a bible of the last translation." The records indicate little discontent with the ways of the old church. The West Country sent at least eighteen families to the new town in Massachusetts, the majority of whom sailed from Bristol Port on the *Lyon,* which made four recorded voyages to the Bay Colony between 1630 and 1632.

Typical of these West Countrymen was John Otis. In 1631 he was nearly fifty years of age and came with his wife and five children. Although born in Glastonbury, he had moved with his family in 1621 to Barnstaple in Devon. His father had been sufficiently stationed at death to have his will proved in the Consistorial Court at Wells in 1611. And John was prosperous enough to pay the heavy cost of migrating to Massachusetts, which came to at least £30. Yet the Otis family was neither the wealthiest nor the most important of the West Country families that came to Bear Cove. The richest would certainly be the Andrews, who along with the Cades repaid the subsidy to King James in 1624. Thomas Andrews, a patriarch in his fifties, must have thought it understandable that his son Joseph should be the town's first clerk, a selectman and for a brief time representative to the General Court.

Then there was Mr. William Walton from Seaton Parish. He was a product of Emmanuel College, the cradle of Puritanism at Cambridge University. It is more than likely that Mr. Walton knew Peter Hobart, also a Cambridge man, who came to Bear Cove as its first pastor. The shipwright James Cade, a Devon man, held lands in Northam Parish. By rural standards this was a wealthy family. In New England Cade utilized the full regnal citation ". . . Lord Charles by the grace of God King of England," a formula distasteful to the majority of the settlers of the Bay Colony, who used the simpler "Caroli Angliae &c." Cade was no rebel. His position as the second son must have been a major factor in his reasons for migrating. The gentleman and rich planter George Strange was his attorney. At Bear Cove they were John Otis's neighbors, as was another West Countryman, Thomas Loring, who became the first deacon and held the license "to sell wine & strong Water." These families are hardly underprivileged. Along with the Strongs, Phippenys, and Betscombes, they were people of record, literate, property owners, and careful husbanders of the soil. Probably the key element in their migration was a desire for greater estates and profits than England offered them. However, these West Country settlers were not to remain alone to fulfill their dreams.

In June of 1633 the *Elizabeth Bonaventure* arrived at Boston from the East Anglian County of Norfolk. It brought to the Bay Colony sixty-three-year-old Edmund Hobart and his family, with their servant Henry Gibbs, as well as the Jacobs and Chubocks. Late that summer this advance guard from old Hingham in Norfolk settled at Bear Cove. They were heralds of a new wave of immigrants that would profoundly change the political and social makeup of that New England town.

In contrast to the general agrarian backgrounds of the West Countrymen, these East Anglians from Norfolk, Essex, and Suffolk represented an area famous for its weaving industries, although the trade itself had been in the grips of depression since the twenties. The land they left was as flat as fine fustian, while the Norfolk Broads periodically suffered from "innundations of water." In fact, it was just such a flood that provided the needed pretext for the citizens of Norwich when they failed to furnish Charles I with £3,000 of ship money in 1635. East Anglia meant dissent in both religion and politics. This region, so very much like Holland, had received heavy influxes of Dutch weavers, whose separatist activities, together with those of the native Puitans, were thorns in the side of at least three High Church bishops. . . .

The continual movement of these East Anglians to Bear Cove during the middle and late 1630s is documented by changes both within and without this plantation. Indicative of the coming direction of things was the renaming of the town as Hingham in 1635, shortly after the Massachusetts General Court accorded municipal recognition. As a legal part of the body politic it was required to maintain a church, enforce law, have a militia unit, while on the provincial level it had to pay taxes and send its representatives to the General Court. Considering that the town had been founded by West Country settlers, and that they constituted the better part of the electorate until 1639, it was only natural that they supplied the first slate of town officers. Joseph Andrews of Devon was the town clerk and constable, and a representative in 1636, 1637, and 1638. Andrews used his influence to obtain the local liquor franchise for his neighbor Thomas Loring. Anthony Eames, a Somerset man, led Hingham's seven man militia requisition during the Pequod Indian difficulties in 1637. He was also the town's representative to the General Court in 1637 and 1638. Mr. Joseph Hull, likewise from Somerset, completed this list by serving as the other representative in 1638.

The year 1639 saw the displacement of the West Countrymen by the East Anglians. From that year until the Otises left Hingham in 1661, the representatives would all be men from East Anglia, save for a single exception in 1643. This should not be interpreted as a planned policy of excluding the West Country planters. Rather it reflects a changing population ratio based upon the continuing influx of settlers from Norfolk and the surrounding areas. The arrival of the *Diligent* in 1638, with more than a hundred East Anglians, meant that numerical superiority rested in the hands of the elders from old Hingham. And due to the community effort of resisting the ecclesiastical policies of the Norwich bishops for better than twenty years, these immigrants came with a sense of purpose and cohesiveness. What could be more natural than for neighbors and relatives to elect their own to the provincial posts—especially when they were Pecks, Hobarts, Allens, Jacobs, and Beales, the very families that had held positions of leadership in the old country!

While this influx had its repercussions in the more distant halls of the Bay Colony's General Court, its effects were most obvious in the twelfth "Church of Christ" gathered at Hingham. Its pastor, Peter Hobart, belonged to the Presbyterian wing of the Puritan reform movement. He held that the pastor, who ministered and instructed (unless there was a teacher who then instructed while the minister dispensed the sacraments), and the two deacons and elders constituted a ruling presbytery. Once these officials had received the "gifts" of office, they formed a council over the church. In Governor Winthrop's unflattering portrait, this was a system in which Pastor Hobart "did manage all affairs without the church's advice." With the coming of Master Peck from old Hingham in 1638, the church divided the ministry by ordaining him as "teacher." These two strong-willed men, who had opposed episcopal interference in England, would be just as willing to challenge the "Congregational" way of the Massachusetts puritans. While that way had started in flux and without a clear-cut policy of separatism from the Church of England, by 1634 it stood for churches "governed by Pastors, Teachers ruling Elders and Deacons" in which the "power lies in the wholl Congregation, and not in the Presbitrye further then for order and precedencye." This was a position directly opposite to the beliefs of Masters Hobart and Peck, and their adherents from Norfolk.

Unlike the Boston churches, which by 1640 included less than half the capital's population, the Hingham church encompassed virtually the entire town's one hundred and forty families. There was thus an identity between townsmen and church members that gave to the pastor a role of unquestioned authority. The Rev. Peter Hobart was the highest paid official in his community, receiving £70 to 100 *per annum* from the town, in addition to special land grants. The many bequests from the faithful testify to the general approval of his society to this status. As pastor, Hobart was in a key position to aid both his family and his adherents. The former, headed by his illiterate father Edmund and his brother Joshua, sought to dominate the political life of Hingham, while the latter sought to reconstruct their traditional way of life. The church presbytery mirrored these aspirations. Peter Hobart was its pastor, Robert Peck its teacher, and by 1641 the deaconships also passed into the hands of East Anglian supporters.

The control of both the two-man Hingham delegation to the General Court and the presbytery by the East Anglians resulted in new judicial and political appointments favorable to their party. Following their election as deputies in 1639, Edmund Hobart, the pastor's father, and Joseph Peck, the teacher's brother, were nominated along with Anthony Eames, as the three commissioners for small causes. This office gave any two of them power to decide at their discretion all legal suits in Hingham in which the damage was under twenty shillings. The deputies then used their positions to award the liquor franchise to neighbors from old Hingham. Of equal import, the three men appointed by the General Court to evaluate property for the province tax came from their adherents, as did the constable elected in 1640. The only important colony office still held by any of the first settlers from the West Country was the militia lieutenancy. With that exception, the East Anglians controlled all major positions of status and profit.

On the town level, the change was equally obvious as may be seen from the personnel which formed the rate-makers, land division, and townsmen committees. In 1637 and 1638 the land grant and rate committees had achieved a kind of parity between West Countrymen and East Anglians. The "great lots division" committee was controlled by the West Countrymen who held five out of the seven places. However, Anthony Eames was the only representative of the West Country settlers on the rate committee. The remaining eight members, headed by the elder Edmund Hobart, as well as Nicholas Jacob, Samuel Ward, and Thomas Underwood, were symptomatic of things to come. East Anglians or their mercantile friends would dominate the committees. By 1644 they held absolute majorities on these three major committees—although the West Country sector could always muster up at least one representative on each committee. By and large, West Country representation meant Anthony Eames and John Otis. The main support of Eames came from his leadership in the militia. He had a team of oxen that he would rent out—certainly an asset in a farming community. Eames also had joined the select circle of Hingham men who pooled their capital to erect a town mill.

The case of John Otis is somewhat different, for he was essentially a farmer. Presumably his knowledge of the local land was excellent. He was almost always a standing member of the divisions committee, and his testimony on boundaries was cited in more than one court case. Otis might be considered the spokesman for the old-timers from Devon. While this could explain his two elections to the rates committee, he must have had the respect of the majority of his neighbors, for he was sent to Boston as a grand juror in 1640, receiving six shillings for this service from the "country." And in 1647 he was elected as one of the nine men in charge of the town. He also served on the church seating committee with Anthony Eames and Nicholas Jacob, which in its own way symbolized the coming together of this society. The inventory of John's estate shows that he had £20 at loan in small sums to various townsmen. As one's vote in the town was a public act before all men these unpaid debts were in one respect political obligations. They undoubtedly increased Otis's influence in Hingham.

Oddly enough, it would be a marriage in the Otis family that raised the first constitutional challenge to "Congregational" rule in the Massachusetts Bay Company. In 1641 John Otis's daughter Margaret presented her husband Thomas Burton, former "clarke of the prothonataries office," with a daughter, Hannah. Burton remained within the Church of England, although inclined to the Presbyterian viewpoint. In Massachusetts he had not taken the covenant in any of its churches as that act would have made him an "Independent" or separatist. As he was not a member of the Hingham Church, "master *Hubbard* Pastor, [and] master *Peck* Teacher" refused to "baptise old Ottis grandchildren [*sic*], an ancient member of their own Church." Otis must have attempted to gain church standing for his grandchild through his own membership and failed. In this instance the Hingham Church followed congregational usage, which limited the sacraments to the "Visible Saints" and their children. This must have been a very difficult decision on the part of the pastor and teacher, who sympathized with Burton's position. Pastor Hobart soon either changed his mind or decided to follow his conscience. He baptized Hannah Otis Burton, although this extension of congregational membership to a grandchild violated the current doctrinal norms. It would exacerbate relations with Boston. This is the background of the third article of Robert Child's *Petition,* countersigned by Thomas Burton, which protested against this exclusive baptismal policy which denied that sacrament to the children of Anglicans. In the eyes of Congregational Massachusetts neither Burton nor Hobart were orthodox. If there were any doubts on this, the Hingham militia controversy removed them.

This dispute involved Anthony Eames, the experienced militia leader and the outstanding West Countryman in Hingham, who alone of the "first" planters had retained his official position in Hingham. In 1640 he had threatened "to looke out for himselfe elswhere" if he did not receive a larger grant of land. However, Eames did not move —unlike several of his friends—perhaps because he expected promotion to captain. That militia post would bring with it an honorarium in the form of a special land grant. And land alone could supply the lack of employment for his oxen, which had led him earlier to think of going elsewhere. In the spring of 1645 Eames was elected to the captaincy. Unfortunately, shortly after this election Eames committed some indiscretion which offended "the greater part of the town." The militia band then held another election and gave the office to the wealthy Norfolk man and "very good friend" of Peter Hobart, Mr. Bozoun Allen. The Boston magistrates, who were the governor's assistants in the Bay Colony and had the right of confirmation, refused to sanction this change until the General Court should meet. All in Hingham were charged to keep their former places. The supporters of Allen now called a training day for the militia. When Eames showed up and told them of the magistrates' position, they accused him of lying and refused to drill under him. The end result was a defection of two-thirds of the band to Allen, while the *de jure* leader Eames, now minus the militia, found himself denounced in church with Pastor Hobart moving for his excommunication.

In the minds of the Bay Colony magistrates, this had become a "slighting of authority" which must be corrected if the commonwealth was not to degenerate into a "mere democracy." John Winthrop called the Hobarts to Boston to answer for their insubordination, whereupon far from expressing sorrow, they rejected his argument and charged him with exceeding his authority. As the deputy governor himself admitted, "many of the deputies were of opinion that the magistrates exercised too much power, and that the people's liberty was thereby in danger." It was precisely this fear that the Hobarts exploited. They introduced a petition, signed by more than eighty of their Hingham supporters, which "complained of their liberties infringed" and asked the deputies for redress. This brilliant maneuver gained the support of fifteen out of thirty-one representatives at its high tide; the issue paralyzed the central government for three months. Finally, doubting deputies were won over to Winthrop's position and fined the Hobarts and their petitioning adherents from the "train band." The Hinghamites had no intention of paying their fines. They were led by their pastor, who intimidated the marshal by "questioning the authority of his warrant because it was not in the king's name." Considering the East Anglians' past observances of the royal writs one might be tempted to doubt Peter Hobart's sincerity—but it struck home at Winthrop and his associates, who had altered the Bay Company's oath so as to remove all reference to the king. Hobart's constitutional point was that "Government here was not more than a Corporation in England" and its action against him and the men of Hingham was not "agreeable to the laws of England." Following the trend of events in 1646 this was the opportune time for a congregation organized along the Presbyterian lines to appeal to England.

It is now that the Hobarts allied themselves with Dr. Robert Child and his petitioners, amongst whom was Thomas Burton—John Otis's son-in-law—who had seen his child initially denied baptism by Peter Hobart in 1641. This petition also declared that the Bay Corporation was but a chartered company and did not have a legal right to govern or to pass laws that infringed the "Naturall rights" of "freeborne subjects of the English nation" (which as a modern critic notes anticipates Locke's position by almost fifty years). The General Court recognized behind this defense of "civil liberty" a plot to weaken the autonomy of the Colony and subject it to English authority. It ordered a day of fast and humiliation so as to implore God's assistance against those *"that seeke to undermyne ye libertyes of Gods people here."* Pastor Peter Hobart refused to comply, holding that his parishioners "would not fast against Dr. Child and against themselves." Doubtlessly Perry Miller is correct in interpreting the *Child Petition* as a planned maneuver "to arouse the then Presbyterian Parliament against the Congregational power" but this does not account for the internal difficulties within Hingham.

While Pastor Peter Hobart, his brother Joshua and their friend Bozoun Allen, posed now as the defenders of home rule, as well as championing the Presbyterian viewpoint, the militia dispute in fact reflected the long smoldering regional and political differences within their town. It has not been possible to locate the eighty-one signatures on the Hingham petition against Captain Eames, but we do have a list of the nine ringleaders, who were fined from £1 to £20, as well as a petition from five of the rank and file, who claimed their "poverty" prevented them from paying their smaller fines. The leaders were the four Hobarts—Edmund, Joshua, Thomas, and the Rev. Peter—Bozoun Allen, Daniel Cushing, William Hersey, and John Towers, all from old Hingham, and Edmound Gold, from Kent, as was his servant John Winchester; the four remaining petitioners were all East Anglians. It is significant that there is not a single West Countryman on either list. The split in the militia unit reflected the regional origins of the Bear Cove planters. Eames of Dorset versus Allen of Norfolk is the West Country against East Anglia. No documents exist to show where John Otis, Sr. stood in this fray, or for that matter his son, who was twenty-five and doubtlessly an active member of the train band. But if in 1646 Otis wanted an excuse to stand clear he had it when his house "burnt to the ground." John Winthrop recorded that fire in his *Journal,* part of his compilation of examples showing the "special providence of God, pointing out his displeasure against some profane persons, who took part with Dr. Child, etc., against the government and churches here."

The Massachusetts General Court's solution to this militia leadership squabble was to impose officers from neighboring towns to take charge of the band. This brought about a closing of ranks within Hingham. By November the two former disputants, Bozoun Allen and Anthony Eames, were back at their milling undertaking. Obviously the desideratum was to regain control of the band and, where dispute and defiance had failed, humility might succeed. In 1648 the "Humble Petions of the Souldiours of Hingham" were submitted to the General Court thanking this honored body for many undeserved favors that they had received ". . . from the Lord, or you his instruments" and requesting the privilege "which we take to be our due, to chouse our owne offesors." They were allowed to elect the lieutenant and ensign, and these posts went to none other than Bozoun Allen and Joshua Hobart. It was not till 1651 that they had authority to elect the captain. This time Bozoun Allen received his coveted prize, and upon his retirement the following year, the post went to Joshua Hobart, thereby completing that family's monopoly of local offices. But the Boston magistrates, determined not to increase the Hobart influence, refused their consent in 1660 to Joshua's application as Hingham's official notary.

By 1650 Hingham had obtained a broad degree of stability. Life as it existed in countless English towns continued its daily pace. Although agriculture constituted the major activity of the inhabitants, there are a handful of extant documents which show that Hingham supplied boards, masts, planks, and small boats for the Boston market. This society could afford such amenities as a fine glass of wine served in silver beakers. It also had carefully arranged marriages in the Elizabethan tradition, for the second generation was now coming into its own. The marriage of John Otis, Jr., to Mary, the daughter of Nicholas Jacob, formerly of old Hingham, is fairly typical, with Otis, Sr. turning over his extensive properties as of 10 May 1649 in "consideration of Tenn pownds p. ann°" and the father-in-law turning over meadow lands to the newlyweds, as well as providing a bequest in his will. This is but one example of how well-to-do Hingham families married each other regardless of their parents' different English backgrounds and past disagreements over policy.

Differences would continue to exist, but on other grounds than West Country against East Anglia. In fact, the Hobarts by their engrossing of local honors helped to bring about a new alignment within the town. Joshua Hobart as militia captain in 1654–1655 received a grant of 300 acres, which was followed in March by a town vote exempting him "from paying any Rates for the public charge of the town" while he held the office of captain. This did not sit well with such leading citizens and ratepayers as Nathaniel Baker, John Jacob, the two John Tuckers, Joseph Jones, Henry Chamberlain, William Hersey, who had been fined £10 for signing the Hobart petition during the militia dispute, and John Otis, Jr. In 1661 these landholders moved unsuccessfully to change the exemption at the January 1st town meeting. No longer are the Hingham lists restricted to West Country men or East Anglians. This protest was a combined attack against Joshua Hobart's special status, with the second generation united by interests and not ethnic diversity. In its own way, this symbolized Hingham's coming of age.

By 1660 Hingham witnessed the disappearance of old-country differences as a major factor in its community life. The daughter of Anthony Eames married John Jacob, Thomas Loring Jr. married Hannah Jacob, and John Otis II took Mary Jacob as his wife. This confirms Crevecoeur's "melting pot" concept of the American as a "new man." However, these are all upper class marriages tending toward the consolidation of position and influence within a small group. Crevecoeur's upwardly mobile "new man" is a stranger in Hingham. For those who follow Frederick Jackson Turner's thesis on the primacy of the environment in the American experience, Hingham exemplifies the retention of old-world forms and values in the wilderness. Its people might meet in the church and mix on the commons, but this did not mean that all could be elected within this community, or that the yeoman's daughter married the village laborer. Its founders were patriarchs. It gave office to its elders, not its youth. Hingham recognized merit; it insisted upon performance from those in office; it believed in hierarchy; and it nurtured an early

American oligarchy. Was Hingham unique in this respect or did other towns follow their old-world paths? The resolution of this question is a challenge to the social historian for additional research into the neglected field of local history in New England's formative period.

Kenneth A. Lockridge
DEDHAM, MASSACHUSETTS

Unobtrusive though it is in his writing, Kenneth A. Lockridge (b. 1940), a professor at the University of Michigan, uses statistical, demographic, and sociological methods in a case study of another New England town to advance our understanding of colonial society. He finds an oligarchy of town, not colony, leaders basing their authority on consensus and bringing Dedham close to realization of a social ideal of unity, order, and peace. But he notes that Dedham's ideal was not entirely a Puritan ideal but was also typical of the traditions of the English village. Nevertheless, in his findings that the town was communitarian and cohesive, with a consensual unity countervailing whatever individualism and popular participation that people evinced, Lockridge disagrees with Rutman's findings of divisive ideas and Shipton's denial of authoritarian elements.

Out of their vision of society and out of the wilderness tract with which they had begun the founders of Dedham had created what might best be described as a Christian Utopian Closed Corporate Community. Christian because they saw Christian love as the force which would most completely unite their community. Utopian because theirs was a highly conscious attempt to build the most perfect possible community, as perfectly united, perfectly at peace, and perfectly ordered as man could arrange. Closed because its membership was selected while outsiders were treated with suspicion or rejected altogether. And Corporate because the commune demanded the loyalty of its members, offering in exchange privileges which could be obtained only through membership, not the least of which were peace and good order. The corporative nature of the town was

Reprinted from *A New England Town, The First Hundred Years,* by Kenneth A. Lockridge. By permission of W. W. Norton & Company, Inc. Copyright © 1970 by W. W. Norton & Company, Inc.

confirmed by the practices of the colony: the typical inhabitant of Massachusetts could obtain land only by belonging to a particular town, since the allotment of most of the land in settled areas had been delegated to the towns by the General Court; and a man was represented in the House of Deputies (the lower house of the General Court) only if he was a member of a town, since representatives were elected from the town corporations rather than from electoral districts containing a certain number of inhabitants.

The obvious origin of the Christian Utopian Closed Corporate Community lay in the Puritan ideology. The very term "Puritan" was coined to describe the desire for perfection which drove many of these otherwise typical Englishmen into martyrdom or exile. Purity in the church itself was the chief goal. The Puritans sought an end to bishops, vestments, ritual—to "papistry" in whatever form it might take. Their consciences required a return to the simple forms of primitive Christianity and a ministry which would preach the unadorned Word of God as it appeared in the Bible. What has often been passed over, however, is the intensity of the drive for social purity which likewise characterized Puritanism. If the Puritan sometimes dreamed of a church whose membership was confined to "visible saints," he also dreamed on occasion of a society dominated by secular saints, men able to live in harmony with their fellowmen as God had commanded.

Most immediately, the policies of perfection in Dedham were the products of a vivid utopian spirit which came to possess most of the leaders and many of the rank and file of the Puritan emigration as they approached America. They were aware that a great opportunity awaited them in the confrontation of the Puritan social ideal with the New World. Here was a chance to begin again, leaving behind the compromises of an established culture. Governor John Winthrop's famous "Modell of Christian Charity," a sermon delivered aboard the *Arabella* on the way to America, is proof of the excitement and trepidation with which he approached the unique opportunity opened to his people. With Gold's help they would build in their colony a "city upon a hill" which would stand as a shining example to all men. The plan of the society Winthrop hoped to construct in Massachusetts was the plan of early Dedham writ large, a holy covenanted corporation mixing mutuality with hierarchy and Christian love with exclusiveness.

But the origins of the Dedham commune ran deeper than the Puritan ideology, deeper even than Christianity. At first glance they seem to run back to the English rural culture which had done so much to shape the social ideals of Puritanism. Any number of institutions and customs found in Dedham were direct transplantations from the English villages of the time. Genuine as this line of descent is, it is also deceptive. For the deepest secular origins of this Utopian Closed Corporate Community lay not merely in English villages but in a major strain of peasant culture also found in medieval and modern villages of France and Spain, and in modern Indian and Javanese villages.

An anthropologist entirely unaware of the internal structure of the New England Town has described the "Closed Corporate Peasant Community" common to all these places and times. His description fits Dedham nicely. Social relationships in these rural communities are "many-stranded and polyadic"; the villagers tend to form a single social coalition which deals with all the issues of village life— land, taxation, regulation, morality. A "Closed Corporate Peasant Community" restricts its membership, retains ultimate authority over the alienation of land, seeks to guarantee its members equal access to resources, and maintains its internal order by enforcing common standards of behavior (by accusations of witchcraft, if all else fails). "The community thus acquires the form of a corporation, an enduring organization of rights and duties held by a stable membership; and it will tend to fight off changes and innovations as potential threats to the internal order that it strives to maintain." Indeed, the constant possibility of disruptions imposed by outside forces generates a powerful hostility toward everything strange, a hostility which further protects the internal order by uniting the villagers in a shared emotional experience. Conscious utopianism may be found in these as in all peasant communities, for from them arise movements centering on a "myth of a social order," looking forward to "the establishment of a new order on earth."

So the utopia of the Puritan émigrés who founded Dedham was in many respects a peasant utopia. The communal ideal of these men repeated so many features of the peasant ideal that their Puritanism seemed a mere continuation of the peasant ethos. The dichotomy of mutual devotion within and hostility without, which had been practiced by a multitude of villages all over the world for thousands of years, was in turn both preached and practiced in Puritan Dedham, and all the characteristic implications of this corporative form were worked out in full detail. Further, the tendency of medieval peasants to look on the villages of an imaginary golden past as their model for the future regeneration of society was repeated in the Puritan idealization of the communes of the primitive Christian church and in the use of these communes as a model for some features of Dedham's organization. Precedents for the peculiar mixture of hierarchy with collectivism manifested in Puritan Dedham could even be found in the history of peasant utopianism. The Puritan source did not simply echo the peasant; they were directly linked. The social ethic of Englishmen of the day still owed much to the peasant experience which had once dominated the English scene, and among the Puritans as among all Englishmen were many men whose families were only a few generations removed from villeinage and still lived in hamlets that were essentially peasant.

Did this really mean that for the men of Dedham Puritanism was nothing more than the continuation of traditional impulses? Not entirely. Puritanism was above all a new religious impulse, part of the Reformation which swept over Europe in the sixteenth and seventeenth centuries and which in its origins and effects was far more than a mere offshoot of the peasant ethos. This new impulse would color the history of Dedham, and indeed it had brought the townsmen there in the first place. Yet somehow when these creatures of the Reformation came to articulate their ideal of social organization, they not only continued but actually perfected and sanctified the ideal of the peasant past. The two sources, Puritan and peasant, were not identical, but by some inscrutable chemistry they came together in a mixture which was as powerful as it was inseparable.

It may be that the catalyst was the American wilderness, whose frightening presence turned the settlers back upon the old ways engrained in them and their forbears. If this was the case, then Puritanism was somewhat incidental to that intensification of the peasant tradition found in Dedham; Puritanism had brought the townsmen face to face with the wilderness and had provided the rhetoric by which their social reaction to this alarming prospect could be sanctified, but it had not directly urged them to their conservative social ideal. Yet it may be also that within Puritanism itself was a fear of the future which tended to send its advocates to the past for their definition of the holy society.

Whatever the exact nature of the mixture, Dedham was at once a Puritan and a peasant utopia. It partook of the desire for a reformed religion which had seized Europeans in all walks of life and at the same time it embraced half-conscious patterns which had arisen in peasant villages long before the discovery of America. It blended these sources into an ideology strong enough to unite men from diverse parts of England into a coherent social organism. Ironically, what was most uniquely "American" about the policies of earliest Dedham was the intensity of their utopianism. For here in the New World the settlers could heed almost without restriction whatever mysterious fears urged them to reconstruct in new perfection the ancient patterns of social organization.

Dedham was not to be a theocracy. By law, the Puritan clergy could not become officers of the civil society here or elsewhere in the colony. In some ways, the local church actually came to occupy a position of isolation. A good many of the lay elders of the congregation would play no role in the leadership of the town, while the town government, though it shared control of the business affairs of the church, had so little to do with religious beliefs that references to the Lord appeared in its records only twice in fifty years.

This superficial isolation did not mean that the church was irrelevant to the life of the new community. Quite the contrary, it was in several ways central to the settlers' experience. In the first place, these Englishmen had not left their homes merely to organize their own township. John Allin, their first minister, spoke for most of them when he wrote that only "the hope of enjoying Christ in his ordinances" could have persuaded the emigrants to "forsake dearest relations, parents, brethren, sisters, Christian friends and acquaintances, overlook the dangers and difficulties of the vast seas, the thought whereof was a terror to many, and . . . go into a wilderness where we could forecast nothing but care and temptation." Even before a church was organized, this overriding concern for the implementation of true Christian faith had been written into the town Covenant, ensuring that the townsmen would be Christians in secular life as well as in church. Once the church was formed, the inhabitants of the town would assemble several times each week to hear sermons or lectures in practical piety, most of them would become members of the church, and church and town officers together would keep watch over the moral tone of the community. So, if anything, the church was to be the focus of that revived Christian spirit which had brought the settlers to America and was to illumine every aspect of their communal life.

At the same time, the church was intimately related to the community of Dedham in that both were organized around the principles of autonomy, exclusiveness, and unity. The local church emerged as an autonomous congregation whose membership excluded persons who could not prove they had received saving grace and in which the members were united by a covenant of love. Although these features were eventually expected of all churches by the religious authorities of the colony, the idea of a self-governing corporation of the saved was not just imposed from above. Founding their church in the years when the spiritual leaders of Massachusetts were still groping their way toward a definition of the true Church, the Dedham townsmen contributed to the growing insistence on what came to be called "congregationalism" and "the church of saints." Their church was organized according to their own vision of religious perfection, a vision which in this respect was very like their vision of social perfection. Both town and church partook of a common utopian form whose sources lay with, yet beneath, Puritan Christianity, in the Bible, yet also in the ancient enduring motives of peasant communities.

The repeated fact that the selectmen were, after all, elected, naturally brings attention back to the town meeting. Surely here was the touchstone of local politics. But it was an elusive touchstone, if indeed there was such a thing in the complex patterns of Dedham's political life. . . .

In theory, the power of the town meeting knew no limit. The town had called the board of selectmen into existence and could as easily abolish the institution altogether. On occasion the town would reaffirm the broad mandate of power given to the board and in the very fact of affirmation confirm the ultimate power of the meeting. In a memorable upset in 1660 the town actually went so far as to negative the proposal, "whether they [the selectmen] should have the same power their predecessors have had" and underlined their dissatisfaction by voting out of office every single incumbent—though the pique soon passed. Theoretical power might be translated in very specific ways into real power any time the townsmen assembled. They might pass bylaws, appoint special committees of their own, or grant small favors to petitioners; they customarily admitted new townsmen and appointed many lower officers. Anything the selectmen could do, they could do. Just to make sure the selectmen did their job well, the meeting would sometimes bring up for approval all the acts and accounts of their executive. The yearly elections gave the town a fine tool for use against its leaders, for not only could an entire board be removed but also any one selectman could be singled out for vengeance and left in limbo for one year, two, three, or forever.

The voting membership of the meeting was generally wide enough to include a fair majority of the townsmen, so most men had a voice in local affairs and most could vote to remove an errant selectman. Though the colony law concerning local suffrage shifted with the changing attiudes of the colonial authorities toward the franchise, and though the consistency of the law's application in the town is questionable, some generalizations are safe. Up to 70 percent of the male taxpayers were eligible under a law in effect to 1647, whose chief requirement was church membership. Whatever the law's requirements, the town meetings of the first few years were informal gatherings in which all men probably voted. As Dedham interpreted a new law of 1647, only men under twenty-four were ineligible to participate, so the legal suffrage rose to over 90 percent of adult males. An additional requirement of twenty pounds taxable estate imposed in 1658 did little to reduce this; a town voting list for 1666 includes the names of eighty-three of the ninety-one male taxpayers. A law of 1670 raised the amount needed to qualify to a stiff eighty pounds, but took effect slowly since it allowed all town voters who had previously qualified under the old law to continue in the privilege regardless of their estates.

Yet broad as its powers and membership were, the town meeting was essentially passive. It lacked initiative, its veto was quiescent, and its theoretical powers were for the most part symbolic. Meeting on the average only twice a year, the town never had a chance to acquire or apply the consistent expertise of the selectmen. Most meetings stayed close to the agenda prepared by the selectmen and were brief in comparison with those of the board. Formal review of the acts and accounts of the executive was sporadic and at best perfunctory. The townsmen seemed glad to leave most decisions to their leaders, often "referring to the selectmen" to "prepare and ripen the answer." Whatever the answer, it would not be challenged; the town never presumed to replace a substantive decision of the selectmen with its own will. The upset of 1660 was the single occasion on which the town used its theoretical right to withdraw the power of the selectmen and the only time the annual election was used to remove an entire panel of seven men. Year after year for half a century the town elected a wealthy and experienced group of respected friends, took their suggestions, obeyed their bylaws, and left them to run the town without interference.

Furthermore, the law of the colony imposed an increasing degree of narrowness on the right to political participation. Even the comparatively generous local suffrage law of 1647 had excluded young men under twenty-four. The law of 1670 was designed to shut out almost all young men coming of age thereafter. A man might easily be forty before he acquired the necessary eighty pounds of taxable estate or he might never acquire that much. By 1686 only a quarter of the male taxpayers could meet the eighty pound minimum, and though some of the rest could vote because they had been voters before the law of 1670 took effect, nearly half of the taxpayers were not eligible to cast a vote in the town meeting. On the level of the provincial suffrage, the colony law continued to insist that full church members alone were eligible to vote for representatives and Assistants, and church membership in Dedham had fallen to half of the male taxpayers by 1662 and continued to fall thereafter. All in all, if the town was a democracy, it was a most peculiar democracy.

The system's prime virtue was that it worked. The very ambivalences of the allotment and use of power produced a marvelously stable politics. No man, group of men, or single institution could run away with the town and generally none wanted to try. Supported at every turn by the policy of mediation introduced by the Covenant, this political system gave Dedham fifty years of tranquil government. But to call the system successful is still not to describe it: "A successful thing unto itself" is hardly satisfactory. What label fits an oligarchy which was not an oligarchy and a democracy which was no democracy? An excursion into the theory of politics in seventeenth-century Massachusetts offers a tentative answer.

Though a new age of revolutionary political theories was even then beginning, order was still the highest political value in the seventeenth century, as it had been for some centuries before. Thomas Hobbes was no innovator when he observed that human society is naturally inclined to chaos. Hobbes' argument in favor of strong rulers merely secularized the old Christian justification of government. God had given man the capacity to sin, Adam and Eve had sinned, thenceforth men were forever imperfect, forever condemned to fall into immorality and discord. As sin was divinely ordained, so was government. The state existed to restrain the sinful impulse and punish the sinner, not simply because sin was wrong, but because the visible church needed an orderly world in which to fulfill its part of God's plan. A society in which violence interrupted the work of the clergy and unbridled license smothered all examples of virtue was not a proper arena for man's struggle for salvation. The much-maligned James I was only invoking the commonplace when he spoke of the divine right of kings, for traditional theory gave divine sanction to the rulers of the state. Likewise Shakespeare's frequent sallies in praise of order were no more than resounding summations of the deep-rooted spirit of his age. And similarly, much of the "reform" thought of the radical English Protestants of the seventeenth century envisioned not a new and mobile society stressing individual opportunity but rather a social commonwealth whose prime features were security and Christian love.

The Puritans of New England had ample reason to hold to and indeed to extend the seventeenth century's faith in order. Their conception of a whole society bound to God by a covenant made the existence of sin an immediate danger, for to allow sin was to breach the contract with God, thereby inviting his wrath down upon them all. Further, their desire to build a perfect visible church accented the need for a state which would give the church an orderly social setting for its work. Circumstance lent practical force to these arguments; England might use any sign of discord in Massachusetts as an excuse to revoke their charter and take over the government in the name of good order. Such a move would shatter the emigrants' covenant and with it their "city on a hill."

But it does not require Hobbesean skepticism, original sin, or Puritan perfectionism to explain the love of order. All were present, but beneath all, as ever, lay the peasant's inbred fear of chaos. Robbery, extortion, war with its legalized murder—few peasant villages had not lived precariously close to these disasters. Only late in the fifteenth century had the Tudor state ended the bloody baronial feuds which had kept England in turmoil for generations, and it would be at least another century before the age of inchoate popular uprisings would come to an end. The confidence generated by uniform legal order imposed by a central monarchy was new to Englishmen's experience. A little below the surface were folk memories of violence and a longing for peace and certainty.

Such was the background of Dedham's peculiar political behavior. A product of its time, the town Covenant had obliged men to pledge obedience and had gone to some lengths to provide mechanisms for the preservation of order. Men of their time, and also men aware of the dangers involved in founding a perfect society in the wilderness, the townsmen of Dedham took the Covenant to heart. They settled their disputes peacefully and used their electoral powers to elevate a handful of substantial men, leaving in their hands the direction of the community. Sanctified by their election, the leaders of Dedham were further sanctified by their success in keeping order, and thereby they gained reelection repeatedly. Today's praise for democracy as the key to opportunity and for dissent as the harbinger of change would have been grotesquely out of place in such a society, where order outranked opportunity and the changes brought by dissent were not expected to be fruitful.

But a narrow-minded passion for order was not the only source of the town's political behavior. Had it been, there would have been no need for a town meeting. The founders or the colony's governor could have imposed a set of lifetime rulers who would name their own successors, a complete oligarchy in short. The Puritans' desire for order was more sophisticated than this. Their intense Christianity led them to see in unity rather than in repression the essence of true order. They "demanded that in society all men, at least all regenerate men, be marshalled in one united array . . . . The theorists of New England thought of society as a unity, bound together by inviolable ties; they thought of it not as an aggregation of individuals, but as an organism, functioning for a definite purpose, with . . . all members contributing a definite share . . . ." Therefore, a degree of popular participation was valued, for it would both symbolize and strengthen the unity of all men in the common Christian society. Consent would strengthen unity and that unity would lead to a higher form of order.

So there was in the Puritan political philosophy a door through which the generality could enter to participate in the workings of government. But, at least on the level of the colony's theoreticians and leaders, it was seen as a very narrow door. It was only the saints who could hope to achieve genuine Christian unity, and therefore it was their participation that was the center of concern. Even in their case, "the commanders were not to trim their policies by the desires of the people . . . the officers were above the common men . . . ." The emphasis was on obedience: "When the Lord sets himself over a people, he frames them unto a willing and voluntary submission unto him . . . they follow Him not forcedly, but as far as they are sanctified by his grace, they submit willingly to his regiment." The chief participatory acts envisioned were the consent to covenants and the election of a few leaders, acts which would enhance the unity of the participating saints and at the same time give extra cachet to the leaders and to the political framework which they had established. Beyond this, participation was likely to be viewed as interference, conducive to disorder.

John Winthrop expressed it in this way: "It is yourselves who have called us to . . . office, and being called by you, we have authority from God." As for liberty, "[the] liberty you are to stand for is a liberty to [do] that only which is good, just, and honest . . . . This liberty is maintained and exercised in a way of subjection to authority." A good subject was to resemble a good wife, for, "the woman's own choice makes such a man her husband; yet being so chosen, he is her lord, and she is to be subject to him, yet in a way of liberty, not of bondage; and a true wife accounts her subjection her honor and freedom . . . ." Though Winthrop's statement exaggerated its authoritarian aspects, the fundamentals on the theory prevailed as the usual ideological justification for popular participation. The colony law continued to insist that church members alone were qualified to vote for colony officers because they alone could be trusted to perceive "that which is good, just, and honest" and to submit themselves to leaders with a like perception.

Perhaps because it was grafted onto a tradition of local consensus and cooperation which had long characterized English peasant communities, the theory had more positive overtones on the local level. The vote was not confined to church members (after 1647) and voters had the right to join in substantive decisions as well as to elect leaders. Still, the town's behavior reveals that the popular voice in Dedham acted in a manner consonant with the Puritan theory of popular participation. Men had signed the Covenant voluntarily and they voluntarily lived according to its commands. Their votes were customarily "by general agreement"—a voluntary consensus. In electing a man, they were asking him to lead a society united in love under the rule of the gospel; in obeying his decisions they were marching together freely in the practice of the "one truth" desired by all. The matching restraint of the selectmen derived more from their own stake in the common unity than from any fear of retaliation. And out of the unity thereby voluntarily achieved, the townsmen also enjoyed an enduring order such as no amount of force could have imposed.

Sixty-nine men of Dedham explicitly approved the prevailing theory in a petition of support sent to the General Court in 1665 to aid the government in its battle against English interference in the affairs of the colony. None of them was qualified to vote in colony elections and some could not participate in the town meeting, yet every last one expressed appreciation of "the great blessing we enjoy . . . in a Godly, righteous, and peaceable government." These men said quite frankly that they valued a government "Godly, righteous, and peaceable" over the limited blessing of the suffrage. In an age in which the suffrage was viewed as one more way of maintaining unity and preserving order, the democrat's worship of the vote was far in the future.

To put it another way, conditions were not ripe for a philosophy of individualism. "The basic sociological findings . . . show that modern individualism depends appreciably upon extensive division of labor, institutional differentiation and cultural diversity." The democracy of differing religions, immigration, urbanization, and contending economic interests was out of the question in the simple society of seventeenth-century Dedham. Diversity had not yet been forced upon men. Until it was, a man's concern would be more with harmonizing himself with the one true way than with protecting his right to vote in a pluralistic world where individual rights had become the only refuge.

The political phenomenon at hand, which might be labeled "Conservative Corporate Voluntarism," actually lies not one but two layers deep in American history. A long distance from the popular democracy of the nineteenth century, it was only beginning to merge into the mechanistic political philosophy which was to characterize eighteenth-century Americans—particularly those eighteenth-century Americans familiar with Enlightenment thought and with contemporary English political theorists. Dedham's political system was intricate, yet ultimately what had made political harmony in Dedham was not a clockwork balance of one power against another but voluntary restraint on the part of all concerned. Eighteenth-century thinkers would deemphasize the notion of an organic society held together by voluntary restraint. In its place would come an emphasis on the balance of political elements, monarchy, aristocracy, and democracy, each with its own virtues and vices. Ideally, each would contribute its virtues while holding in check the vices of the others. Democracy would contribute the representation of a certain class of interests and the innate good sense of the commonry. The instability of democracy would be cancelled partially by restricting the suffrage to propertied men, partially by the stability of the monarchical and aristocratic elements. The theory of the eighteenth century allowed popular participation at once a greater and a lesser role than its predecessor. By justifying the participation of the commonry in a legislative role and by freeing the suffrage of religious restrictions, it opened a door to the later deification of democracy. Yet by destroying the Puritan notion of popular participation as a holy recognition of the organic unity of men (or at least of all believers) in their society, the eighteenth-century outlook stripped the popular voice of a mystical level of human significance which it has since regained, alas, largely in the perverted world of plebescitary totalitarianism.

"Conservative Corporate Voluntarism" in politics, like the closed corporate community in which it operated, was "American" chiefly in that it was a uniquely intense expression of Old World ideals. Only in the most tenuous sense can the roots of modern American democracy be traced back to the political experience of seventeenth-century Dedham. Its limitations and conservative theoretical context notwithstanding, the suffrage *was* significantly wider in Dedham than in England. Both in Dedham and in Massachusetts at large the many officers subject to election by this wider electorate exercised powers which were in the aggregate greater than the powers exercised by elected officers in England. In such innovations lay the deepest foundation of an American participatory mentality, a mentality born of a widened public role in government, which eventually would lead increasing numbers of men to demand a still wider role in their own governance. In this context perhaps the brief political upset in the town of Dedham in 1660 might be seen as the first faint movement of an awakening giant. And perhaps it is possible to see in the divine sanction with which all New England Puritans endowed a limited popular voice the beginnings of the later secular sanctification of Everyman's right to participate which paved the way for the triumph of democracy as a supreme virtue. But it must not be forgotten that modern democracy whether in practice or in theory was a long way in the future. It took far more than moderately wide participation, occasional popular protests, or veiled scriptural justifications to create that democracy.

IV WITCHCRAFT

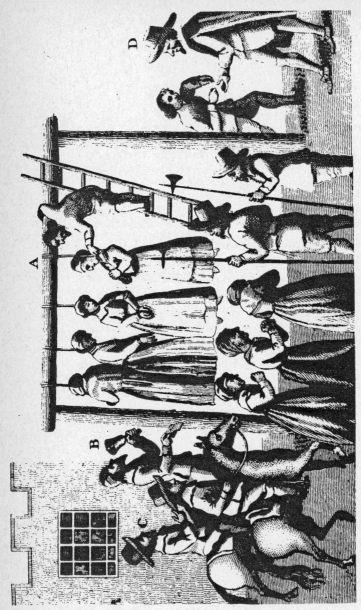

FIGURE 6. A witch-hanging in England in the seventeenth century, similar to those in New England. Letters identify: A. hangman B. bellman C. two sergeants D. witch-finder taking fee.

John Demos

UNDERLYING THEMES IN NEW ENGLAND WITCHCRAFT

Applying the techniques of anthropology and psychology to the Salem out-break of 1692, John Demos (b. 1937) seeks to find insights into the problem of how a society manages the tensions created by change, a problem central to any social structure, whether created by New England settlers or in our own times. Demos is less concerned to know who brought on the witch-craft frenzy than he is to find out how the social and political institutions of New England reacted to it. His conclusions square with studies of other late seventeenth-century problems, that the problems stem from difficulties en-countered by social and political institutions which are not changing rapidly enough to meet new conditions. Did the widespread impact of the Salem disturbance result from a lack of satisfactory outlets for normal aggressive tendencies in the Puritan state, from broader inadequacies in the social and political system than merely a repressive intellectual or religious outlook, which many historians have charged?

It is faintly embarrassing for a historian to summon his colleagues to still another consideration of early New England witchcraft. Here, surely, is a topic which previous generations of writers have suffi-ciently worked, indeed overworked. Samuel Eliot Morison once com-mented that the Salem witch-hunt was, after all, "but a small incident in the history of a great superstition"; and Perry Miller noted that with only minor qualifications "the intellectual history of New Eng-land can be written as though no such thing ever happened. It had no effect on the ecclesiastical or political situation, it does not figure in the institutional or ideological development." Popular interest in the subject is, then, badly out of proportion to its actual historical significance, and perhaps the sane course for the future would be silence.

This assessment seems, on the face of it, eminently sound. Witch-craft was not an important matter from the standpoint of the larger historical process; it exerted only limited influence on the unfolding sequence of events in colonial New England. Moreover, the literature on the subject *does* seem to have reached a point of diminishing

From John Demos, "Underlying Themes in the Witchcraft of Seventeenth-Century New England" in the *American Historical Review* 75 (1970): 1311–1326. Used by permission of the author.

returns. Details of fact have been endlessly canvassed, and the main outlines of the story—particularly the story of Salem—are well and widely known.

There is, to be sure, continuing debate over one set of issues: the roles played by the various persons most directly involved. Indeed the historiography of Salem can be viewed, in large measure, as an unending effort to *judge* the participants—and above all, to affix blame. A number of verdicts have been fashionable at one time or another. Thus, the ministers were really the people at fault; or Cotton Mather in particular; or the whole culture of Puritanism; or the core-group of "afflicted girls" (if their "fits" are construed as conscious fraud). The most recent and in some ways most sophisticated study of the Salem trials plunges right into the middle of the same contro- versy—and with yet another conclusion. Not the girls, not the clergy, not Puritanism, but the accused witches themselves are now the chief culprits. For "witchcraft actually did exist and was widely prac- ticed in seventeenth century New England"; and women like Goody Glover, Bridget Bishop, and Mammy Redd were "in all probability" guilty as charged.

Clearly these questions can still generate lively interest, but are they the most fruitful, the most important questions to raise about witchcraft? Will such a debate ever be finally settled? Are its partisan terms and moral tone appropriate to historical scholarship? And if, with Morison and Miller, we agree that witchcraft does not loom large as historians usually measure events, what significance remains for the old arguments about personal credit and blame? The outlook, on all counts, seems discouraging.

But this situation is not a hopeless one if only we are willing to look beyond the limits of our own discipline. There is, in particular, a substantial body of interesting and relevant work by anthropologists. Many recent studies of "primitive" societies contain chapters about witchcraft, and there are several entire monographs on the subject. The approach they follow differs strikingly from anything in the historical literature. Broadly speaking, the anthropological work is far more analytic, striving always to *use* materials on witchcraft as a set of clues or "symptoms." The subject is important not in its own right, but as a means of exploring certain larger questions about the society and the individuals directly concerned. Thus witchcraft throws light on social structure, or the organization of families, or the inner dynamics of personality. The substance of such investigation is, of course, highly variable from one culture to another, but the framework, the informing purposes are roughly the same. To apply this framework and these purposes to historical materials is not inherently difficult. The data may be inadequate in a given case, but the analytic categories themselves are designed for any society, whether simple or complex, Western or non-Western, past or contemporary.

Consider, by way of illustration, the strategy proposed for the main body of this essay. The whole enterprise turns on a set of complex relationships between the alleged witches and their victims. The former group includes (for these purposes) all the persons accused of practicing witchcraft; and from henceforth let them be called, simply, "witches." The category of victims, on the other hand, comprises everyone who claimed to have suffered from witchcraft. But note, too, an important distinction between different *kinds* of victims. As every schoolchild knows, some of them experienced "fits"—bizarre seizures that, in the language of modern psychiatry, closely approximate the clinical picture for hysteria. These people may be called "accusers," since their sufferings and their accusations seem to have carried the greatest weight in generating formal proceedings against witches. A second, much larger group of victims includes people who attributed to witchcraft some particular misfortune they had suffered: most typically, an injury or illness, the sudden death of domestic animals, the loss of personal property, or repeated failure in important day-to-day activities like farming, fishing, and hunting. This type of evidence was of secondary importance in actual trials of witches and was usually brought forward after the accusers had pressed their own more damaging charges. For people testifying to such experiences, therefore, the short-hand term "witnesses" seems reasonably appropriate.

Witches, accusers, and witnesses: here, then, are the three basic categories of participants in witchcraft proceedings. But just who were they? And how did their lives intersect with one another? And, most important, what attributes were generally characteristic of each group? These will be the organizing questions in the pages that follow. They will, however, demand answers of two distinct kinds, one that corresponds roughly to actual circumstances in the lives of the persons involved, and another which treats imaginary (or "irrational") materials. In short, the questions will point towards two most fundamental levels of human experience—external and internal, objective and subjective, social and psychological, define them as you will.

Consider, for example, the specific case of the witches. It is important to discover, if at all possible, their age, marital status, socio-economic position, visible personality traits, and so forth. And it is equally important to examine the chief characteristics *attributed* to witches by others (flying about at night, for instance, and transforming themselves into animals). In short, we can construct a picture of witches in fact and in fantasy; and we can make comparable efforts with accusers and witnesses as well. Analysis directed to the level of fact or "external reality" helps to locate certain points of tension or conflict in the social structure of a community. The fantasy-picture, on the other hand, reveals more directly the psychological dimension of life, the inner preoccupations, anxieties, and conflicts of individual members of that community.

An outline such as this looks deceptively simple—even, perhaps, easy to put into practice. In fact, it demands an unusual degree of caution, from writer and reader alike. The approach is explicitly cross-disciplinary, reaching out to anthropology for a strategy, and to psychology for theory. There is, of course, nothing new about the *idea* of a working relationship between history and the behavioral sciences. It is more than ten years since William Langer's famous summons to his colleagues, to consider this as their "next assignment." But the record of actual output is still very meager. Hence all such efforts remain quite experimental—designed more to stimulate discussion than to prove a definitive case.

There is a final point about context and the larger purposes of this form of inquiry. Historians have traditionally worked with purposeful, conscious events, "restricting themselves," in Langer's words, "to recorded fact and to strictly rational motivation." They have not necessarily wished to exclude nonrational, or irrational behavior; but it has mainly worked out that way in practice. Surely in our own post-Freudian era there is both need and opportunity to develop a more balanced picture. It is to these long-range ends that further study of witchcraft should be dedicated. For witchcraft is, if nothing else, an open window on the irrational.

The first witchcraft trial of which any record survives occurred at Windsor, Connecticut, in 1647, and during the remainder of the century the total of cases ran to nearly 100. Thirty-eight people were executed as witches during this span of time; and a few more, though convicted, managed somehow to escape the death penalty. There was, of course, a variety of other outcomes as well: full dress trials resulting in acquittal, hung juries, convictions reversed on appeal, "complaints" filed but not followed up. Finally, no doubt, there were many unrecorded episodes touching on witchcraft, episodes of private suspicion or public gossip that never eventuated in legal action at all.

This long series of witchcraft cases needs emphasis lest the Salem outbreak completely dominate our field of vision. Salem differed radically from previous episodes in sheer scope; it developed a degree of self-reinforcing momentum present in no other instance. But it was very similar in many qualitative aspects: the types of people concerned, the nature of the charges, the fits, and so forth. Indeed, from an analytic standpoint, all these cases can be regarded as roughly equivalent and interchangeable. They are pieces of a single, larger phenomenon: a "system" of witchcraft belief that was generally prevalent in early New England. The evidence for such a system, must, of course, be drawn from a variety of cases in order to produce representative conclusions. For most questions this is quite feasible: there is more evidence from a greater range of cases than can ever be presented in a single study.

Yet in one particular matter the advantages of concentrating on Salem are overwhelming. It affords a unique opportunity to portray the demography of witchcraft, to establish a kind of profile for each of the three basic categories of people involved in witchcraft, in terms of sex, age, and marital status. Thus the statistical tables that follow derive entirely from detailed work on the Salem materials. The earlier cases do not yield the breadth of data necessary for this type of quantitative investigation. They do, however, provide many fragments of evidence that are generally consistent with the Salem picture.

There is at least minimal information about 165 people accused as witches during the entire period of the Salem outbreak. (See Tables 1, 2, and 3.) These figures point to an important general conclusion:

TABLE 1

Sex	Total
Male	42
Female	120
Total	162

TABLE 2

Marital Status	Male	Female	Total
Single	8	29	37
Married	15	61	76
Widowed	1	20	21
Total	24	110	134

TABLE 3

Age	Male	Female	Total
Under 20	6	18	24
21–30	3	7	10
31–40	3	8	11
41–50	6	18	24
51–60	5	23	28
61–70	4	8	12
Over 70	3	6	9
Total	30	88	118

the witches were predominantly married or widowed women, between the ages of forty-one and sixty. The exceptions add up to a considerable number; but, significantly, most of them belonged to the *families* of middle-aged, female witches. Virtually all the young persons in the group can be identified as the children of previously suspected women, and most of the men as their husbands. In fact this pattern conformed to an assumption then widely prevalent that the transmission of witchcraft would naturally follow the lines of family or of close friendship. An official statement from the government of Connecticut included among the "grounds for Examination of a Witch" the following:

> *If ye party suspected be ye son or daughter the servt or familiar friend; neer Neighbor or old Companion of a Knowne or Convicted witch this alsoe a presumton for witchcraft is an art yt may be learned & Convayd from man to man & oft it falleth out yt a witch dying leaveth som of ye aforesd. heirs of her witchcraft.*

In short, young witches and male witches belonged to a kind of derivative category. They were not the prime targets in these situations; they were, in a literal sense, rendered suspect by association. The deepest suspicions, the most intense anxieties, remained fixed on middle-aged women.

Thirty-four persons experienced fits of one sort or another during the Salem trials and qualify thereby as accusers. (See Tables 4, 5, and 6.)

TABLE 4

Sex	Total
Male	5
Female	29
Total	34

TABLE 5

Marital Status	Male	Female	Total
Single	5	23	28
Married	0	6	6
Widowed	0	0	0
Total	5	29	34

TABLE 6

Age	Male	Female	Total
Under 11	0	1	1
11–15	1	7	8
16–20	1	13	14
21–25	0	1	1
26–30	0	1	1
Over 30	0	4	4
Total	2	27	29

Here again the sample shows a powerful cluster. The vast majority of the accusers were single girls between eleven and twenty years old. The exceptions in this case (two boys, three males of undetermined age, four adult women) are rather difficult to explain, for there is little evidence about any of them. By and large, however, they played only a minor role in the trials. Perhaps the matter can be left this way: the core group of accusers was entirely composed of adolescent girls, but the inner conflicts so manifest in their fits found an echo in at least a few persons of other ages or of the opposite sex.

Eighty-four persons came forward as "witnesses" at one time or another during the Salem trials. (See Tables 7, 8, and 9.) Here the

TABLE 7

Sex	Total
Male	63
Female	21
Total	84

TABLE 8

Marital Status	Male	Female	Total
Single	11	3	14
Married	39	16	55
Widowed	3	1	4
Total	53	20	73

TABLE 9

Age	Male	Female	Total
Under 20	3	2	5
21–30	13	4	17
31–40	14	6	20
41–50	18	7	25
51–60	11	1	12
61–70	2	1	3
Over 70	2	0	2
Total	63	21	84

results seem relatively inconclusive. Three-fourths of the witnesses were men, but a close examination of the trial records suggests a simple reason for this: men were more likely in seventeenth-century New England, to take an active part in legal proceedings of any type. When a husband and wife were victimized together by some sort of witchcraft, the former would normally come forward to testify. As to the ages of the witnesses, there is a fairly broad distribution between twenty and sixty years. Probably, then, this category reflects the generalized belief in witchcraft among all elements of the community in a way that makes it qualitatively different from the groupings of witches and accusers.

There is much more to ask about "external realities" in the lives of such people, particularly with regard to their social and economic position. Unfortunately, however, the evidence is somewhat limited here, and permits only a few impressionistic observations. It seems clear that many witches came from the lower levels of the social structure; but there were too many exceptions to regard this as a really significant pattern. The first three accused at Salem were Tituba, a Negro slave, Sarah Good, the wife of a poor laborer, and Sarah Osbourne, who possessed a very considerable estate. Elizabeth Godman, tried at New Haven in 1653, seems to have been poor and perhaps a beggar; but Nathaniel and Rebecca Greensmith, who were convicted and executed at Hartford eight years later, were quite well-to-do. And "Mistress" Ann Hibbens, executed at Boston in 1656, was the widow of a wealthy merchant and former magistrate of the Bay Colony.

What appears to have been common to nearly all these people, irrespective of their economic position, was some kind of personal eccentricity, some deviant or even criminal behavior that had long since marked them out as suspect. Some of them had previously been tried for theft or battery or slander. Others were known for their interest in dubious activities like fortune-telling or certain kinds of folk-healing. The "witch Glover" of Boston, on whom Cotton Mather reports at some length, was Irish and Catholic, and spoke Gaelic; and a Dutch family in Hartford came under suspicion at the time the Greensmiths were tried.

More generally, many of the accused seem to have been unusually irascible and contentious in their personal relations. Years before her conviction for witchcraft Mrs. Hibbens had obtained a reputation for "natural crabbedness of . . . temper"; indeed she had been excommunicated by the Boston church in 1640, following a long and acrimonious ecclesiastical trial. William Hubbard, whose *General History of New England* was published in 1680, cited her case to make the general point that "persons of hard favor and turbulent passions are apt to be condemned by the common people as witches, upon very slight grounds." In the trial of Mercy Desborough, at Fairfield, Connecticut, in 1692, the court received numerous reports of her quarrelsome behavior. She had, for example, told one neighbor "yt shee would make him bare as a bird's tale," and to another she had repeatedly said "many hard words." Goodwife Clawson, tried at the same time, was confronted with testimony such as the following:

Abigail Wescot saith that as shee was going along the street goody Clason came out to her and they had some words together and goody Clason took up stones and threw at her: and at another time as shee went along the street before sd Clasons dore goody Clason caled to mee and asked me what was in my Chamber last Sabbath day night; and I doe afirme that I was not there that night: and at another time as I was in her sone Steephens house being neere her one hous shee folowed me in and con-

*tended with me becase I did not com into her hous caling of me proud
slut what—are you proud of your fine cloths and you love to be mistres
but you neuer shal be and several other provoking speeches.*

The case of Mary and Hugh Parsons, tried at Springfield in 1651 affords a further look at some of these same questions. There is, for example, the record of a tax-rating taken at Springfield in 1646, which shows the land-holdings of most of the principals in the witchcraft prosecutions of five years later. When the list is arranged according to wealth, Parsons falls near the middle (twenty-fourth out of forty-two), and those who testified against him come from the top, middle, *and* bottom. This outcome tends to confirm the general point that economic position is not, for present purposes, a significant datum. What seems, on the basis of the actual testimonies at the trial, to have been much more important is the whole dimension of eccentric and antisocial behavior. Mary Parsons was very nearly insane. She succumbed repeatedly to periods of massive depression; and during the witchcraft investigations she began by testifying against her husband, and ended by convicting herself of the murder of their infant child. Hugh Parsons was a sawyer and brickmaker by trade, and there are indications that in performing these services he was sometimes suspected of charging extortionate rates. But what may have weighed most heavily against him was his propensity for prolonged and bitter quarreling; many examples of his "threatening speeches" were reported in court.

One other aspect of this particular episode is worth noting: namely, the apparent influence of spatial proximity. When the names of Parsons and his "victims" are checked against a map of Springfield in this period, it becomes very clear that the latter were mostly his nearest neighbors. In fact, nearly all the people who took a direct part in the trial came from the southern half of the town. No other witchcraft episode yields such a detailed picture in this respect, but many separate pieces of evidence suggest that neighborhood antagonism was usually an aggravating factor.

We can summarize the major characteristics of this—the "external"—side of New England witchcraft as follows. First, the witches themselves were chiefly women of middle age, and their accusers were girls of about one full generation younger. This may reflect the kind of situation which anthropologists would call a "structural conflict"—that is, some focus of tension created by the specific ways in which a community arranges the lives of its individual members. In a broad sense it is quite probable that adolescent girls in early New England were particularly subject to the control of older women, and this may well have given rise to a powerful underlying resentment. By contrast, the situation must have been less difficult for boys, since their work often took them out of the household and their behavior generally was less restricted.

There are, moreover, direct intimations of generational conflict in the witchcraft records themselves. Consider a little speech flung out by one of the afflicted girls during a fit and meticulously taken down by Cotton Mather. The words are addressed to the "spectre" of a witch, with whom the girl has been having a heated argument:

> What's that? Must the younger Women, do yee say, hearken to the Elder?
> —They must be another Sort of Elder Women than You then! they must
> not bee Elder Witches, I am sure. Pray, do you for once Hearken to mee.
> —What a dreadful Sight are You! An Old Woman, an Old Servant of the
> Divel!

Second, it seems notable that most witches were deviant persons —eccentric or conspicuously antisocial or both. This suggests very clearly the impact of witchcraft belief as a form of control in the social ordering of New England communities. Here indeed is one of the most widely found social functions of witchcraft; its importance has been documented for many societies all over the world. The process operates in a fairly straightforward way on any individual who contemplates actions of which the community disapproves. He knows that if he goes ahead, he will make himself more vulnerable either to a direct attack by witchcraft or to the charge that he is himself a witch. Such knowledge is a powerful inducement to self-constraint.

What can be said of our third basic conclusion, that witchcraft charges particularly involved neighbors? Very briefly, it must be fitted with other aspects of the social setting in these early New England communities. That there was a great deal of contentiousness among these people is suggested by innumerable court cases from the period, dealing with disputes about land, lost cattle, trespass, debt, and so forth. Most men seem to have felt that the New World offered them a unique opportunity to increase their properties, and this may have served to heighten competitive feelings and pressures. On the other hand, cooperation was still the norm in many areas of life—not only in local government, but for a variety of agricultural tasks as well. In such ambivalent circumstances it is hardly surprising that relations between close neighbors were often tense or downright abrasive.

"In all the Witchcraft which now Grievously Vexes us, I know not whether any thing be more Unaccountable, than the Trick which the Witches have, to render themselves and their Tools Invisible." Thus wrote Cotton Mather in 1692; and three centuries later it is still the "invisible" part of witchcraft that holds a special fascination. Time has greatly altered the language for such phenomena—"shapes" and "spectres" have become "hallucinations"; "enchantments" are now a form of "suggestion"; the Devil himself seems a fantasy—and there is a corresponding change of meanings. Yet here was something truly remarkable, a kind of irreducible core of the entire range of witchcraft phenomena. And how much of it remains "unaccountable"? To ask the question is to face directly the other side of our subject: witchcraft viewed as psychic process, as a function of "internal reality."

These phrases are obvious signposts on the road from history to psychology, and they suggest the need for another brief comment on method. Ordinarily, the biggest obstacles to a joining of history and psychology are practical ones, involving severe limitations of historical data. Yet for witchcraft the situation is, on just these grounds, uniquely promising. Even a casual look at writings like Cotton Mather's *Memorable Providences* or Samuel Willard's *A briefe account*, discloses material so rich in psychological detail as to be nearly the equivalent of clinical case reports. The court records on witchcraft are also remarkably full in this respect. The clergy, the judges, all the leaders whose positions carried special responsibility for combatting witchcraft, regarded publicity as a most important weapon. Witchcraft would yield to careful study and the written exchange of information. Both Mather and Willard received "afflicted girls" into their own homes and recorded "possession" behavior over long periods of time.

Of course, a wealth of evidence does not by itself win the case for a psychological approach to witchcraft. Further problems remain problems of language, for example, and of validation. There is, moreover, the very basic problem of selecting from among a variety of *different* theoretical models. Psychology is not a monolith, and every "psycho-historian" must declare a preference. In opting for psycho-analytic theory (as in the following pages), he performs, in part, an act of faith—faith that this theory provides deeper, fuller insights into human behavior than any other. In the long run the merit of such choices will probably be measured on pragmatic grounds. Does the interpretation "work"? Does it serve to explain materials which would otherwise lie inert? Is it consistent with different evidence in related subject-areas?

If, then, the proof lies in the doing, let us turn back to the New England witches and especially to their "Trick . . . to render themselves and their tools Invisible." What was the character of these spectral witches? What qualities were attributed to them by the culture at large?

First and definitely foremost in the minds of most New Englanders was the idea that witches gave free rein to a whole gamut of hostile and aggressive feelings. In fact most witchcraft episodes began after some sort of actual quarrel. The fits of Mercy Short (reported by Cotton Mather) followed an abusive encounter with the convicted witch Sarah Good. The witch Glover was thought to have attacked Martha Goodwin after an argument about some missing clothes. Many such examples could be accumulated here, but the central message seems immediately obvious: never antagonize witches, for they will invariably strike back hard. Their compulsion to attack was, of course, most dramatically visible in the fits experienced by some of their victims. These fits were treated as tortures imposed directly and in every detail, by witches or by the Devil himself. It is also significant that witches often assumed the shape of animals in order to carry out their attacks. Animals, presumably, are not subject to constraints of either an internal or external kind; their aggressive impulses are immediately translated into action.

Another important facet of the lives of witches was their activity in company with each other. In part, this consisted of long and earnest conferences on plans to overthrow the kingdom of God and replace it with the reign of the Devil. Often, however, these meetings merged with "feasts"—the witches' main form of self-indulgence. Details are a bit thin here, but it is clear that the focus was on eating and drinking. The usual beverage was wine or beer (occasionally described as bearing a suspicious resemblance to blood); and the food was bread or meat. It is also worth noting what did *not* happen on these occasions. There were a few reports of dancing and "sport," but very little of the wild excitements associated with witch revels in continental Europe. Most striking of all is the absence of allusions to sex; there is no nakedness, no promiscuity, no obscene contact with the Devil. This seems to provide strong support for the general proposition that the psychological conflicts underlying the belief in witchcraft in early New England had much more to do with aggressive impulses than with libidinal ones.

The persons who acted as accusers also merit the closest possible attention, for the descriptions of what they suffered in their fits are perhaps the most revealing of all source materials for present purposes. They experienced, in the first place, severe pressures to go over to the Devil's side themselves. Witches approached them again and again, mixing threats and bribes in an effort to break down their Christian loyalties. Thus Elizabeth Knapp, bewitched at Groton, Massachusetts, in 1671, was alternately tortured and plied with offers of "money, silkes, fine cloaths, ease from labor"; in 1692 Ann Foster of Andover confessed to being won over by a general promise of "prosperity"; and in the same year Andrew Carrier accepted the lure of "a house and land in Andover." The same pattern appears most vividly in Cotton Mather's record of another of Mercy Short's confrontations with a spectral witch:

> *"Fine promises!" she says, "You'l bestow an Husband upon mee, if I'l bee your Servant. An Husband! What? A Divel! I shall then bee finely fitted with an Husband: . . . Fine Clothes! What? Such as Your Friend Sarah Good had, who hardly had Rags to cover her! . . . Never Dy! What? Is my Life in Your Hands? No, if it had, You had killed mee long before this Time!—What's that?—So you can!—Do it then, if You can. Come, I dare you: Here, I challenge You to do it. Kill mee if you can."*

Some of these promises attributed to the Devil touch the most basic human concerns (such as death), and others reflect the special preoccupations of adolescent girls (such as future husbands). All of them imply a kind of covetousness generally consistent with the pattern of neighborhood conflict and tension mentioned earlier.

But the fits express other themes more powerfully still; and once again problems of aggression seem to occupy the central place. The seizures themselves have the essential character of attacks: in one sense, physical attacks by the witches on the persons of the accusers; and, in another sense, verbal attacks by the accusers on the reputations and indeed the very lives of the witches. This points directly toward one of the most important inner processes involved in the witchcraft, the process that psychologists call "projection" and define roughly as follows: "Projection is escape from repressed conflict by attributing . . . emotional drives to the external world." In short, the dynamic core of belief in witchcraft in early New England was the difficulty experienced by many individuals in finding ways to handle their own aggressive impulses. Such impulses were not readily acceptable in terms of their culture and upbringing; but witchcraft accusations did provide one approved means of resolving the problem. Aggression was in this manner denied in the self and attributed directly to others. The accuser says, in effect, "I am not attacking you; you are attacking me!" In reality, however, the accuser *is* attacking the witch, and in an extremely dangerous fashion too. Thus witchcraft enables him to have it both ways: the impulse is denied and gratified at the same time.

And yet, too, the situation has another side, for the seizures of the afflicted children also permitted them to engage in a considerable amount of direct aggression. Of course, they were not held personally responsible; it was always the fault of the Devil at work inside them. Sometimes these impulses were aimed against the most important—and obvious—figures of authority. A child in a fit might act in a very disobedient way towards his parents, or revile the clergy who came to pray for his recovery. The Reverend Willard of Groton, who ministered to Elizabeth Knapp during the time of her most severe fits, noted that the Devil "urged upon her constant temptations to murder her p'rents, her neighbors, our children . . . and even to make away with herselfe & once she was going to drowne herselfe in ye well." The attacking impulses were quite random here, so much so that even suicide seemed a possibility. Cotton Mather reports a slight variant on this type of behavior in connection with the fits of Martha Goodwin. She would, he writes, "fetch very terrible Blowes with her Fist, and Kicks with her Foot at the man that prayed; but still . . . her Fist and Foot would alwaies recoil, when they came within a few hairs breadths of him just as if

Rebounding against a Wall." This little paradigm of aggression attempted, and then at the last moment inhibited, expresses perfectly the severe inner conflict that many of these people were acting out.

One last, extremely pervasive theme in the witchcraft data is more difficult to handle without having direct recourse to clinical models; and the summary word for it is "orality." It is helpful to recall at this point the importance of "feasts" in the standard imaginary picture of the witches, but the experience of the accusers speaks even more powerfully to the same point. The evidence is of several kinds. First, the character of the "tortures" inflicted by the witches was most often described in terms of biting, pinching, pricking; and, in a psychiatric sense, these modes of attack all have an oral foundation. The pattern showed up with great vividness, for example, in the trial of George Burroughs:

> It was Remarkable that whereas Biting was one of the ways which the Witches used for the vexing of the Sufferers, when they cry'd out of G.B. biting them, the print of the Teeth would be seen on the Flesh of the Complainers, and just such a sett of Teeth as G.B.'s would then appear upon them, which could be distinguished from those of some other mens.

Second, the accusers repeatedly charged that they could see the witches suckling certain animal "familiars." The following testimony by one of the Salem girls, in reference to an unidentified witch, was quite typical: "She had two little things like young cats and she put them to her brest and suckled them they had no hair on them and had ears like a man." People assumed that witches were specially equipped for these purposes and searched their bodies for the evidence. In 1656 the constable of Salisbury, New Hampshire, deposed in the case of Eunice Cole,

> That being about to stripp [her] to bee whipt (by the judgment of the Court att Salisbury) lookeing upon hir brests under one of hir brests (I thinke hir left brest) I saw a blew thing like unto a teate hanging downeward about three quarters of an inche longe not very thick, and haveing a great suspition in my mind about it (she being suspected for a witche) desiered the Court to sende some women to looke of it.

The court accepted this proposal and appointed a committee of three women to administer to Goodwife Cole the standard form of examination. Their report made no mention of a "teate" under her breast, but noted instead "a place in her leg which was proveable wher she Had bin sucktt by Imps or the like." The women also stated "thatt they Heard the whining of puppies or such like under Her Coats as though they had a desire to sucke."

Third, many of the accusers underwent serious eating disturbances during and after their fits. "Long fastings" were frequently imposed on them. Cotton Mather writes of one such episode in his account of the bewitching of Margaret Rule: "Tho she had a very eager Hunger upon her Stomach, yet if any refreshment were brought unto her, her teeth would be set, and she would be thrown into many Miseries." But also she would "sometimes have her Jaws forcibly pulled open, whereupon something invisible would be poured down her throat. . . . She cried out of it as of Scalding Brimstone poured into her." These descriptions and others like them would repay a much more detailed analysis than can be offered here, but the general point should be obvious. Among all the zones of the body, the mouth seems to have been charged with a special kind of importance for victims of witchcraft.

In closing, it may be appropriate to offer a few suggestions of a more theoretical nature. The reason for doing so is to indicate both the way in which an interpretation of New England witchcraft might be attempted and the kind of conclusions one can hope to draw from the witchcraft materials about the culture at large. But this is meant only as the most tentative beginning of a new approach to such questions.

Consider, first, an interesting set of findings included by two anthropologists as part of a broad survey of child-rearing practices in over fifty cultures around the world. They report that witchcraft belief is powerfully correlated with the training a society imposes on young children in regard to the control of aggressive impulses. That is, wherever this training is severe and restrictive, there is a strong likelihood that the culture will make much of witchcraft. The correlation seems to suggest that aggression, if forcibly suppressed, will seek indirect outlets of the sort that witchcraft belief provides. Unfortunately, there is relatively little concrete evidence about child-rearing practices in early New England; but it seems at least con-

sistent with what is known of Puritan culture generally to imagine
that quite a harsh attitude would have been taken towards any substantial show of aggression in the young.

The concept of "projection" has been sufficiently discussed already; but now it may be useful to speak also of the allied notion
of "displacement." Only very few cases of witchcraft accusations
occurred between members of the same family. But, as noted previously, the typical pattern involved adolescent girls accusing middle-
aged women. It seems plausible, at least from a clinical standpoint,
to think that this pattern masked deep problems stemming ultimately
from the relationship of mother and daughter. Perhaps, then, the
afflicted girls were both projecting their aggression and diverting or
"displacing" it from its real target. Considered from this perspective,
displacement represents another form of avoidance or denial; and so
the charges of the accusers may be seen as a kind of double defense
against the actual conflicts.

But how to locate the *source* of these conflicts is a more difficult
and frankly speculative kind of issue. Indeed it leads farther and
farther from the usual canons of historical explanation; the proof,
such as it is, must come by way of parallels to certain findings of
recent psychological research and, above all, to a great mass of
clinical data. More specifically, it is to psychoanalytic theory that
one may turn for insights of an especially useful sort.

Actually, the historical record does provide one more strong clue
with the prominence it gives to oral themes and anxieties. This suggests that the disturbances which culminated in charges of witchcraft must be traced to the earliest phase of personality development.
It would be very convenient to have some shred of information to
insert here about breast-feeding practices among the early New
Englanders. Possibly their methods of weaning were highly traumatic; but hard evidence does not exist, and there is simply no
way to be sure. What does seem plausible—if, once again, we accept the psychoanalytic model—is that many New England children
were faced with some unspecified but extremely difficult psychic
tasks in the first year or so of life. The outcome was that their aggressive drives were tied especially closely to the oral mode, and driven
underground. Then, years later, in accordance with changes normal
for adolescence, instinctual energies of all types were greatly augmented; and this tended, as it so often does, to reactivate the earliest

conflicts. (The process is what Freud called, in a vivid phrase, "the return of the repressed.") But these conflicts were no easier to deal with in adolescence than they had been earlier; hence the need for the twin defenses of projection and displacement.

One final problem must be recognized. The conflicts on which this discussion has focused were, of course, most vividly expressed in the fits of the accusers. But the vast majority of people in early New England—subjected, one assumes, to roughly similar influences as children—managed to get through to adulthood without experiencing fits. Does this pose any serious difficulties for the above interpretations? The question can be argued to a negative conclusion, in at least two different but complementary ways. First, the materials on witchcraft, and in particular on the fits of the accusers, span a considerable length of time in New England's early history. When taken all together, they strongly suggest that aggression and orality were more or less constant themes in the pathology of the period. Second, even in the far less bizarre testimonies of the witnesses—that category which has been taken to represent the community at large—the same sort of focus appears. Above all, it is significant that the specific complaints of the accusers were so completely credible to so many others around them. The accusers, then, can be viewed as those individuals who were somehow especially sensitive to the problems created by their environment; they were the ones who were pushed over the line, so to speak, into serious illness. But their behavior clearly struck an answering chord in a much larger group of people. In this sense, nearly everyone in seventeenth-century New England was at some level an accuser.

˙Chadwick Hansen
WITCHCRAFT AT SALEM

*That Chadwick Hansen (b. 1926) could write a book in 1969 maintaining the
reality of witchcraft, and that it became a best-seller, is testimony to the
persistent fascination of the subject. Hansen, a professor of English at Pennsylvania State University, sees importance in the subject, as does Demos,
for the light it sheds on the socio-cultural nature of Puritanism. In the selections reprinted from his book he challenges prevailing views that accuse the
clergy for the Salem outbreak. They opposed the reliance of the judges on
"spectral evidence," the belief, as the judges used it, that the Devil could
take the "shapes" of persons who were seen to afflict the victims, even
though such persons were unaware of this use of their "shapes" and considered themselves innocent of intent to harm.*

The purpose of this book is to try to set straight the record of the
witchcraft phenomena at Salem, Massachusetts, in the year 1692,
about which much has been written and much misunderstood. The
more I studied the documents of what actually took place in the community, and what was actually said and written by the participants,
the more I found myself in opposition to the traditional interpretation
of these events. It seemed to me that a serious reconsideration of
them was in order. But I could see no point in employing the common revisionist technique of quarreling with my predecessors item
by item and person by person, for to do so would be to bury the
account of what did happen in an immense and tedious analysis of
what did not. What was needed was a fresh and objective review of
the entire matter.

The traditional interpretation of what happened at Salem is as
much the product of casual journalism and imaginative literature as
it is of historical scholarship. It might be summarized as follows:
(1) no witchcraft was practiced in Massachusetts; (2) the behavior
of the "afflicted" persons, including their convulsive fits, was fraudulent and designed chiefly to call attention to themselves; (3) the
afflicted persons were inspired, stimulated, and encouraged by the
clergy (especially Cotton Mather), who used the fear of witchcraft
as a means of bolstering their flagging power in the community;

(4) the clergy whipped the general populace into a state of "mass hysteria" with their sermons and writings on witchcraft; (5) the only significant opposition to the proceedings at Salem came from the merchant class, specifically from Thomas Brattle and Robert Calef; and (6) the executions were unique in Western civilization, and therefore monstrous, and attributable to some narrowness or fanaticism or repressiveness peculiar to Puritans.

Yet the facts are quite contrary to these common assumptions. To begin with, witchcraft actually did exist and was widely practiced in seventeenth-century New England, as it was in Europe at that time (and still is, for that matter, among the unlearned majority of mankind). It worked then as it works now in witchcraft societies like those of the West Indies, through psychogenic rather than occult means, commonly producing hysterical symptoms as a result of the victim's fear, and sometimes, when fear was succeeded by a profound sense of hopelessness, even producing death.

The behavior of the afflicted persons was not fraudulent but pathological. They were hysterics, and in the clinical rather than the popular sense of that term. These people were not merely over-excited; they were mentally ill. Furthermore, they were ill long before any clergyman got to them.

The general populace did reach that state of public excitement inaccurately called "mass hysteria," but this was due to the popular fear of witchcraft rather than to the preachings of the clergy. The public excitement continued well after the leadership, both clerical and secular, had called a halt to the witchcraft proceedings. In fact the clergy were, from beginning to end, the chief opponents to the events at Salem. In particular, Cotton Mather was anything but the wild-eyed fanatic of tradition. Throughout most of the proceedings he was a model of restraint and caution, and at one point he went further than any of his colleagues dared go in proposing a method to protect the innocent.

The writings of Brattle and Calef came too late to have any significant influence on the course of events in Massachusetts.

Finally, the executions at Salem were by no means unique. Belief in witchcraft was quite as common among seventeenth-century Anglicans, Quakers, Lutherans, and Catholics as it was among Puritans. Executions for witchcraft reached their height in Western civilization during the seventeenth century and continued in Europe until the end of the following century, more than a hundred years after the outbreak at Salem.

Many writers have taken exception to one point or another in the traditional interpretation. The point raised most often has been that witchcraft trials were not at all unusual in the seventeenth century; that they were in fact typical of Western civilization at that time. George Lyman Kittredge has put it best:

> The Salem outbreak was not due to Puritanism; it is not assignable to any peculiar temper on the part of our New England ancestors; it is no sign of exceptional bigotry or abnormal superstition. Our forefathers believed in witchcraft, not because they were Puritans, not because they were Colonials, not because they were New Englanders,—but because they were men of their time. They shared the feelings and beliefs of the best hearts and wisest heads of the seventeenth century. What more can be asked of them?

And he added that

> it is hard to satisfy modern writers on witchcraft, who insist on censuring the sixteenth and seventeenth century on a basis of modern rationalism. It is quite certain that if some of those who now sit in judgment on the witch-prosecutors had been witch judges, no defendant would ever have escaped.

The same issue has been raised, with varying degrees of incisiveness, by John Fiske, Edward Eggleston, W. F. Poole, Kenneth B. Murdock, Samuel Eliot Morison, and many others, including Perry Miller, who protested that on this point further refutation had become a bore. But boring or not, the refutation has not taken hold. The common scholar as well as the common man has continued to believe that there was something peculiarly puritanical about the Salem trials.

A second exception has been that Cotton Mather was not, as Calef put it, "very forward" in carrying on witchcraft examinations, that in fact he counseled moderation throughout the trials. W. F. Poole saw this. So, among others, did Longfellow, Barrett Wendell, Samuel Eliot Morison, and Marion L. Starkey. But none of them seems to have recognized how very far the younger Mather went in attempting to protect the innocent, nor how thoroughly Calef lied about Mather's treatment of Margaret Rule. Starkey, for one, accepts Calef's lies at face value and consequently makes Mather out to be little better than a fool.

A third departure from the traditional interpretation has been to call the behavior of the afflicted persons hysterical. George M. Beard was the first to do so, and he has been followed by John Fiske, Winfield S. Nevins, Perry Miller, and Marion L. Starkey, among others. Yet no one who has used the word "hysterical" seems to have fully realized its implications. The difficulty lies in the fact that the word has different meanings in common usage from those it has in medical usage. In the former it means little more than a state of excitement in which the subject may temporarily lose self-control. The afflicted persons at Salem were in a far worse state than that. Their condition was pathological, and much more serious than has previously been supposed. Marion L. Starkey makes a diagnosis of hysteria the very basis of *The Devil in Massachusetts*. Yet because she confuses the popular and the medical meanings of the term she regards the Salem girls' behavior as more fraudulent than pathological, and in the long run her interpretation differs only in detail from that of Upham. In her case and in others this popular usage has led finally to little more than inaccurate talk about "mass hysteria."

Finally, and most significantly, a few persons have recognized that image magic was actually employed in Massachusetts, and at least two have wondered whether there might not have been something behind the charges of witchcraft after all. Poole tells us that Longfellow examined some of the seventeenth-century narratives before composing his play on the Salem trials, *Giles Corey of the Salem Farms*. Longfellow was learned enough to recognize that Cotton Mather's suspicions had been aroused by concrete evidence of image magic. He also recognized that Mather had counseled judicial caution. That was as far as he got, but it was much farther than most. *Giles Corey* is a bad play, but it is much better history than most of the historians have written. Barrett Wendell also knew there had been image magic at Salem and was startled to discover that nineteenth-century spiritualists were believers in the possibility of accomplishing harm through such means. He went so far as to compare the Salem trial evidence to his own experiences with spiritualism; this comparison is the central substance of his article, "Were the Salem Witches Guiltless?" and of his handling of witchcraft in his biography of Cotton Mather. But spiritualism was a blind alley, and Wendell never got further than wondering whether there might not have been something to the charges after all.

David R. Proper, formerly librarian of Essex Institute, tells me that Kittredge suspected there might have been witchcraft practiced at Salem. However, he did not pursue his suspicions; at least I have not been able to discover any further evidence that would lead me to believe otherwise. Finally, the late dean of twentieth-century New England studies, Perry Miller, knew there had been image magic in the Glover case of 1688 at Boston, yet he was unable to take seriously a practice he found so contemptible. But it has to be taken seriously. One cannot fully understand any aspect of the events at Salem without a recognition of the genuine power of witchcraft in a society that believes in it. The failure to appreciate this fact has vitiated all previous accounts of witchcraft at Salem. . . .

There were various reasons for the shift in opinion that took place at the end of the summer of 1692. There was the opinion that those who died on August 19 died so well. There were the various protests against the procedures of the Court of Oyer and Terminer. And there was the fact that the court's procedures seemed to be aggravating the witchcraft troubles rather than allaying them. But most important of all, as the witch hunt spread and the accusations flew, people were accused whom nobody could think guilty.

One such accusation had been made early; at the second session of the court, at the beginning of July, the Reverend Samuel Willard of Boston had been cried out on. Nobody could think him guilty, but a ready explanation occurred to someone. John Willard of Salem Village was then in prison awaiting trial; perhaps the girl had gotten the wrong Willard? The court decided this was so. As the summer wore on several were accused whom many thought innocent. These included Captain John Alden; Hezekiah Usher, a prominent Boston merchant; Nathaniel Saltonstall, the judge who had resigned from the court; Phillip English, a Salem merchant (and like Judge Hathorne an ancestor of Nathaniel Hawthorne) and his wife; Dudley Bradstreet, the Andover Justice of the Peace.

By the end of the summer the accusations were becoming preposterous. They included the Secretary of Connecticut; Mrs. Margaret Thatcher, who was the widow of a Boston clergyman and the mother-in-law of Judge Corwin; and "members of [the governor's] Council." According to rumor there were even more startling accusations, including the wife of Governor Phips and the wife of Increase Mather. But these were probably only rumors. It was Robert Calef (a person given to false insinuations, as we shall see) who suggested Lady Phips had been accused, and Cotton Mather called the suggestion "a putrid slander." And if Mrs. Mather was accused, it was not until after October 3. This was the date Increase Mather read to the Boston clergy, for their approbation, the manuscript of *Cases of Conscience,* the little book which put an end to the witch hunt, and in that book he wrote that "it was never the portion allotted to me nor to any relation of mine" to be falsely represented by the Devil.

Throughout the summer Mather had been moving in the traditional New England pattern, presenting his opinions yet trying to accommodate them to an eventual consensus. But if debate aimed at unanimous consensus had always been the New England way, this did not imply that any man was expected to abandon the truth. The Puritans were radical protestants, with the radical protestant's belief in a free and unforced conscience. Although the very basis of their community was a belief in the possibility of reaching unanimous consensus on all fundamental matters, they also acknowledged that there were some matters in which such a consensus could not easily be reached, and an honest minority might disagree with the course the community was taking; some matters were, as they put it, "cases of conscience." So when Increase Mather called his manuscript *Cases of Conscience Concerning Evil Spirits Personating Men* everyone who heard the title knew immediately that he was issuing a flat and direct challenge to the opinions on spectral evidence held officially—held, that is, by the Special Court of Oyer and Terminer.

He reasserted all the Boston clergy's old doubts, but with a new thoroughness and vigor that virtually amounted to a new argument. To begin with, he made it absolutely clear that anybody can be falsely accused of witchcraft and that all such accusations should be taken skeptically.

Mather had no doubt of what should be done in such a situation. He put forward a principle that has always been inimical to witch hunts: "It were better that ten suspected witches should escape than that one innocent person should be condemned." Furthermore, he cast as much doubt on the testimony of confessors as on spectral evidence. One might, he thought, accept a witch's confession of her own guilt,

> *but as for the testimony of confessing witches against others, the case is not so clear as against themselves. They are not such credible witnesses as in a case of life and death is to be desired. It is beyond dispute that the Devil makes his witches to dream strange things of themselves and others which are not so.*

He strongly condemned some of the tests the magistrates had used at preliminary examinations and trials; they were in themselves, he said, a kind of witchcraft.

> *For my own part, I should be loath to say to a man that I knew or thought was a witch, "Do you look on such a person, and see if you can witch them into a fit," and "There is such an afflicted person; do you take them by the hand and see if you can witch them well again." If it is by virtue of some contract with the Devil that witches have power to do such things, it is hard to conceive how they can be bid to do them without being too much concerned in that Hellish covenant. . . . We ought not to practice witchcraft to discover witches.*

But Mather was by no means ready to recognize that the court had already shed innocent blood. He recognized only that the court must be stopped because, given its mistaken ideas on spectral evidence and its mistaken procedures, and given the accusation of obviously innocent persons, innocent blood might be shed in the future.

> *The Devils have of late accused some eminent persons. It is an awful thing which the Lord has done [i.e., permitted] to convince some among us of their error. This then I declare and testify, that to take away the life of anyone merely because a specter or Devil in a bewitched or possessed person does accuse them will bring the guilt of innocent blood on the land where such a thing shall be done. Mercy forbid that it should (and I trust that as it has not it never will be so) in New England. What does such an evidence amount unto more than this: either such an one did afflict such an one, or the Devil in his likeness, or his eyes were bewitched.*

It is not hard to see why Mather was able to persuade himself that the innocent had not yet suffered. He knew the judges to be sensible and honorable men, and they had assured him there was more than specter evidence against all those who had been condemned.

> *The Judges affirm that they have not convicted anyone merely on the account of what specters have said or of what has been represented to the eyes or imaginations of the sick, bewitched persons.*

But in many cases the judges had, because of their belief in specter evidence, accepted confirmatory evidence so slender that it could not possibly have stood by itself. Still, Mather could not have known that. His personal experience of the trials had been limited to that of George Burroughs, where there *had* been more than specter evidence.

Although the clergy had now made a stand, and the governor had begun to act, and there was substantial popular opposition to the court, the popular majority still seems to have been on the side of the witch hunt. This would seem to be the only conclusion to be drawn from Judge Sewall's diary entry of October 15:

> *Went to Cambridge and visited Mr. Danforth, and discoursed with him about the witchcraft. [He] thinks there cannot be a procedure in the court except there be some better consent of ministers and people.*

The ministers, as we have seen, and as Brattle had pointed out, were now thoroughly dissatisfied with the court's methods. If the people were on the opposite side, the majority must still have been supporting the court. The same conclusion may be drawn from the vote of the people's representatives on October 26. Sewall tells us what happened in the General Court on that day:

> *A bill is sent in about calling a fast, and convocation of ministers, that [we] may be led in the right way as to the witchcrafts. The season and manner of doing it is such that the Court of Oyer and Terminer count themselves thereby dismissed. 29 Nos and 33 Yeas to the bill. Capt. Bradstreet and Lieut. True, William Hutchins and several other interested persons there in the affirmative.*

The bill called for a fast day and for a convocation of ministers in order that Massachusetts might be "led in the right way as to the witchcrafts." The implication, of course, was that the court had been proceeding in the wrong way, and was therefore dismissed. The vote was extremely close, and Sewall makes it plain that the bill passed only because a number of the representatives were "interested"—that is, had relatives among the accused. Without the presence of these "interested" persons the legislature would have voted for rather than against the court.

Sewall was plainly not satisfied with this vote, and on October 28 he asked, as he "had done several times before . . . the advice of the Governor and Council" about whether the court should sit again next week, as it had intended at its adjournment in September. He added that he would not raise the issue again. The only response was a "great silence," which he correctly took as instructions not to continue. Sewall did not raise the issue again, but the following day someone else put the question to the governor more contentiously: "Mr. Russell asked whether the Court of Oyer and Terminer should sit, expressing some fear of inconvenience by its fall. [The] governor said it must fall." With its fall the witch hunt was over; the clergy's cases of conscience over spectral evidence had prevailed.

Cases of Conscience was not simply an expression of personal opinion on the part of Increase Mather. Cotton Mather tells us that the book was written at the request of "the ministers of the province," who were afraid that without such a positive statement of principles their advice on specter evidence would "not be duly followed." We can assume that since the elder Mather was being asked, in effect, for a fuller and more positive exposition of views he had already expressed, he found the task a congenial one. In the fall of 1692 Cotton Mather was also happily accepting the opportunity to write; Governor Phips had asked him to draw up an account of some of the Salem trials.

We should recall at this point how sane and temperate Cotton Mather had been in his previous dealings with witchcraft. His handling of the afflicted Goodwin children in 1688 had been exemplary. He had managed both to cure them and to suppress the accusations they made after they came under his care. He had offered to undertake the cure of half-a-dozen of the Salem girls early in 1692, but unfortunately his offer had been rejected. He had several times warned against accepting specter evidence at face value, and when he found the judges stubbornly maintaining the opposite opinion he wrote to a member of the governor's council suggesting that abuse of specter evidence might be prevented by placing an eminent minister or two on the bench. If his suggestion had been followed he would probably have practiced what he preached; he had always discounted specter evidence in 1688. It is necessary to recall his sanity and temperance now because the book he wrote in October of 1692, *The Wonders of the Invisible World,* was anything but temperate, and some of Mather's more excitable enemies among historians have gone so far as to call it insane.

To understand Mather's position we must recognize that our prevailing view of the Salem witchcraft trials has been, to put it bluntly, simple-minded. Both the majority of historians and the majority of imaginative writers who have dealt with the subject have asked us to accept a view of Massachusetts during the witchcraft that divides the community into two parties: on the one hand the ministers and magistrates, a group of wild-eyed fanatics using the trials as a means to bolster their own flagging powers; on the other a little band of stalwart citizens who opposed the witchcraft as nonsense from the beginning; in between these two parties the public. That such a view is grossly in error should by now go without saying.

There was a full spectrum of opinion about witchcraft in Massachusetts, ranging from those who accepted every bit of specter evidence as the revealed truth, through those who discounted spectral evidence but were inclined to believe there had been some witchcraft at Salem, to those who would not believe there had ever been a genuine case of witchcraft in Massachusetts. These last were an extremely small minority, and since they wrote nothing that has survived until the witch hunt was over we have heard nothing of them so far. But they were apparently beginning to talk, at least, and rather loudly, by the end of the summer. And the substance of their talk was apparently a sharp condemnation of the judges.

Although Mather had consistently opposed the judges' methods, he knew and respected them as persons, and thus his immediate instinct was to defend them against criticism.

> *I saw in most of the judges a most charming instance of prudence and patience, and I knew their exemplary piety and the agony of soul with which they sought the direction of heaven. . . . For this cause, though I could not allow the principles that some of the judges had espoused, yet I could not but speak honorably of their persons on all occasions.*

On September 20 he wrote to Stephen Sewall, the clerk of the court, to ask (apparently for the second time) for "a narrative of the evidences given in at the trials of half a dozen, or if you please a dozen, of the principal witches that have been condemned." And he made it plain that he intended to put the trial evidence to partisan use. He was willing, he wrote, "to expose myself to the utmost for the sake of my friends." He urged on Sewall a similarly partisan stance:

> *I shall be content if you draw up the desired letter by way of a letter to me . . . [and] I am willing that, when you write, you should imagine me as obstinate a Sadducee and witch-advocate as any among us. Address me as one that believed nothing reasonable. . . .*

Two days later, according to Judge Sewall's diary, Mather, Stoughton, Hathorne, Captain John Higginson, and Stephen and Samuel Sewall met at the latter's house to discuss "publishing some trials of the witches." Mather put the book together in less than three weeks, because on October 11 Stoughton and Sewall attested that they had read it and found "the matters of fact and evidence truly reported."

In all cases Mather's data squares with the data in the surviving trial documents. But it is also true that Mather, as Calef put it, "wrote more like an advocate than an historian." He reported five trials, and included among them those two which depended least on specter evidence: those of Bridget Bishop and George Burroughs. Two of the remainder were of persons with long and unsavory reputations: Susanna Martin and Martha Carrier. And he gave no attention to persons, like Rebecca Nurse and John Procter, who now seem most obviously innocent.

He still maintains the inadequacy of specter evidence. He thinks that "among the persons represented by the specters which now afflict our neighbors there will be found some that never explicitly contracted with any of the evil angels." But this cautionary advice, which had previously been the main burden of his writings on Salem, is now virtually lost in the process of justifying the court. In his desire to defend his friends he is frequently abusive. He calls Martha Carrier "this rampant hag," and while the phrase is not original with Mather—it occurs in several seventeenth-century English witchcraft narratives, including *Saducismus Triumphatus,* by the Oxford scholar Joseph Glanvill—one still cannot forgive him for it. And when his language is not abusive it is generally overwrought. For in defending his friends Mather accepted the idea that the events at Salem were part of "an horrible plot against the country by witchcraft." The court, then, had been doing battle with "an Army of Devils," a "terrible plague of Evil Angels."

Thus Cotton Mather converted himself from a man who, during the trials, had been one of the most cogent critics of the court's methods to the man who, once the trials were over, became their chief apologist. Neither *The Wonders of the Invisible World* nor *Cases of Conscience* was published until 1693, presumably because of Phips' moratorium on witchcraft publications. But the governor sent a copy of the former along with his letter to the clerk of the Privy Council. And presumably both circulated widely in manuscript. Because by the time they were printed people were already beginning to think of Increase Mather as the man who had criticized the court and of his son as the man who defended it, and the father therefore added the following postscript to his book:

> *Some I hear have taken up a notion that the book newly published by my son is contradictory to this of mine. 'Tis strange that such imaginations should enter into the minds of men. I perused and approved of that book before it was printed, and nothing but my relation to him hindered me from recommending it to the world [i.e., in a preface]. . . .*

Increase Mather was, of course, correct. Father and son agreed in condemning the court's methods—and in refusing to condemn the members of the court.

Suggestions for Additional Reading

A convenient anthology of the writing of the New Englanders is Perry Miller and Thomas H. Johnson, *The Puritans,* 2 volumes (New York and Evanston, Ill., 1963) which includes masterly introductions and a bibliography prepared by George McCandlish.

Thomas Hutchinson, *History of the Colony and Province of Massachusetts Bay,* edited by Lawrence Shaw Mayo (Cambridge, Mass., 1936), is a straightforward eighteenth-century history by a later leader of the colony. Still useful as a detailed, general history is James Truslow Adams, *The Founding of New England* (Boston, 1921), although his interpretation is outmoded. One who, like Adams, sees New England bound by tyranny, narrow conformity, and religious formalism is Vernon Louis Parrington, *Main Currents in American Thought,* vol. I (New York, 1927–1930). A similar interpretation is in Thomas Jefferson Wertenbaker, *The Puritan Oligarchy* (New York, 1947).

Among general works on the colonial period, the first two volumes of Charles M. Andrews, *The Colonial Period of American History,* 4 volumes (New Haven, 1934–1938) provide a detailed account of New England institutions. More recently, Clarence L. VerSteeg, *The Formative Years 1607–1763* (New York, 1964) is one of the best treatments of the colonial period and includes an excellent analysis of New England in the broader setting of the other colonies. Daniel Boorstin, in *The Americans: The Colonial Experience* (New York, 1958) offers another interpretation based on the belief that their orthodoxy freed the Puritans from doctrinal disputes and left them able to work out the practical methods of achieving their ideals in the wilderness environment unhampered by ideological controversy.

Perry Miller's works are preeminent in Puritan studies. In addition to the selections printed in this volume, see his major work, *The New England Mind: The Seventeenth Century* (New York, 1937), and *The New England Mind: From Colony to Province* (Cambridge, Mass., 1953). Also valuable is *Orthodoxy in Massachusetts* (Cambridge, Mass., 1933), and two of the essays reprinted in his *Errand Into the Wilderness* (Cambridge, Mass., 1956), both the title essay and "Thomas Hooker and the Democracy of Connecticut."

Another eminent figure of the "Harvard school" is Samuel Eliot Morison, whose *Builders of the Bay Colony* (Boston and New York,

1930) is one of the most readable accounts of the New England leaders. In *The Intellectual Life of Colonial New England* (New York, 1956), originally printed in 1936 as *The Puritan Pronaos,* Morison defends the Puritans against charges of intellectual sterility and stagnation. In his histories of Harvard, *The Founding of Harvard College* (Cambridge, Mass., 1935), and *Harvard College in the Seventeenth Century* (Cambridge, Mass., 1936), he offers further delightful insights into the life of the period. In the same vein, *Puritanism and Democracy* (New York, 1944), by Ralph Barton Perry, surveys and refutes the earlier characterizations by Adams and Parrington.

Among those who have examined the New England mind and modified Miller to some extent are Kenneth B. Murdock, *Literature and Theology in Colonial New England* (Cambridge, Mass., 1949); Edmund B. Morgan, *The Puritan Dilemma: The Story of John Winthrop* (Boston, 1958), a widely read and deservedly popular book, and his valuable *Visible Saints: The History of a Puritan Idea* (New York, 1963); and Norman Pettit, *The Heart Prepared: Grace and Conversion in Puritan Spiritual Life* (New Haven, 1966). Two recent works following the influence of Morgan develop special aspects of the Puritans' thought: T. H. Breen, *The Character of the Good Ruler: A Study of Puritan Political Ideas in New England 1630–1730* (New Haven, 1970); and Stephen Foster, *Their Solitary Way: The Puritan Social Ethic in the First Century of Settlement in New England* (New Haven, 1971).

Alan Simpson, in a very useful book, *Puritanism in Old and New England* (Chicago, 1955), relates English and American Puritanism and discerns a broader entity than that portrayed by Miller and his followers, one less monolithic and less American-centered. So does James Fulton Maclear, "The Heart of New England Rent—the Mystical Element in Early Puritan History," *Mississippi Valley Historical Review* 42 (1955–1956): 621–652. In his most recent book, *American Puritanism: Faith and Practice* (Philadelphia and New York, 1970), Darrett B. Rutman subjects Puritan ideas to comparison with actual practice. The work also provides a good bibliographical essay on current Puritan studies.

Three writers using the biographical approach to the nature of New England leadership are Richard S. Dunn, *Puritans and Yankees: The Winthrop Dynasty of New England 1603–1717* (Princeton, 1962); Larzer Ziff, *The Career of John Cotton: Puritanism and the American*

Experience (Princeton, 1962); and Robert Middlekauff, *The Mathers: Three Generations of Puritan Intellectuals* (New York, 1971).

On the question of the transition of Puritan society in the later colonial period, see Richard L. Bushman, *Puritan to Yankee: Character and the Social Order in Connecticut 1690–1765* (Cambridge, Mass., 1967); and the study of changes in town government by Michael Zuckerman, *Peaceable Kingdoms: New England Towns in the Eighteenth Century* (New York, 1970).

The treatment of dissenters and the issues involved are the subjects of Emery Battis, *Saints and Sectaries: Anne Hutchinson and the Antinomian Controversy* (Chapel Hill, 1962); Perry Miller, *Roger Williams* (Indianapolis, 1953); Samuel H. Brockunier, *The Irrepressible Democrat: Roger Williams* (New York, 1940); and Edmund S. Morgan, *Roger Williams: The Church and the State* (New York, 1967). Selections of readings dealing with the controversy over Roger Williams are conveniently brought together in *The Problems in American Civilization* volume edited by Theodore P. Greene, *Roger Williams and the Massachusetts Magistrates* (Boston, 1964).

The extent to which business practices squared with the religious views of the colonists is explored in Bernard Bailyn, *The New England Merchants in the Seventeenth Century* (Cambridge, Mass., 1955); and an often overlooked but especially valuable treatment of general economic ideas by Edgar A.J. Johnson, *American Economic Thought in the Seventeenth Century* (New York, 1932).

Recent town histories are Philip Greven, Jr., *Four Generations: Population, Land and Family in Colonial Andover, Massachusetts* (Ithaca, 1970); John Demos, "Notes on Life in Plymouth Colony," *William and Mary Quarterly* 22 (1965); and his "Families in Colonial Bristol, Rhode Island," *William and Mary Quarterly* 25 (1968).

An important book on the problem of social control is Kai T. Erikson, *Wayward Puritans: A Study in the Sociology of Deviance* (New York, 1966), supplemented by Emil Oberholzer, Jr., *Delinquent Saints: Disciplinary Action in the Early Congregational Churches of Massachusetts* (New York, 1956); and Edmund S. Morgan, "The Puritans and Sex," *New England Quarterly* 25 (December 1942): 591–607. Two additional articles are useful, Jules Zanger, "Crime and Punishment in Early Massachusetts," *William and Mary Quarterly* 22 (1965); and Lawrence W. Towner, "A Fondness for Freedom: Servant Protest in Puritan Society," *William and Mary Quarterly* 19 (1962).